Memories of Maggie

❧❧

A Portrait of
Margaret Thatcher

Edited by

Iain Dale

DA
591
.T47
M46
2000

For Eleanor Daniels

Published in Great Britain 2000
by Politico's Publishing
8 Artillery Row
Westminster
London
SWiP iRZ

Tel 020 7931 0090
Fax 020 7828 8111
Email publishing@politicos.co.uk
Website http://www.politicos.co.uk/publishing

First published in hardback 2000

A catalogue record of this book is available from the British Library.

ISBN 1 902301 51 X

Printed and bound in Great Britain by St Edmundsbury Press

CONTRIBUTORS

Introduction by Iain Dale	vii	Angela Browning	85
Lord Biffen	1	Cheryl Gillan	86
Adam Boulton	6	Lord Bellwin	87
Sir Archie Hamilton	11	Nicholas Ridley	91
Hugo Young	17	Nick Hawkins	94
Gillian Shephard	21	Oliver Letwin	97
Lord Whitelaw	23	John Redwood	100
Sir Alfred Sherman	28	Sir Malcolm Rifkind	104
Baroness Miller of Hendon	33	Sir Robin Butler	106
The Earl of Caithness	36	Alan Clark	110
Lord Powell of Bayswater	38	Sir Robin Day	117
David Prior	42	Ronald Reagan	122
Sir George Gardiner	43	Sir Ronald Millar	124
Lord Mackay of Clashfern	48	Sir John Junor	127
Matthew Parris	51	Lord Howe of Aberavon	130
Lord Owen	53	Lord Crickhowell	137
Sir Michael Spicer	59	Baroness Trumpington	142
Lord Jenkin of Roding	62	Lord Jopling	144
Patrick Nicholls	69	Baroness Fookes	146
Sir Peter Emery	70	Lord Lamont of Lerwick	147
Lord Armstrong of Ilminster	71	Sir Christopher Lawson	150
Sebastian Coe	73	Lord Baker of Dorking	152
Admiral Sir John Woodward	75	Alexander Haig	158
Sir Teddy Taylor	77	Sir David Steel	160
Vàclav Klaus	80	Edward Pearce	161
Alex Aiken	83	Neil Hamilton	164

Christine Hamilton	166		Lord Tebbit	259
Sir Mark Lennox-Boyd	168		Patrick Minford	261
Michael Dobbs	170		Quentin Davies	263
Sir Richard Needham	173		Sir Richard Body	267
Sally Pipes	175		Robert Key	270
Lord Wakeham	178		Sir John Stanley	275
Bernard Jenkin	182		John Whittingdale	277
Peter Lilley	183		Ann Widdecombe	281
Bob Hawke	184		Michael Brunson	282
Terry Major-Ball	187		Sir Edward Du Cann	285
Mikhail Gorbachev	190		Baroness Nicholson	289
Harvey Thomas	197		Sir Brian Mawhinney	293
Sir Rex Hunt	200		Michael Howard	295
Eleanor Laing	212		Paul Elliot	298
Sir Norman Fowler	213		Michael Cockerell	302
Lord Waddington	217		Julia Langdon	305
Viscount Tonypandy	220		William Hague	309
Baroness Cox	222			
Lord Young of Graffham	225			
Baroness Seccombe	228			
Major Gen. Julian Thompson	230			
John Blundell	232			
David Davis	238			
Alan Duncan	239			
Andrew Rowe	240			
Sir David Mitchell	242			
Edwina Currie	244			
Eric Forth	247			
Howard Flight	249			
Lawrence Robertson	251			
Lord Denham	253			
Lord Harris	255			

INTRODUCTION

The idea for this book came on a holiday to the United States when I came across a marvellous book called 'Recollections of Reagan: A Portrait of Ronald Reagan' (edited by Peter Hannaford and published by Morrow in 1997). Using the premise that if it was good enough for Ronald Reagan it was good enough for Margaret Thatcher I stored the idea at the back of my mind and eventually decided that the book should appear to coincide with the tenth anniversary of her resignation (or perhaps more accurately, overthrow) as Prime Minister. Just as people remember where they were when Kennedy was shot, most people in Britain remember exactly where they were when they heard Margaret Thatcher had resigned.

This book has been a pleasure to compile, edit and indeed publish. I am indebted to the contributors whose anecdotes are entertaining, informative and, on occasion, quite moving. They all provided their contributions on the understanding that royalties from the book would be donated to one of Lady Thatcher's favourite charities, the National Society for the Prevention of Cruelty to Children (NSPCC) and we are delighted to have received their co-operation.

Parts of this book are available to read on the new Margaret Thatcher Internet Website http://www.margaret-thatcher.com. There is also an opportunity on the site to add your own particular memories. Or you may do this be emailing your contribution (of between 400 and 1500 words) to memories@margaret-thatcher.com.

There is a danger with a book like this – particularly when it has a title like 'Memories of Maggie' – is that it is viewed almost as a tribute to someone who is with us no longer. Margaret Thatcher is most definitely still a part of the political tapestry of this country and long may she remain so. Her views are perhaps even more relevant today than ever. The tragedy is that whenever she expresses opinions they are inevitably interpreted as attacks on her successors and she therefore rarely makes pronouncements on domestic politics. In this country we are never quite sure what to do with ex Prime Ministers, so our media spends its time on the search for splits and controversy. If only we could find a proper role for ex Prime Ministers the political lives of their successors might be a little more comfortable.

This book contains anecdotes from world leaders, former Cabinet Ministers, Members of Parliament, journalists, civil servants and many other people who have experienced memorable encounters with the Iron Lady. We have also received co-operation from several leading publishers which has allowed us to reprint relevant passages from the memoirs of the Ronald Reagan, Mikhail Gorbachev and the late Alan Clark among others.

In the introduction to my previous book on Margaret Thatcher, *As I Said to Denis: The Margaret Thatcher Book of Quotations* (Robson Books, 1997) I said that an aim of the book was to give the reader insight into the character of Margaret Thatcher and her political views. It is even more the case with this book and I hope it goes some way to destroying the myth of a hard, uncaring and ill-meaning politician. I hope that you, the reader, will enjoy the anecdotes in this book and will forgive me for getting the ball rolling with my own!

രംഹ

My first encounter with Margaret Thatcher came in 1983 when she invited the chairmen of the various University Conservative Associations to a reception at Number Ten. For a country boy like me, it was unbelievable to have been invited and it was something I had been looking forward to for months. Just to climb those stairs, with the portraits of all past Prime Ministers on the walls was worth the trip on its own. And there at the top of the stairs was the Prime Minister. She had obviously perfected the art of welcoming people to receptions and as she shook you by the hand and wished you a good evening, she moved you on into the room without you even knowing she was doing it. Most of the Cabinet were there – I remember discussing with Cecil Parkinson the number of free running shoes he had been sent after a recent profile had announced to the world that he was a keen runner. He offered me a pair but it turned out his feet were much smaller than mine! We were constantly plied with wine and I made a mental note to stop at two glasses. But after the second glass was emptied I felt rather self-conscious without a glass in my hand so grabbed another. Just as the Prime Minister walked by I took a sip. All I remember is my stomach heaving and me thinking that I was about to throw up at the Prime Minister's feet, thus ending a glorious political career which had hardly got off the ground. Luckily I managed to control my stomach and all was well. It turned out that it was whisky in the glass, rather than white wine.

Later in the evening, as I was talking to my local MP, Alan Haselhurst, the division bell sounded. Although there were at least 40 MPs there, none made a move to leave to go and vote over the road in the House of Commons. Mrs Thatcher started to look rather irritated and was obviously none too impressed. In the end she walked to the middle of the room, took off one of her shoes and banged it on the floor. There was instance silence. The Prime Minister then spoke. 'Would all Conservative MPs kindly leave the building immediately,' she instructed. 'And the rest of us will stay and enjoy ourselves!' Naturally we all laughed uproariously, enjoying the sight of the MPs trooping out of the room in a somewhat sheepish manner.

After I graduated I went to work at the House of Commons as a researcher for a Norfolk Member of Parliament. He was not a particularly well known MP and never courted publicity. He had a marginal seat and devoted himself to his constituency rather than join the rent-a-quote mob. It served him well as he held his seat for the next two elections. If ever there was an MP less likely to be involved in sleaze it was him. But one day, a careless error by me left him open to charges of dirty dealing. We ran a businessmen's club in the constituency, called The Westminster Circle. It served two purposes – one to keep the MP in touch with local businesses, and secondly to raise a little money for the very poor constituency association. For £100 a year business people joined and were given a dinner in the House of Commons, usually addressed by a Cabinet Minister, and another dinner in the constituency, addressed by a more junior Minister. These clubs were common in all parties up and down the country. But in a publicity leaflet designed to attract new members I had used the phrase 'with direct access to government ministers'. By this I had meant that they would be able to meet and speak to a government minister at the dinner. In those pre 'cash for questions' days we were all rather innocent. But it proved to be my undoing – and very nearly my employer's.

Early one Tuesday afternoon he found out that at that day's Prime Minister's Question Time, the Liberal leader, David Steel, would raise this subject with the Prime Minister. He immediately went to see her in her office behind the Speaker's Chair. He must have been quaking in his boots but he later told me she had been brilliant. She sat him down, offered him a coffee and heard him out. She did not disguise her dislike for Steel and thought it typical of him to operate in this manner. She told him she would let Steel have both barrels, and of course she did! He returned to the Office after PM's Question Time and related the events of the day to me. I had been completely oblivious, which was just as well as I would no doubt have been having a premonition of what a P45 looks like.

A few months later I was having lunch with a couple of Tory MPs in the Members' Cafeteria. We had just finished our lunch when in walked Mrs T and her entourage. She grabbed a tray and chose a light lunch of Welsh Rarebit. Unfortunately, as we had finished, I did not have cause to hang around too much longer so left the room, cursing that we had decided to have an early lunch. A few minutes later I realised I had left some papers and magazines on the table in the cafeteria and returned to retrieve them. As luck would have it, the Thatcher group had sat themselves at the table we had been sitting at and Mrs T had her elbow plonked on my papers. I decided to summon up the courage and interrupt them to ask for my papers. Just as I had started I looked down at the pile of papers and to my horror saw that my copy of the new issue of Private Eye was on the top of them and the front cover had a particularly nasty photo of Denis Thatcher. Mrs Thatcher cottoned on to what I wanted, removed her elbow and gazed down at the offending magazine. My heart stopped. 'Oh, Private Eye, Denis loves it,' she gushed. To my eternal shame, I just picked it up, along with the rest of the papers, made my excuses and left. What a wimp.

In 1995 I took an American friend, Daniel Forrester, to the T E Utley Young Journalist of the Year awards at the Reform Club. Lady Thatcher had been invited to present the awards. She treated us to a half hour impromptu speech on political issues of the moment, which seemed to go by in about five minutes – quite an achievement as her entire audience had to remain standing throughout. After she had finished Daniel whispered to me: 'I have to meet her, what should I do?' Knowing of her penchant for strapping 6 feet tall dark haired American men I encouraged him to go and introduce himself. He suddenly got cold feet so eventually I dragged him over to where she was talking to several of the award winners. In typically American style he launched into a sycophantic introduction which immediately attracted her attention. 'Mrs Thatcher,' he began. I kicked him. 'Er, Lady Thatcher,' he hurriedly corrected himself, 'May I say how much our country misses your leadership….' and he continued in that vain for a few seconds. While he was speaking, the diminutive figure of the Iron Lady (for she is much smaller in height than most people imagine) stared up at him, her eyes never leaving his. When he had finally finished having his say, Lady Thatcher hardly paused for breath. 'Your President, President Clinton.' She paused, heightening the drama for our American friend. 'He is a great communicator.' Up came the forefinger, almost prodding Daniel's chest. Then in a particularly contemptuous tone, came the pièce de résistance. 'The trouble is, he has absolutely nothing to communicate.' With that she was away. It was almost a flounce. Daniel eventually came down from whichever cloud he had been on – probably nine – and said, 'I'll remember that for the rest of my life' – and as a well-known critic of Bill Clinton, has been dining out on it ever since.

My latest encounter came at a retirement party for ITN's much missed political editor Michael Brunson. My friend Alan Duncan, the Tory MP for Rutland, started a conversation with her and she suddenly asked where Denis had disappeared off to as they had to leave for a dinner. Being of diminutive stature, and me being over six feet tall he asked me to scan the room. Both of them looked at me expectantly. To my horror I spied Denis on the other side of the room talking to Michael Heseltine. I summoned up all the courage at my disposal and explained where he was. Lady Thatcher's eyes became even bluer than normal and she exclaimed: 'Denis and I are having dinner with Cap Weinberger tonight. I think he's rather more important than THAT man, don't you! If Denis isn't over here within one minute I shall go over and stare at them.' Luckily for Michael Heseltine, she didn't have to.

What memories! What a woman! What a Prime Minister!

IAIN DALE

August 2000

LORD BIFFEN

CABINET MINISTER 1979–87

John Biffen, now Lord Biffen, served as a Cabinet Minister under Margaret Thatcher from 1979 until 1987, initially as Chief Secretary to the Treasury then later as Secretary of State for Trade, Lord President and Leader of the House of Commons and finally as Lord Privy Seal.

৵৵৻

Unbending Leadership

The career and character of Margaret Thatcher will fascinate historians for decades to come. Her achievements and limitations will bear constant re-interpretation. This short piece would not seek such an academic task, but only offer a personal recollection.

Her actions never betrayed the trivial or banal. She was puritanical and committed to the work ethic. She despised the worldly and cynical politics of many Tories. I suspect she looked upon the Macmillan period with some unease and felt that his sunset years, from Profumo onwards, showed the consequence of a lack of political purpose. Her decision to stand against Edward Heath for the Conservative leadership in 1975 was an example of cool courage. No member of Heath's Cabinet, and more particularly William Whitelaw, was prepared to stand against him. She, alone, broke rank, although Keith Joseph might have done so had he possessed the suitable temperament. Margaret Thatcher was not foolhardy in her venture. She had self-confidence and a deep sense that the Conservative politics of the Heath Government needed reversing. Thirty years later it is difficult to recapture how demoralised the Tories had become by U-turns and ineffective trade union legislation.

Doubtless this inspired Margaret Thatcher to convert a defeated party into a government in exile. Rarely have policy groups worked so assiduously to propose measures 'proof against U-turn'. The trade union plans were recast to avoid the ignominy of the unenforceable Industrial Relations Act of Geoffrey Howe and Robert Carr. A host of City executives and academics, and notably Arthur Cockfield, toiled to produce a fiscal and monetary policy that would restore liberal economics and escape the thraldom of price, income and exchange control. The technical financial skills accumulated in Opposition fully matched the resources of the Treasury under Denis Healey.

Margaret Thatcher was not a commanding Commons speaker, certainly not equal to James Callaghan, but she was a formidable party leader. For her politics was not a game for amateurs: everything was played in earnest. This austere drive inspired the Parliamentary party, and even more raised the morale of the Conservative activists in the country. Her rhetoric became sharper and more effective as she was able to tone down her natural shrillness. The Soviets dismissed her as 'the Iron Maiden'. She grasped the epithet and turned it into a compliment. The irony was that in many ways her commitment to firm government was reminiscent of her predecessor whom she had toppled. 'Ted Heath in drag' observed Denis Healey; but she was determined to succeed in economic and trade union policies where he had been ill served by fortune.

The redoubtable character of Margaret Thatcher became increasingly apparent in the early years of her premiership. Britain had a Premier in a hurry. She was calculating and determined, placing her known supporters in the key Treasury and economic posts. The relative isolation of the pragmatists – later derided as 'wets' – was a high-risk strategy; but it paid off. There were no resignations on account of policy, and the Cabinet was gradually reshaped with younger and more sympathetic members. Her Chancellor, Geoffrey Howe, loyally carried out the essential tenets of the new liberal economics. Exchange controls were abolished along with regulated prices and incomes. Public spending was stabilised and taxation was changed to enable income tax reductions to be financed by increases in Value Added Tax. It is no disparagement of Howe to say that he could not have achieved such major changes without the full-hearted support and prodding of his Prime Minister. No Cabinet cabal of spenders could prize apart the Downing Street partners. Alas it was not always to be the case.

Margaret Thatcher's single mindedness was best demonstrated in the latter half of 1981. Unemployment had risen sharply; there were the usual government 'mid term blues'; the academic world was almost unanimous in calling for 'moderation' and a return to some kind of Keynesian economic policy. She persisted with her plans despite her growing adverse reputation for stubbornness. The sobriquet coined by Ronnie Millar, surely the decade's most elegant spinner, was 'the lady's not for turning'.

This view of her determined courage was emphasised by the Falklands dispute with Argentina. That conflict has been well documented. The task of recapturing the islands was a logistic nightmare. Success has subsequently created the false impression of comparative ease. Margaret Thatcher knew only too well the hazards of distance to the South Atlantic and the ambivalence of some of our NATO allies. Politically the campaign was conducted by a small inner Cabinet. There was general domestic political support for the venture but it would have been dissipated if there had been defeat or misfortune. Margaret Thatcher knew this and kept her nerve. There was no shortage of those who vainly sought a compromise settlement. If victory goes to the brave she certainly deserved her triumph. In the Commons, Enoch Powell – no stranger to courage and purpose – commented 'Is the Right Hon Lady aware that the report has now been received from the public analyst . . . It shows that the substance under test consisted of ferrous matter of the highest quality, that it is of exceptional tensile strength, is highly resistant to wear and tear and to stress, and may be used with advantage for all national purposes?'

There can be a nemesis which may mock the quality of determination and courage. Self-confidence becomes self-righteousness, and commitment becomes stubbornness and a vision becomes an obsession. Furthermore, as Churchill discovered, the British electorate is often short on gratitude. It was an experience that Margaret Thatcher suffered unhappily in her premiership between 1987–90. One particular measure focussed growing hostility – the community charge, popularly described as the 'Poll Tax'. The radical agitators took to the streets and incensed members of the middle classes bombarded Tory MPs with hostile correspondence. Undeterred Margaret Thatcher pronounced the tax as the 'flagship' of government policy and planned that it should raise more revenue than the rating system it was scheduled to replace. Such a reaction had panache but little electoral guile, ostensibly it was firm government but lacked political touch.

We live too near the events to judge properly the various factors that impelled Margaret Thatcher to lose control of the Conservative Parliamentary party. My instinctive judgement is that the Poll Tax was the major issue, not least because it had a lightning conductor attraction for other items of lesser discontent. Of course there were also major matters including the poor relations with the Chancellor, Nigel Lawson, and their divergent economic views. Her unhappy years with Geoffrey Howe over Europe have been well chronicled, and, though important, were not decisive in balancing Tory opinion in the Commons. At any rate a Prime Minister, however iron her resolution and fearless her politics, is unwise to quarrel simultaneously with her Chancellor and Foreign Secretary. The outstanding qualities of course that Margaret Thatcher bestowed upon the Conservative Party in the mid1970s–80s simply had to be adjusted to meet Britain's changing economic and social circumstances. 'Not for turning' was no longer a compelling Thatcher slogan. Of course this reluctance to bend meant a somewhat poignant epitaph to her premiership, but it can never deny the overall quality of courage and perseverance that distinguish her politics.

ADAM BOULTON

POLITICAL JOURNALIST

Adam Boulton is the Political Editor of Sky News and was formerly the political editor of TV-am. He has been a Lobby Correspondent since 1983.

രൂൔ

Maggie & Me

I doubt even Bill Clinton has had a British Prime Minister on hands and knees before him but it's happened to me, and it was the mighty Iron Lady as well. We were in her constituency office in Finchley preparing for an interview. When the crew moved a desk they exposed the generations of fluff and paper-clips gathered in a pit in the carpet pile. It was too much for the grocer's daughter; the Housewife Prime Minister was kneeling in a split second to tidy things up. Whatever you think of her that's vintage Margaret Thatcher: she lived in her own world and honoured her own values with never a thought for the concerns, or pomposities of others. At times her personal cocoon may have made her insensitive, but if you got to deal with her face-to-face it also meant she was unprejudiced without airs and graces.

For the most part though, I had only a passing acquaintance with 'Prime Minister Thatcher', passing me on a thousand doorsteps, in planes, in corridors, always on the way to something more important.

Or was it really something more important? Certainly Margaret Thatcher always gave full value on the doorstep. The impression at least was that she would stop, think and voice a spontaneous reaction to the questions unceremoniously shouted at her by the hack-pack. It's a marked contrast to Tony Blair. 'The Prime Minister doesn't do doorsteps!' is one of Alastair Campbell's proudest boasts – by which he means that even if you asked Mr Blair what he thought about the Second Coming now underway, he'd still walk past your cries, consult with his advisors and, maybe, come back out with a carefully crafted soundbite on his lips.

Maggie wasn't like that. Indeed the best bit of advice I ever got about her, was the first I ever received, from Andy Webb, then my boss and Political Editor of *TV-am*. 'She takes everything at face value,' he said, 'so think before you speak. If you say 'good morning', she's quite likely to reply 'is it?' and go into a full appraisal of current meteorological conditions.' This, of course, made her fantastic television for reporters like me. She could always take you aback, for example likening the 'ANC to IRA killers' even as the one-day South African President Thabo Mbeki was being feted under the same roof at the 1987 Vancouver Commonwealth Conference.

At work and study in the USA from 1980–82, I missed out on the rise of Thatcherism at home. I sat out the Falklands in Washington: my most vivid memory of her then is of an over-stimulated Secretary of State Alexander Haig speculating luridly with the White House Corps about the precise intimate nature of the relationship between Thatcher and Reagan given their frequent one-on-one meetings. So I suppose I didn't know any better and was fair game to be sent into the Iron Lady's den as a Lobby correspondent shortly after joining *TV-am* in 1983.

Thatcher's other-worldliness, or at least her determination to live in her own world, worked in my favour. She didn't read the newspapers and her ability to discriminate between TV networks depended entirely on who she recognised with her basilisk eyes.

Indeed, when she remembered it, she tended to get my name right. Perhaps because 'Mr Boulton' gave her the chance to exercise her elocution on the long 'o'. My more illustrious rivals John Cole and Michael Brunson usually had to settle for the not-quite-right 'Mr Brunston' and 'Mr Coles'.

Mind you, you were never quite sure she knew who you were. Sometimes she didn't seem to distinguish between journalists and her hard-pressed hand-bag carriers. Working on a David Frost interview during the 1987 election, I was a little bemused to find the Prime Minister's finger poking into my chest in the Green Room, telling me 'the message you've got to get out.'

I have no doubt that she was an instinctive 'gut' politician, what in politer circles is called 'a conviction politician'. But I still don't know what to make of one incident. In the 1987 General Election Campaign Labour had made much of the case of Mark Burgess, a 10 year old boy awaiting an NHS operation for a hole-in-the-heart. Several years later, long after Margaret Thatcher's third election victory, Mark, very sadly, died.

This coincided with the end of a European Council in Denmark, when Mrs. Thatcher was due to give a series of television interviews. You would not be allowed to eavesdrop today, but in those days , with the latest deadline, I was allowed to wait my turn in the interview room itself. And so I heard four separate uneasy interviewers ask the same final question: 'I know it's got nothing to do with the summit, but my newsdesk insist . . . your reaction to Mark's death'. And I saw the same emotional reaction repeated four times: the hand to the heart, the catch in the throat . . . the 'as a mother I know how terrible this must be.'

True or bluff? I still don't know.

I do know how sensitive she is about her family. Even after her enforced retirement, the affairs of her son Mark remained the only subject absolutely off-limits in interviews tied to her memoirs. By contrast, her husband Denis is no buffoon, brief encounters left no doubt how sharp he is, and how fiercely right-wing.

Chris Moncrieff of the *Press Association* is rightly the reporter most associated with the Thatcher years. One day I hope he delivers on his promise to publish his memoirs. His working title is 'Maggie Thatcher's Flying Circus'. It's a good one because we used to get closest to her on her numerous foreign trips. There were drawbacks because where her successors have favoured commercial charters, Mrs Thatcher insisted on using the ageing VC 10s in the Queen's Flight. The acoustics were so poor that only the person bold enough to sit in the seat next to her ever heard the briefings which she gave in the soft voice reserved for social occasions.

Bernard Ingham would always ensure that the print journalists had plenty of time for sight seeing, shopping and golf, with a briefing conveniently timed for deadlines. But for those of us who had to record the visit on tape, the pace was more hectic. The day usually started with a dawn call for a wreath laying. I've visited practically every British War Cemetery in the world with Maggie; including in Turkey the graves from the Crimean War (the more recent Gallipoli battlefield was held back for a visit of its own the next year). Turkey was also a first for the one-and-only recorded cultural stop on a Thatcher tour. I had expected the visit to the British-made Istanbul sewage works, and the gas plant where the gasometers were painted with giant portraits of PMs Ozal and Thatcher. Even the courtesy call on the General widely whispered to be the government's 'head of torture' was not a surprise. But I never thought I'd accompany Mrs Thatcher on a canter through St. Sofia and the Okapi Palace. A British Embassy Official explained: 'she struck it out of the programme but we told her there would be an international diplomatic incident if she didn't come'.

There was a real crusading spirit about those foreign trips. Downing Street did not boast a White House style advance team, and no one seemed quite certain what was going to happen. Suspense was at its highest in her ground breaking forays behind the Iron Curtain. Here again she not only bolstered politicians like Lech Walesa and Mikhail Gorbachev, she also sought out dissidents in their freezing flats. Margaret Thatcher, clad in her new Aquascutum wardrobe, careering round the outer-Moscow tenement blocks is still the most impressive exercise in political canvassing I've seen. Thatcher certainly worked hard on her foreign policy. The most shaken I ever saw her was in Brussels – ashen and near tears when the new President Bush made clear Helmut Kohl was his preferred special relation in Europe. A couple of years later of course, she'd won Bush back, as he took up her strong line against Saddam Hussein.

With hindsight, we in the Westminster Press corps were as well placed as anyone to see the end coming. Cabinet Ministers complained she stopped listening. With us she stopped engaging. The gleam faded in her eyes and the fresh response to questions was replaced by a rambling monologue. 'On and on and on' was too long as she began to believe her own publicity. In the way that generals tend to fight the last war, I'm sure Tony Blair has learnt this lesson. Unless it all goes to his head before then, I expect him to resign in a second term.

It was a splendid exit: 'We fight on, we fight to win' on the doorstep of Downing Street; the tears in the car. Transitions of power are difficult for impartial reporters to cover: it's about people you know, you can feel the elation of the victors and the desolation of the vanquished.

Finally I'd like to confess that I've returned the compliment and been on my hands and knees before Margaret Thatcher – crawling quite literally under a live camera before an interview. Ever frank she cried 'You look like a giant mouse.'

Last year a *Guardian* reporter rang to ask me to nominate an icon of the Twentieth Century. There was an intake of breath on the line when I said 'I assume you've already got the obvious ones like Thatcher'. I chose her anyway.

SIR ARCHIE HAMILTON

MARGARET THATCHER'S PPS 1987–88

Sir Archie Hamilton has been the Member of Parliament for Epsom and Ewell since 1978. After serving as a Government Whip and as Parliamentary Under Secretary of State for Defence Procurement he became Margaret Thatcher's Parliamentary Private Secretary (PPS) in 1987, remaining with her until 1988 when she made him a Minister of State at the Ministry of Defence.

৵৽৽

Life with the Leader

I first met Margaret Thatcher when she came as Leader of the Opposition to support me in my by-election in 1978 when I was first elected as MP for Epsom and Ewell.

At the end of a full day of walkabouts and opportunities to meet my prospective constituents, we had a press conference. The questions from our local newspapers were not exactly challenging and the last one was particularly sycophantic.

'Mrs Thatcher, it looks very much as if you might win the forthcoming General Election. If you do, will you find a place for Archie Hamilton in your government?'

I was expecting a reply that, while being non-committal, would sing the praises of the candidate hoping to enter Parliament. Not a bit of it.

'Oh no! It's much too early to consider that.'

Knowing her as I now do, I suspect that she was much more concerned about appearing to take the outcome of the forthcoming election for granted, than being committed to having Archie Hamilton in her Government.

 споре

I was PPS to Margaret Thatcher as Prime Minster for the 15 months following the 1987 Election.

We were sitting one evening in her rooms in the House of Commons and she raised the question of women priests in the Church of England. Although brought up a Methodist, she had become an Anglican and was troubled that ordaining women would split the Church.

I took issue with her and argued that as a woman Prime Minister she really could not be seen to be against women entering the priesthood.

'Anyway', I said, ' I don't know why you are so worried. I think women are capable of greater spirituality than men and also they are less inclined to succumb to sexual temptation.'

'Oh, I don't know about that', said the Prime Minister.

As with so many arguments, she would never cede any ground and, on occasions, one was left wondering whether one had gone too far and upset her.

It was a week later that I read a short excerpt in the paper, headed 'Thatcher backs women priests'.

споре

Weekdays in Number 10 started with a meeting to discuss forthcoming events and what was in the newspapers.

Staff in Bernard Ingham's press office must have got up very early to produce an extraordinarily succinct summary of all the stories in the newspapers on a couple of sides of foolscap. Closely argued articles from the broadsheets would be reduced to three lines.

I asked Margaret Thatcher one day whether she ever read the daily papers.

'Oh no!' she replied, 'they make such hurtful and damaging remarks about me and my family, that if I read the papers every day, I could never get on with the job I am here to do.'

Some years later, when John Major was Prime Minister and having serious problems with the press, I repeated Margaret Thatcher's remark to him.

He did not respond but just gave me one of those pitying looks that people reserve for the feeble-minded.

ॐ

Margaret Thatcher did not read the daily papers but she invariably studied the Sundays during her weekends at Chequers.

She always took great heart from Woodrow Wyatt's articles in the *News of the World*.

Monday morning meetings with Cabinet colleagues often started with the Prime Minister saying 'Did you see Woodrow's marvellous article in the *News of the World*?' Many Cabinet ministers found that it became almost compulsory to add the *News of the World* to their Sunday morning reading.

ॐ

As her Parliamentary Private Secretary, I used to sit behind Margaret Thatcher at Cabinet meetings, on a chair against the wall.

On the whole, Cabinet meetings were rather formal and dull affairs, and policy formulation was reserved for smaller ad hoc meetings with Cabinet Ministers and Cabinet sub-committees.

At these meetings the Prime Minister dispensed with preamble and launched into the contentious elements of the policy paper, often with the help of a briefing from the Policy Unit, in which she had highlighted the most significant passages.

On one occasion, a heated argument ensued between her and a favoured Cabinet Minister. This prolonged and acrimonious discussion left everyone exhausted and some rather bruised.

Finally, she announced:

'Of course, I agree with everything you are trying to do here. I just wanted to play devil's advocate to ensure that you were prepared for all the counter-arguments.'

❧

Margaret Thatcher was always known to be an avid listener of the *Today* programme, which she had on the radio whilst she got up.

I remember her telling me that the coverage of *Today* regularly infuriated her husband Denis, and she used to hear him shouting 'Bastards!' as he lay in bed, listening to the programme.

❧

Margaret Thatcher had a rather odd belief that it was impossible to write a speech for the Party Conference until the conference itself was underway and the 'atmosphere' of the gathering had been accurately assessed.

The result was that most of her conference speech had to be written at the end of a series of hard days among the party faithful and would stretch on until the early hours of the morning. Contributions came in from all and sundry but invariably only small bits were selected with the rest being torn up by the Prime Minister amid cries of 'Nothing fresh here!'

There was an occasion when one of Margaret Thatcher's Cabinet Ministers had asked himself to Sunday lunch at Chequers. The Prime Minister did not want to be subjected to unremitting pressure from this man for most of her Sunday, so she asked me, as her PPS, to join the two of them, plus Denis, for lunch.

I gladly accepted the invitation, although slightly worried that I was neglecting my family at home.

A few days later, the Prime Minister realised that her invitation might have disrupted a family weekend.

'Why don't you bring your wife Anne too?' she asked.

'The problem is, Prime Minister', I replied, 'that she has our three teenage daughters at home that weekend.'

'Bring them all', she said.

Later on, life was made even more complicated when it became apparent that my youngest fourteen year-old had also invited a friend home from school.

'I am afraid Prime Minister that my youngest daughter has invited her friend Abigail for the weekend as well.'

'Bring her too!'

I admired the Secretary of State who arrived for what he imagined was to be a *tête-a-tête* with the Prime Minister only to be confronted with the Hamilton family and a row of teenage girls. It must have resembled a scene out of St Trinians. Not a flicker of emotion crossed his face; he was charm itself.

Conversation at the ensuing meal was somewhat strained. The Minister struggled in vain for a hearing, as one daughter, in that uncompromising teenage mode which is determined not to be overawed, rolled up her sleeves, and putting her elbows on the table, embarked on what seemed an interminable anecdote. The PM drummed her fingers on the table, while another daughter, benefiting from the adult distraction, dipped her finger in the jug of cream. Her friend Abigail sat immobilised as if she were a rabbit caught in the headlights.

It crossed my mind that Mrs Thatcher might have regretted her generous invitation.

ᔥᔤ

To understand the exceptional qualities of Margaret Thatcher as a politician, one should think of her as an evangelical.

She was born a woman with immense powers of concentration, a prodigious memory and an exceptionally analytical mind.

What made her one of the greatest Prime Ministers of the last century was the conviction with which she drove her policies and the way she was prepared to risk serious short-term unpopularity for doing things which she knew were right in the long-term.

Although prepared ultimately to compromise, she always dragged the argument further than most into her own territory.

I often wondered whether her determination to press her own point of view could be attributed to the fact that she was a woman. All I do know is that all the men I have met and worked with in politics have shown themselves more ready to compromise than she.

HUGO YOUNG

POLITICAL JOURNALIST

Hugo Young was Political Editor of the Sunday Times from 1973 until 1984, and is now a columnist for the Guardian. He has written for numerous foreign magazines. His biography of Margaret Thatcher One of Us *is regarded as the one of the definitive accounts of her life.*

అ~6

Only One of Us

Margaret Thatcher knew from the start that I wasn't likely to be One of Us. I worked for the *Sunday Times*, then an independent and liberal paper not under the suzerainty of an owner who was one of her cheer-leaders. I had all the wrong instincts, being neither a Conservative nor someone who believed any political journalist should have other than sceptical connections with politicians. But despite these bad basics, we got on quite well, which was more to her credit than to mine.

It was partly, no doubt, a matter of prudence. The *Sunday Times* was a very big paper with a lot of politically uncommitted readers, and any interview in its pages reached an important audience. I did several of them when she was Prime Minister. The first, I well recall, was preceded by her personal search for Nescafé to get some cups of coffee together. If that happened at Number 10 today, you could be sure there had been a meeting of the spin-doctors beforehand, to assess precisely what impression should be made on this or that journalist who was coming in. Nothing happens by accident now. But the early Thatcher was a cosmetic artefact only when she appeared on television. Her personal coffee-making wasn't, I thought, done for effect. Like her obsession with turning off the Downing Street lights, it was the extension of Grantham housekeeping into the prime ministerial world.

The reason I survived for ten years as an acceptable interviewer, and occasional off-the-record conversationalist, was, I think, twofold.

First, Mrs Thatcher always liked an argument. Although argument was not what this interviewer particularly sought, it was a mode of discourse she found irresistible. Somewhere along the line, the very fact that I was so plainly not in her camp became a virtue. I was bestowed with 'convictions', and even principles. When Matthew Parris left her service as an MP, he once wrote that he was especially counselled to read my stuff as a way of keeping in touch with the world he was deserting, perhaps to know who the enemy was.

Once allotted this label, I never seemed to lose it. One of the things Mrs Thatcher said, intimidatingly, to an early civil servant was that she usually made up her mind about a man in ten seconds – 'and I rarely change it'. So, perhaps, it was with me. One of her attractive virtues was that she never, in those days, showed any side. The grandeur of the post-imperial years was nowhere to be seen. Argument could flow on almost equal terms. She was utterly convinced that, in the course of such discussion, any reasonable person was certain to be persuaded to the way she thought: which is the trait she most specifically shares with Tony Blair.

Her encompassing of me within her invincible power of persuasion was due, however, to the second feature of our relationship. I'm sure she never read a word I wrote. I retained my place in the tent of the acceptable because she never knew what I really thought, since she was a stranger to my columns. These became, as the years went by, critical to the point of savagery. I questioned her honesty as much as her wisdom (over Westland, for example). I impugned her motives, ridiculed her judgement and even cast doubt on her sanity. I remained, unread, within the pale: an ambiguous fate, but one which gave me scarcity value at my new employers, *The Guardian*, which otherwise seemed to have no contact of any kind with the Thatcher people.

One thing Mrs Thatcher certainly did not read was my biography of her, 'One of Us'. This was an unofficial work in every sense. It drew on my talks with her over the years, but I never asked for a biographical interview. Members of her entourage told me, in due course, that they thought the book rather good. Perhaps because my columns were spiky, they expected a more polemical work between hard covers, and were relieved when that wasn't quite the book I wrote. But from herself – nothing. And after all, why should she? Who would want to read what purported to be a detailed account of their life and thought, when knowing that every nuance, however honestly chronicled, was bound to be not quite how it really was. Besides, by that time, I was permanently excluded from the bunker that had become her residence, the closed world that eventually produced her downfall.

The last time I met her was in what could, nonetheless, be called a biographical context. The occasion was the annual Christmas party given by the American ambassador. A long queue was lining up to shake his hand, and suddenly my wife and I found that Lady Thatcher and her husband had materialised beside us. This wasn't long after she had ceased to be prime minister, and she could still not quite credit that she had to queue at all. A frisson of doubt on her face plainly revealed an inner impulse to march up to the front and be greeted without delay. But Denis decided against such a display of amnesia as to who they now were, and the two of them therefore faced ten minutes imprisoned in our company.

The talk, led by her, immediately turned to writing. This was a subject which used to attract little but her scorn. She once asked me in very public company when I was going to get down to some proper work – building wealth, creating jobs etc. – instead of wasting my time with journalism. It was one of the little regrets of my life that I had lacked the presence of mind to say, given such an opportunity: 'After you, Prime Minister'.

But now, she told me, she had just completed the first volume of her memoirs. Naturally, this became the sole subject of our ten-minute shuffle in the queue. She was now a writer. The book had been a great labour, she recalled. But I wouldn't know anything about that, would I? Because I was a professional journalist. I was incredibly lucky, she said with patent reproach. A note of envy was even detectable. It was all so easy for me. She, on the other hand, had had to labour at getting it all down. She had written every line of the first draft herself, she said, although that nice John O'Sullivan had helped her rearrange some of the words into a better order. But it was essentially all her own work. And there would be another volume to come, on which her researchers were already hard at work. Meanwhile, what mattered was who owned the copyright to the over-matter in her television interviews. Here Denis stepped in with a commercial reckoning as to the value of what lay, untransmitted, in David Frost's archives. This was serious author talk.

In recent years, she has taken up her life as a politician, albeit surrounded by a court rather than colleagues, and certainly not by journalists invited to give her an argument. Long ago, I resumed my original distance, and she, in more exaggerated form than ever, the delusions of unchallengeable, world-correcting rightness that marked her last months in office. But I bask in the moment when, with ego pumping in a new direction, she was briefly one of us, absolving us writers, just for a year or two, from being One of Them.

GILLIAN SHEPHARD

CABINET MINISTER 1990–7

Gillian Shephard has been MP for South West Norfolk since 1987. She served under Margaret Thatcher as Parliamentary Under Secretary of State for the Department of Social Security from 1989–90 and was subsequently a member of John Major's Cabinet from 1992–7.

೪৹৶

Maggie's Minister

Mrs Thatcher appointed me to my first Ministerial post in July 1989. It was on the day of a Number 10 Reception. Conservative PMs used to hold these after Buckingham Palace Garden Parties, when spouses were likely to be in London.

When we arrived, Tom and I became conscious of a number of meaningful glances and smiles from the Chief Whip, David Waddington. Although the air was thick with reshuffle gossip, I had no clue that his demeanour and my future were linked. Eventually, however, he came over and said, 'The Prime Minister would like a word with you' and showed me into a small sitting room. In swept Mrs Thatcher, resplendent in party gear.

'Dear,' she said (her usual form of address when she was not quite sure of your name – she still calls me 'dear'), 'I want to bring you into the Government and you will be going into the job I began with, Under Secretary of State at the Department of Social Security. There is a lot of detail to master, it is important to do that. You will be working for Tony Newton, as John Moore is leaving the Government. Now you had better get back to your husband'.

Amazed, I crept back into the reception, where I found Tom deep in conversation with Mark Thatcher. 'I just called in, only to find Ma shuffling', he said, irreverently, I thought, in the circumstances. Within seconds the Chief Whip bounded up and within a few seconds more the whole room knew. It was a memorable way to get one's first Government job – I did not realise at the time that doing it in this way merely saved the Prime Minister some time on the following day – and such was her professionalism, she gave no hint either.

However, the next day, I arrived at the office, wondering what to do next, only to find (it was 8.30am) that Number 10 had already been on to my constituency secretary, my office and my Norfolk house. Cowed, and thinking that it had been a very short Ministerial career, I rang Number 10. 'Dear,' said Mrs Thatcher, 'Just to be quite clear and confirm what I said last night' and went on to re-state her offer. She added, 'If I were you, I would get straight on round to the Department – there's sure to be plenty to do'.

I did, giving officials the shock of their lives and forcing the very genial Permanent Secretary to spend the next hour with me while my predecessor Peter Lloyd packed his bags for the Home Office. You cannot, after all, have two Ministers in one job at the same time.

☙❧

In the early 1980s, Ministers and, in particular, the Prime Minister, were followed by demonstrators wherever they went. When Mrs Thatcher visited Norfolk County Hall, she swept in in a motorcade. The statutory demonstrators let loose all their tomatoes and eggs at the first two or three cars, only to be dumbfounded, not to say enraged, by the sight of Mrs Thatcher, unscathed and waving from the fifth car.

It seemed to me to be such a good tactic that I recommended it to Martine Aubry when she, as my opposite number, the French Employment Minister, was similarly dogged by demonstrators. She thought it a great wheeze and said she would adopt it too. History does not relate the French outcome.

LORD WHITELAW

DEPUTY PRIME MINISTER 1979–88

Willie Whitelaw served as Leader of the House and Secretary of State for Northern Ireland under Edward Heath and as Chairman of the Conservative Party. In Margaret Thatcher's Cabinet he was Home Secretary, Lord President of the Council and Leader of the House of Lords. He served as Deputy Prime Minister under Mrs Thatcher until his retirement in 1988. Lord Whitelaw died in 1999. This passage is taken from his book, 'The Whitelaw Memoirs' (Aurum, 1989).

࿎

Loyalty to the Leader

I have often wondered how two such different people managed to get on so well together. Of course, as Prime Minister and Party Leader, it was in her hands to decide how she treated me and used me. I must therefore say at the start that it was her personal kindness and constant understanding which gave me the opportunity to help her. For my part, I hope I always remembered that she was the Leader, who had to face all the ultimate pressures and take the final decisions. Life at the top is very lonely and extremely demanding. Anyone in an immediately subordinate position should never forget the exceptional pressures which a Leader faces, and the personal reactions which they provoke. I believe we both started from these particular positions, and understood them.

Second, we both had a passionate belief in our party and so in its Government. We probably had somewhat different perceptions of

23

how we would like to see it react in particular circumstances. On such occasions I would certainly have the chance to argue my case, but of course I had to accept that in the final event Margaret Thatcher was the Leader and had the ultimate right to decide. I do not think I ever left her in any doubt that I understood that relationship.

Third, we both knew that we were very different people with varying backgrounds, interests and thus reactions. As a result we had never been close personal friends before we were brought together in this particular political relationship.

I am often asked what it is like serving a woman Leader. In general I would say it is no different from serving a man, except that it would be futile not to appreciate that women are always ready to use their feminine charms, and indeed their feminine qualities, to get their way. Margaret Thatcher is no exception, nor could any one fail to recognise her great personal charm. Perhaps it was easy for me to work with a woman as I had been brought up by my mother and spent much time alone with her. No one who knew her could deny that my mother was a powerful character.

I was reminded the other day by the hostess who brought my mother and Margaret Thatcher together of their only meeting not long before my mother died. No one knew how it would turn out, since my mother was immensely protective of me and, naturally perhaps, proud of my performance. She was therefore very suspicious of this woman Margaret Thatcher, who had been preferred to her son as Leader of the Conservative Party. In the event, I am told, for I certainly was not present, that they got on famously together. My mother subsequently became an immense fan of Margaret Thatcher, even to the extent of upbraiding me for failing to support her more effectively. Alas, she died before she could see Margaret Thatcher as Prime Minister and her son as Home Secretary. I know she would have been far more critical of the latter than the former.

On another topic, I am asked if Margaret Thatcher ever listens to points of view other than her own. This question, with its perception of her, angers me, for it is grossly unfair. I think she probably enjoys an argument more than most people, and the more vigorous it is, the better, as far as she is concerned. She is by nature a conviction politician and so has very strong views, yet she can certainly be swayed and influenced by good arguments in the final event. I wish the critics would realise that no one could have presided over such a successful team as Leader unless they had been prepared to take account of internal discussions. Of course it is not easy to convert her, but that should surely be the case with a powerful Leader. She is certainly the type of chairman who leads from the front and from the start of a discussion makes no secret of her own feelings and views. But all chairmen have their different methods, even if most successful ones like to get their way in the end. I know that I am totally different from Margaret Thatcher in the way that I handle meetings, and that some people regard me as too conciliatory. But I have to acknowledge the truth of the remark which Norman Tebbit alleges that I made to him: 'My image is emollient – and so I am, but only when I am getting my own way.' I suspect too that Margaret Thatcher did not always find me easy to deal with. She had to experience – which I must say she did stoically on occasions – my sudden and unexpected outbursts of rage when crossed in argument. She often accepted, although I imagine she sometimes found it irritating, my cautious approach to parliamentary difficulties and tendency towards compromise. She seldom interfered with my conduct of sensitive Home Office issues, although she must have disliked some of my decisions on the treatment of offenders, and perhaps particularly on broadcasting matters where we have never quite seen eye to eye.

In particular we tended to have different views on the bias of BBC programmes. Naturally, Prime Ministers feel particularly sensitive to criticism which they consider unfair, since they are constantly in the firing line. My feelings about the BBC, on the other hand, were conditioned by my experience in dealing with broadcasting matters as Opposition Chief Whip during the 1960s. When I argued our party's case at that time I felt that I was treated most fairly by the BBC, sometimes to the intense irritation of Harold Wilson and the then Labour Government.

My experience and so perhaps inevitably my views were very different from those of the Prime Minister and the overwhelming majority of my colleagues. And so when there were controversies over different television or radio programmes, I tended to come out as a defender of the BBC. In addition to my natural instincts, I also felt that as Home Secretary it was my duty to stand up for their point of view. This led to spirited discussions on occasions. As is well known, Margaret is a regular listener to the BBC's *Today* programme and, waking early as she does, is extremely well-informed of every detail in the news each morning. So she naturally came to some meetings with that day's programme in the forefront of her mind. I have to say that on occasions I wished I had stronger grounds on which to stand up for a BBC programme. I recognise that I had some bad mornings when I abandoned defence of the indefensible. But generally I stood my ground for I felt it was good for me and for my other colleagues, including the Prime Minister, to test our views against each other. Anyway, we probably all rather enjoyed the arguments and perhaps sometimes they did affect subsequent Government reactions.

I suppose the Prime Minister listened to me most, on parliamentary and party matters, where I obviously had a great experience, and least on economic and foreign policy, where I did not claim any special knowledge and where other senior Ministers bore the responsibility.

She was always very generous with her time in giving me opportunities privately to express my feelings on any subject. She also consulted me frequently and kept me fully informed on major issues. I therefore seldom had any reason to argue with her in wider ministerial meetings and usually intervened only if I felt I could be of general assistance.

I can only conclude with a general observation. Margaret Thatcher is a remarkable and powerful Leader in every way. Of course, like everyone in her position, she has her critics and detractors. No doubt she has made mistakes, but no one can deny her incredible achievements, nor should anyone neglect the great contribution that Denis Thatcher has made to them, as the country as a whole has increasingly recognised.

SIR ALFRED SHERMAN

ADVISER TO MARGARET THATCHER

Sir Alfred Sherman co-founded the Centre for Policy Studies with Sir Keith Joseph and Margaret Thatcher in 1974 where he acted as a formative influence on Thatcherite political and economic thinking. He served as a speech writer and aide to Margaret Thatcher from 1974 until 1983.

All that is real is rational

Those who reached the top of the greasy pole this century can be counted on your fingers; identifying qualities which brought them to the top where many others failed remains infinitely challenging. I had personally identified Margaret Thatcher as a potential successor to Heath under certain circumstances back in Autumn 1973, when asked by two friends, Basil (now Lord) Feldman, a leading party figure, and Barry Rose, publisher and one-time Conservative council-leader. Basil called this far-fetched. How right he was. That it came to pass does not make it any less so. That an almost unknown middle-aged lady from a lower middle-class background whose political career had been unspectacular could within sixteen months reach the top in the Tory interest seemed inconceivable. Nor were her chances of leading her party to electoral victory, once precariously established as Leader, rated highly until the Callaghan government's last few months beset by difficulties of its own making. Yet in a short time she became one of the few twentieth-century leaders of whom it could be said that she 'bestrode our narrow world like a colossus.' But per Hegel: 'all that is real is rational'; there must have been valid reasons for her achievement.

When I forecast that Margaret might receive the mandate of Heaven, I had never met her, and only once even seen her. What struck me then was the fervour of her beliefs. The Spanish political philosopher, José Ortega Y Gasset, distinguished between ideas and beliefs, complaining that historians and political writers over-emphasised the importance of the former at the expense of the latter. Current sensitivity among Conservatives about what they pejoratively dub 'ideology', by which they mean ideas or conceptual frameworks, reflects the fact that for generations Conservatives managed on the basis of implicit beliefs incorporating practices which had evolved over time and ideas derived from classical philosophy and Protestant Christianity. As Nigel Lawson was later to argue in a CPS pamphlet, Conservatives had managed quite well without a structure of explicit ideas until Liberals and Labour elaborated theirs, following which the Conservatives had no alternative but to match them. MT filled the gap by her Conservative beliefs: the puritan ethic; personal responsibility; patriotism. Conversion of these beliefs into ideas as a basis for policies was left till later, too late.

I did not meet her till the Spring of 1974, under Keith Joseph's auspices, after he had accepted my outline for the 'we were wrong' Upminster Speech in June, which was to become the first in his series on 'Reversing the Trend', rejecting Butskellism and advocating radical Tory counter-revolution. The speech was designed to launch his new think-tank (soon to be named the Centre for Policy Studies) which Heath had suggested after Keith had declined the shadow cabinet portfolio offered, in the hope that it would keep him busy and out of mischief expounding Butskellism and Europhilia, but which I had persuaded him – I am still not sure how – to devote to expounding radical Conservatism, which eventually became known as Thatcherism.

He decided to offer Margaret Thatcher the deputy-chairmanship. She was then fifty, with grown-up children, but there was then something girlish about her: her enthusiasms; the simplicity of her beliefs; her trusting nature. She reminded me of nineteenth century explorers, aware that their ambiance was strange and dangerous but unquestioningly confident in themselves. At the time, she believed strongly that Keith should become Party leader, and that only Lady Joseph's reluctance to give him full support was preventing this. Since Keith had always been the antithesis of a leader, this convinced me that she was a bad judge of character.

She was unapologetically aware that her grasp of ideas, politics and economics was insufficient for the role in which she was subconsciously casting herself, and had no hesitation in casting me as a second John the Baptist after Keith.

When we first met, her chosen persona was as an upper middle class Tory lady in twin-set and pearls. But her first reactions to Keith's epoch-making 'we were wrong' Upminster speech, praising it for its 'economy with words', suggested to me an alternative persona, the puritan grocer's daughter, bringing faith and common sense to the convoluted world of public affairs and economic controversy: 'economics is Greek for running a household.' Peel's dictum that a Prime Minister must be 'an uncommon common man' was relevant. Her outward demeanour as a housewife shopping at Marks and Spencers reassured many who are basically suspicious both of politicians and of political ideas, believing that politics and government ought to be much simpler.

In opposition, and to some extent in government, we worked closely for hours on end, often à deux, sometimes with her PPS's. During the day, we worked in the Leader of the Opposition's office, overlooking Boudicca's statue, evenings and weekends we worked at her home in Flood Street, Chelsea, in the dining room, with a typewriter on the table. When we had progressed, she would go into the kitchen to prepare food, giving instructions though the linking door, exemplifying her dual roles. In her flat at Number 10 – living over the shop – she was in and out of the kitchen, as no other Premier ever was.

It is not easy for labourers in the vineyard to get into the minds of the great, who achieve greatness precisely because their mind and spirit work distinctively. I found that she possessed a razor-sharp mind and great application, but because they had been honed in natural science and the law her thinking was linear rather than lateral. But it was her will which marked her out. Though power wrought its effects on her in time, she remained free to the end from the side and self-importance which it inflicts on so many politicians. I remember an occasion when I had arranged to bring an American to see her, who ran a media-monitoring unit, which I believed we should emulate. As we waited in the ground-floor reception at Number 10, she suddenly appeared in the doorway in stockinged feet and took us up to her study. Conversely, she never fully acquired the art of suffering fools gladly, so essential in democratic politics. It was her body language rather than her politics which so enraged Geoffrey Howe that he steeled himself to resign his benefice and stab her in the back.

In the course of time her enthusiasm for ideas seemed to lapse, while the ironclad self confidence, which had been so essential when she was an outsider storming the citadel became an impediment. The leadership election, which she had lost by four votes, epitomised the personal dimension in her trajectory. Had she stayed and fought it, personally meeting waverers and lukewarm supporters, and impressing on enthusiastic supporters not to disqualify their vote by writing slogans on their ballot paper, and hence spoiling it, she would have come home comfortably. Instead, misled by naïve canvass reports which took voting promises at face value (since many MPs, character-istically, backed themselves both ways) and hankerings after the glory of the prestigious Paris end of the cold war summit which coincided with the leadership contest, she went to Paris and left re-election to look after itself. Her fall, like her rise, was the stuff of which cautionary fables are made.

As I argued earlier, Margaret Thatcher's rise to power had come about by the interplay of chance and 'necessity' (Hegel's rendering of the Greek *ananke*) between the accidental, incidental and inherent, per Aristotle. I had been catalyst to this process. When, after her 1983 election victory (which looked much larger than it actually was) Margaret Thatcher was persuaded to dispense with people and ideas which had brought her to power in the first place, it was not apparent to her that she might be eroding the ideal cement of her own power base, that her native hue of resolution might depend on the ideas which had fed into Thatcherism. In the event, de-Shermanisation of the CPS and its milieu, which had been the seed-bed of Thatcherism, set in motion de-Thatcherisation, leaving her bereft of a lodestar and vulnerable to her colleagues-cum-enemies. Legend and literature contain many such instances.

BARONESS MILLER OF HENDON

CHAIRMAN OF THE WOMEN INTO PUBLIC LIFE CAMPAIGN
1986–92

Doreen Miller was raised to the peerage in 1993 after serving as the Chairman of the Women into Public Life Campaign and the Chairman of Barnet Family Health Services Authority. She is currently the Opposition Spokesman for Employment and an Opposition Spokesman on Trade & Industry.

కళ

Whipping Margaret

It is sometimes said that Margaret Thatcher did not do enough to promote the interests of women in political and public life – especially in regard to appointments to her Government.

However, her attitude to women in both spheres was entirely consistent with her general political philosophy: people as well as businesses make progress according to ability; no special favours, no quotas. Market forces, if you wish.

My own personal experiences of her was quite different.

In 1979, just prior to the election, I was given the opportunity of playing a major part in the production of a pamphlet for her constituency, in the form of a newspaper called 'The Finchley Leader', one edition of which had the prescient front page headline 'We shall be the next Government'.

Time moved on, and while Prime Minister she took time to encourage the work of the 300 Group, an all-party organisation dedicated to getting more women into the House of Commons of which I was Chairman – not, you will notice, Chair or Chairwoman or Chairperson! In 1991, at the invitation of David Astor and the 300 Group she unveiled a plaque at the house where Nancy Astor lived while she was an MP.

In 1990, it was at her special request in her capacity, not as Prime Minister, but as a local MP, and with the concurrence of the other three local MPs, that I became the Chairman of the Barnet Family Health Services Authority because, as she explained, since its area included her own constituency of Finchley, she regarded it as a politically sensitive appointment which was likely to be targetted by pressure groups and required someone with experience in politics as well as the organisational ability to perform the task.

This was the first of three public appointments which I have no doubt contributed to my CV coming to the notice of 'the powers that be', contributing to my elevation to the House of Lords, so I shall always be grateful for that particular nomination.

As a Whip in the House of Lords, she was not amongst the group of peers for whom I was responsible. Ex Prime Ministers get someone far more senior than the absolutely lowest office holder in the government hierarchy (because that is where government whips in the Lords stand on the organisation chart – and for a long time I was the most junior of them).

Nevertheless, as someone who had the unique opportunity of being both in touch with the government on the one side and the grass roots on the other I sometimes wanted to remind her of the contents of the current hymn sheet when as sometimes happened she departed from it. But how?

There is a riddle which asks, 'how does a porcupine make love?' The answer is 'very gingerly'.

I have to say that when I tactfully and as casually as I could 'had a word', explaining what the activists in the field were thinking, she listened carefully, nodded – and continued to go about on her own way. The point is that there was never any suggestion of 'who do you think you are talking to?'

Perhaps that says something about her character and what made her the great Prime Minister that she was. There was time to hear a different opinion, but in the end it would be she who made up her own mind and her own decision.

Fortunately for this country her instincts were many more times often right than wrong.

I have no doubt that many other contributors to this collection of anecdotes, with a far closer connection with Margaret Thatcher will be able to give a detailed picture of her in her high office.

All I can do is to speak of her as a colleague in local politics, in her little publicised capacity as a supporter of women's interests and as a member of the greatest legislative chamber in the world that anyone can have the privilege of belonging to.

I believe that when she is judged by history – history that which will be written far removed from the hurly-burly of current politics and political disputes – her many achievements for the benefit of our country will outlive the 'little local difficulties' in which she is still occasionally involved.

THE EARL OF CAITHNESS

MINISTER 1985–94

Malcolm Caithness served as a junior minister under Margaret Thatcher from 1985 and then later under John Major until 1994. His Government career spanned numerous departments including the Department of Transport, the Home Office, the Department of the Environment, the Treasury and the Foreign and Commonwealth Office. He currently serves as an elected hereditary peer in the House of Lords.

ॐॐ

A very 'big' person

It is hard to think back and picture accurately Britain twenty-one years ago. The West had lost its sense of purpose and the State dictated vast areas of our lives. We seemed to be in a quagmire from which no Government could extract us. Margaret Thatcher was the first leader in Europe to stand up and say there was a better way. Her governments were pioneers in changing the role of the State and enhancing the freedom of the individual to what we, and most of the rest of the world, now take for granted. The reforms were bitterly contested, mostly by those who are now advocating the same policies. At times she was portrayed as uncaring and seeming not to listen. However I found a different side to her.

Just after I had been appointed a whip in the early summer of 1984 she held a reception at 10 Downing Street to which I was asked. I had never been there, nor had I met my Prime Minister. She was receiving her guests at the top of the stairs and, in due turn, I was introduced to her. She stopped receiving her guests and took time to show me, the most junior member of her team and youngest in the room, some of the pictures in the house and explain its history to me. She then went back to her other guests. That action is the mark of a very 'big' person and considerate hostess.

My first important working meeting with my Prime Minister was after about six months as Minister for Prisons in the Home Office. I thought I had a reasonable understanding of my brief by then. In our discussions it was soon apparent that she knew more of the detail and 'nitty gritty' of the policy than I did. It amazed me that someone with so many other issues to contend with had such detailed knowledge and cared so much about one aspect of a junior Minister's portfolio. I realised then that if, in future, I did not know more than her at every meeting concerned with areas of my responsibility I would not last long in her government.

Some years later in 1989, as a Minister in the Department of the Environment, I was due to attend a very difficult negotiation in Brussels over emissions of 'greenhouse' gases. Nick Ridley, the Secretary of State, had backed my proposals for a tightening of standards leading to a reduction in emissions, but this would be costly to our industries as expensive new equipment would be needed. We produced a paper on it and all the other departments briefed against it so a meeting was called to decide what to do. Nick was tied up in the Chamber of the House of Commons on the Housing Bill, so I had to argue the case with a serried rank of Cabinet Ministers opposed to me. Against the wishes of some of her most senior Ministers she backed Nick and my proposals and that became the new Government position. Rightly she then espoused the policy in typically forthright terms. Since then the standards have been tightened yet again, but at the time she was making a bold new move by backing a minority view.

LORD POWELL OF BAYSWATER

PRIME MINISTER'S ADVISER ON FOREIGN AFFAIRS AND DEFENCE 1984–91

Charles Powell served as a diplomat in Washington, Bonn and EC Brussels before becoming the Prime Minister's private secretary and adviser on foreign affairs and defence, a position that he held from 1984 until 1991.

'My God, that man is so German'

After a previous Foreign Office career spanning twenty years during most of which Britain's standing and influence in the world steadily declined, I found working for Margaret Thatcher on foreign affairs an exhilarating if sometimes tempestuous experience. Her extraordinary will-power and leadership broke the seemingly endless and inevitable cycle of national decline, restored the nation's confidence and gave us the feeling that Britain once again counted in the world.

It was not exactly a tranquil experience. She was non-stop and so was the turbulence created by her legendary hand-bag. Foreign visits were invariably conducted at the double: I think our record was seven countries – Malaysia, Singapore, Brunei, Indonesia, Sri Lanka, India and Saudi Arabia – in eight days. Yet only once in twelve years did a slip of the tongue give away that she forgot which country she was in. That had been more of a problem for one of her predecessors, Sir Alec Douglas-Home, whose wife used to follow him down the aircraft steps on foreign visits chanting: 'China, Alec, China' or whatever the country was.

Of course it helped being a woman: that made her more easily identifiable amongst world leaders. But it was the personality and the policies which counted. The strong and unyielding stand against Communism, in partnership with Ronald Reagan, which led to the West's triumph in the Cold War: victory in the Falklands: getting 'our money' back from Europe: extricating Rhodesia from illegality to independence: standing by our American allies over Libya when others turned their backs: ensuring a resolute response to Saddam's invasion of Kuwait. All these turned her into a heroic figure, the Iron Lady of legend. She did not win all her battles, with German reunification the prime example. And she fought some unnecessary ones, mainly with her own colleagues in Government. But she indisputably raised Britain's international profile; and whatever the pained expressions and snooty comments of old-style diplomats, she advanced Britain's interests. In the simplest terms, we were taken a lot more seriously in 1990 than in 1980.

Margaret Thatcher was never a diplomat and proud not to be one. She had no time for courtly phrases and carefully drafted compromises. She was ready to go toe to toe with any world leader from Gorbachev to Deng Xiaoping. She had the huge advantage of being unembarrassable, a quality not always shared by her Private Secretary. I recall a meeting with President Mitterrand in Paris during which the President took her for a stroll in the Elysée garden. I sat down in the sun for a blissful moment of peace with my French opposite number, only to be shaken from my reverie by the sight of Mitterrand hurrying back, clutching a blood-stained handkerchief to himself. For a moment of panic I thought: 'she's gone too far this time, she's bitten him!' It turned out to have been an over-enthusiastic puppy which did the damage, but it was a nasty moment.

She was deeply suspicious of the Foreign Office as an institution, believing that its tribal culture led it to give too much weight to the foreigners and too little to Britain's interests, as well as having its own agenda on European integration. She would gleefully recount the old chestnut of the man asking a policeman in Whitehall during the Second World War black-out, which side the Foreign Office was on and being told: 'the other'. There were some memorable rages, as when she demanded to inspect the gift which the Foreign Office had thoughtfully procured for her to take to Gorbachev and discovered a handsome pair of silver-backed hair-brushes.

'But he's completely bald', she stormed, and a messenger had to be sent out from London with a replacement gift.

Fortunately the prejudice against the institution was matched by a high regard for many of its most distinguished servants, who were granted a sort of amnesty for the misdeeds – real or imagined – of their *alma mater*.

Margaret Thatcher's diplomacy was less concerned with making friends than with winning battles. That had a downside in her relationship with Chancellor Kohl, who went to great pains to win her friendship. This extended to inviting her to spend a weekend in his home-town in the Rhineland, including a visit to his favourite tavern to sample his favourite dish of pig's stomach. Margaret Thatcher's appetite seemed mysteriously to fade as Chancellor Kohl went back for seconds and thirds. We moved on to the great crypt of the Romanesque Cathedral of Speyer where Margaret Thatcher was invited to inspect the tombs of Holy Roman Emperors, precursors of earlier attempts at European Union. While she undertook this task without visible enthusiasm, Chancellor Kohl took me behind a pillar: 'now she's seen me here in my own home-town, right at the heart of Europe and on the border with France', he said, 'surely she will understand that I am not just German, I am European. You must convince her'. I accepted the assignment with trepidation. As soon as we boarded our aircraft for the return to Britain, Margaret Thatcher threw herself into her seat, kicked off her shoes and announced with the finality which was her trade-mark: 'My God that man is so German.' Gutless, I aborted my mission to persuade her otherwise.

Margaret Thatcher captured the imagination of people outside Britain even more than at home. One only had to witness the rapturous welcome which she received from huge crowds in Poland, Russia, Georgia and Armenia in the late 1980s to realise that she symbolised their hope for relief from Communist tyranny. Or to experience her ability to rouse an American audience with her forthright rhetoric on democracy, the rule of law and the need for strong defence. Or to be swept away by the ecstatic welcome of crowds in Africa, despite fatalistic Foreign Office warnings that she would be shunned.

A sometimes embattled but always defiant figure, she invariably stood up for Britain. And just as she galvanised Britain itself, so she galvanised other countries' view of Britain as once again a strong, dependable, worthwhile ally and a country which gives a lead in world affairs. We still benefit from that.

DAVID PRIOR

MP FOR NORTH NORFOLK

David Prior was elected to Parliament as MP for North Norfolk in 1997 and currently serves as the Deputy Chairman of the Conservative Party.

જ⊷ઙ

A Natural Curiosity

I can count the number of times I have met Margaret Thatcher on the fingers of one hand, and I doubt she would remember me. The first time I met her was in 1982 when I was working for Sir Ian MacGregor, when he was Chairman of British Steel. I was asked to go to Number 10 Downing Street to brief Mrs Thatcher, as she then was, about the overlap between the nationalised British Steel and the private special steel companies in Sheffield. She was giving a speech later that week in Sheffield.

All I remember is that she had a keen interest in metallurgy, and the whole process of special steel making, which greatly surprised me. She seemed to have more genuine interest in the effects of molybdenum and vanadium on the properties of the final product than she did the squabbles between British Steel and the private steel sector. She had the natural curiosity of the scientist and inventor, as well as her strong beliefs in freedom and responsibility, which made her such a great Prime Minister.

SIR GEORGE GARDINER

MP FOR REIGATE 1974–97

Sir George Gardiner was the Conservative MP for Reigate from 1974 until March 1997 when he joined the Referendum Party. He is the Author of Margaret Thatcher: From Childhood to Leadership *(1975) and* A Bastard's Tale *(Aurum, 1999).*

꩜

A cell of revolutionaries

The 1975 Thatcher Campaign Team used to meet in a subterranean Committee Room below the Commons under the shrewd chairmanship of Airey Neave. Our task was to conduct a discreet canvass of how most of the 276 Conservative MPs intended to vote in the leadership ballot, all duly recorded by William Shelton. We were an odd bunch: backbench worthies like Julian Ridsdale, John Stokes, and Angus Maude; hard-hitters like Norman Tebbit and Nicholas Ridley; the lovable rogue Billy Rees-Davies, severely war-wounded and minus an arm; and a few like myself, products of the previous year's elections. Airey then reported to Margaret's sponsor, Sir Keith Joseph. We were as unlikely a cell of revolutionaries as ever you could find – yet did we realise quite what a hurricane force we were about to release on the British people, a woman who would break the miserable mould of post-war politics together with its complacent and stifling corporatism? Did we hell!

Few of us then could envisage a time when the mighty union leaders could no longer aspire to dictate Cabinet policy or indeed bring down Governments. In a speech nine days after her election as Leader she dealt with the issue very cautiously: often when you find a solid rock blocking your path, she said, it was best not to charge it head on, but to move round or undermine it. What on earth, we asked, did she mean?

Not until we were into the following Parliament did we begin to get an inkling of what we had done. The first Thatcher manifesto, after all, was a pretty cautious document – new laws to curb picketing, slight tightening of the law on the closed shop, fresh curbs on immigration, more incentives through taxation – but not much more.

At the time the leadership election was called I was on christian name terms with Margaret, but nothing more. Then a publisher asked me to write her biography, and she agreed to co-operate. So it was that in spring that year I went regularly on Saturdays to her flat in Chelsea's Flood Street with my tape-recorder. During these sessions I came to realise just how much her roots in Grantham meant to her. She was eloquent in describing her father, Alderman Alfred Roberts, the grocers' shop run by her family over which they lived, the local Methodist Church and its culture, and how the privations and hopes of World War II made her what she was. Only years later did she amplify this in her own memoirs.

From then until her downfall in 1990 I was one of her foremost backbench supporters, and for the final six years of her Premiership saw her regularly as Chairman of the '92', a group of around 100 right-of-centre Tory MPs.

If you stood by Margaret in tough times she was supportive and loyal in return. But I am always amazed by the Press caricature of her as an impetuous bully, happily handbagging everyone in sight. In fact, she was immensely cautious. So anxious was she to pacify the old Wets and supporters of her predecessor, Edward Heath, that after victory in 1979 she gave them preponderance in her Cabinet for eighteen months until she reshaped it more in the image of the Party as a whole. Peter Walker, who ran Heath's leadership campaign, was brought into her Cabinet, and even while he was delivering coded speeches attacking her policies she kept him there. Privatisation of the public utilities was barely heard of until just before the 1983 election. When miners' leader Arthur Scargill first challenged her on pit closures she backed off; not until she was equipped to beat him did she come back fighting.

Contrary to Press myth, she was tolerant of other points of view, provided they were well argued. I flouted three-line whips many times, but never did she see this as an attack upon herself, nor did it affect our trusting relationship The totalitarianism that crept into the Party after her downfall had no roots in her. In Opposition, when I was among those advising her twice a week in preparation for Prime Minister's Questions, I helped to organise a rebellion on the renewal of economic sanctions against what was then Rhodesia. We inflicted humiliation on the Tory Whips, yet when I turned up somewhat abashed to help advise her next day (along with Geoffrey Pattie, who had rebelled too) she was in teasing mood: 'What's the matter with you two? Have you lost your tongues?' She knew our rebellion was based on principle.

Never did she allow her high office to diminish her concern for her friends. Once, during her first Parliament as Prime Minister, I called one evening at Downing Street to compare notes with Ian Gow, then her PPS. I met him in her flat, where we watched the TV news. Our intention was to go on to his club for dinner – until Margaret arrived unexpectedly early. 'You two boys must be hungry.' Despite our protests she disappeared into the little kitchen, took chicken kievs, peas and carrots from the fridge – then insisted we sat at the kitchen table to join her for supper. Before we were finished Denis arrived, and he made coffee. Was there any other significant nation in the world, I asked myself, whose Prime Minister (or President, as the case may be) would insist on cooking supper for unexpected visitors?

When I was in hospital in 1992 awaiting bypass surgery she sent encouraging messages every few days. The weekend before my operation I wrote a leader-page article for the Sunday Express; no sooner was I out of my anaesthetic than there was a note from Margaret saying how spot-on my piece had been. When I was a lunch guest at Chequers one Sunday I watched her crouching beside Margaret Tebbit's wheelchair lifting food on a fork to her mouth. She felt it deeply that the IRA's Brighton bomb, which left Margaret Tebbit paralysed, was in fact intended for her.

It often seemed that the media were determined never to present this human side to her character. There was the time I persuaded her to perform the official opening of the new East Surrey Hospital in my constituency. It was the first hospital she had ever opened; Geoffrey Howe, Kenneth Baker and I joined her, since the hospital served our constituencies; Health Secretary Norman Fowler and Reigate's Mayor were also there. The afternoon's itinerary was way behind as Margaret spent far more time than was scheduled at bedsides, listening to individual cases and sympathising. Likewise she spent far longer with staff than had been planned, asking and answering probing questions. Cameras followed her all the way. Yet what did the BBC report? Only that some trade unionist at a tiny demonstration outside had thrown an egg at her car! Big deal.

Her final downfall could not have been more brutal. Over the preceding year I and officers of the '92' often warned her of the dangers lurking, but she always believed she could face her critics down. Then Geoffrey Howe plunged the first dagger over European policy, opening the way for Michael Heseltine's challenge; Heseltine said he had a better alternative to the poll tax, which was deeply unpopular, and as the election drew near many Tory MPs were anxious.

She had a so-called Campaign Team, but there was no evidence of a proper campaign; utterly complacent, they gave her totally wrong advice. Worse still, she was in Paris for the election. Not until evening the day after the first ballot (which she led, though just short of an outright win) were I and others in the '92' able to get through to her. But by then it was too late; her resolution had been broken by Cabinet colleagues pledging support while telling her she could never win – 'treachery with a smile on its face,' as she put it later. I will never forget her then, on the verge of tears as we pleaded with her to stay in the race, which I am convinced to this day she would have won with a last-minute campaign worthy of the name.

I doubt whether we shall see the like of her as Prime Minister again. Yet the woman who sent packing the likes of Scargill, General Galtieri and the hooded assassins of the IRA, who restored pride to her country after years of creeping socialism, and who with President Reagan hastened the end of the evil Soviet Empire, was brought down by a clutch of her own MPs in a blue funk over a looming election, and by Ministers who owed her everything.

LORD MACKAY OF CLASHFERN

LORD CHANCELLOR 1987–97

*After a distinguished legal career in Scotland, James Mackay was raised to the
peerage in 1979. He served as Lord Advocate from 1979 until 1984 and then as
Lord Chancellor from 1987 until1997.*

ॐॐ

An offer I couldn't refuse

I had the privilege of being appointed to serve as Lord Advocate in
Margaret Thatcher's first administration in May 1979. We had
never met and my appointment was offered and accepted over the
telephone. I was privileged to continue as Lord Advocate into her
second administration when I became a Judge of the Supreme Courts
of Scotland. On her recommendation I was appointed a Lord of
Appeal in Ordinary, one of the two Scottish full time judges in the
House of Lords in October 1985.

In October 1987 I was listening to a debate in the House on the
Criminal Justice Bill after the judicial sitting had terminated when I
received a message from the Secretary of the then Leader of the
House, Viscount Whitelaw, to ring urgently the Prime Minister's
private secretary. That I did and was invited immediately to come over
to meet the Prime Minister.

I duly went over to Number 10 thinking the Prime Minister had
an inquiry of some kind that she wished me to undertake. Whenever
I arrived at Number 10 I was ushered into the Prime Minister's study.
She arose to welcome me, immediately asked me to sit down and sat

in the chair opposite. She informed me that Lord Havers, the Lord Chancellor, had come to see her a little earlier that day and had tendered his resignation as Lord Chancellor on the grounds of ill health. She asked me to become Lord Chancellor in succession to him. As you can imagine, this was an extraordinary surprise and I answered that she knew my commitment to Sunday as a special day, to which she replied that she was also of the view that it should be a special day and that there would be no difficulty on that score. I then said that I would need to consult my wife but the Prime Minister knew better than any that when one is in an important public office there are profound effects for wife and family. She said 'certainly, please go and ring her up' so I was duly presented with the telephone at the other end of the table from that at which we were sitting and I telephoned home, only to find that my wife was out. The Prime Minister said 'we are very anxious to put the news out tonight of the new appointment along with Lord Havers' resignation and therefore I am very keen to have your answer as soon as possible'. I left promising to let her know as soon as I could.

As you can imagine, I kept ringing home to Edinburgh at frequent intervals and eventually my wife came in and when I told her my message she said 'oh well, you can hardly refuse that offer'. I duly telephoned to the Prime Minister's private secretary but he declined to take the message and put me through to the Prime Minister herself. I told her my wife's reply and in view of that reply I was happy and honoured to accept her invitation. She kindly said that she was delighted and that arrangements would be made for the intimation as soon as possible. The intimation was in fact made on the seven o'clock news that evening.

Shortly thereafter my wife was in London and we met the Prime Minister in Speakers' House. When we met I said to the Prime Minister. 'This was the lady for whose reply we were waiting the other day'. And with that charm and grace which was so characteristic of the

Prime Minister she gave a very nice bow and said to my wife: 'We were very delighted with your reply.'

In the order of precedence which is established for State occasions the Lord Chancellor takes precedence immediately after the Archbishop of Canterbury, before the Archbishop of York and before the Prime Minister. I hope it is easy to imagine that I felt very embarrassed, and so did my wife, at the idea of preceding the Prime Minister. Again, her charm and grace always showed and on such occasions she would always encourage us to take our proper place in front of her making it a lot easier for us to do so than if we had not been shown that charm. I remained as Lord Chancellor during the remainder of the tenure of Margaret Thatcher as Prime Minister and she was always most respectful and very clear about the importance of the Executive, not interfering in the work and affairs of the judiciary.

MATTHEW PARRIS

BROADCASTER AND COLUMNIST

After working for the Conservative Research Department and in Mrs Thatcher's Private Office, Matthew Parris became the MP for West Derbyshire in 1979, a position he held until 1986. Since then he has worked as a television presenter and most famously as a parliamentary sketch writer for The Times.

చ్ళ

I have never dared ask . . .

When I was a Branch Chairman of South Battersea Conservative Association we welcomed Margaret Thatcher, as Leader of the Opposition, on an official visit to our neighbourhood. I and others were deputed to guide her on a walkabout down the Northcote Road (a little market) for the local Press. This was about 1978.

She spotted a council workman driving a motorised street cleaner. After speaking to him she began to climb into the driver's seat crying: 'Show me how this thing works and I will clean the street. Only a woman knows how to get into corners men cannot reach'.

చ్ళ

In 1978 the RSPCA asked Mrs Thatcher to present me (at the time I was her Correspondence Secretary) with their award for bravery in rescuing a dog from the River Thames.

The ceremony took place on Westminster Bridge in the presence of a number of officials, the dog (Jason) and some photographers. Privately, Mrs Thatcher thought I had been mad to rescue the dog. But she was a kindly employer and no doubt spotted a good photo opportunity too.

During the ceremony the dog began (as little male dogs too often do) to mate with her elegantly-stockinged leg. She took absolutely no notice and carried on smiling for the cameras. To this day I have never been quite sure whether she realised what was going on down below, and have never dared ask her.

LORD OWEN

LEADER OF THE SDP 1983–92

Dr David Owen served as Foreign Secretary under James Callaghan from 1977 until 1979. In 1981 he resigned from the Labour Party to form the Social Democratic Party with Roy Jenkins, Bill Rodgers and Shirley Williams. He became leader of the SDP after the 1983 election, resigning in 1987 over the merger with the Liberal Party. He was re-elected Leader of the SDP in 1988 and remained in that position until 1992 when he became Chairman of the International Conference on former Yugoslavia. Lord Owen now sits as a cross-bencher in the House of Lords.

கூஷ்

Expensive scent and alcohol

M y first personal memory of Margaret Thatcher was as Secretary of State for Education in the early 1970s. A medical friend had come to dinner with her in the House of Commons to discuss a young patient and when she bumped into me in the division lobby she asked if I would go and have a drink with them. It was a revealing occasion, for as the conversation developed Margaret Thatcher's best and worst qualities were on display: consideration for a young constituent and the wish to get to the bottom of a problem coupled with a total inability to comprehend how any seventeen year old could be depressed.

As Foreign Secretary we met at many official functions. In April 1979 I was interviewed in the *Daily Mirror* and said, 'I saw her the other evening the House of Commons and for the first time she looked really rather attractive. She'd had a couple of whiskies and was quite glowing, in the nicest possible way. She came over, smiling that special smile of hers, and wafted a combination of expensive scent and alcohol over me'.

This was described by an angry Conservative Party as the first dirty trick of the forthcoming election campaign. It was mild compared to President Mitterrand's remark later that 'she has the lips of Marilyn Monroe and the smile of Caligula'. But John Junor, the editor of the *Sunday Express*, who had lunch with her next day, found her relaxed, even flattered. It was at about this time that I had realised that we faced in her a far more formidable opponent than it was fashionable for most Labour politicians to admit.

In addressing Margaret Thatcher's leadership I believe the 1984 miners' dispute showed her at her best. She had cut her losses and settled when challenged by Joe Gormley in 1981 and had then planned ahead for the inevitable confrontation with Arthur Scargill. When the pit deputies union, NACODS, threatened sympathetic strike action at the end of October 1984 I was extremely worried that any concession to them could be used by Scargill as a face-saver. I took the opportunity of being in the same room as Margaret Thatcher to have a private talk with her. She seemed genuinely pleased to find that my worries about letting Arthur Scargill off the hook were exactly the same as hers. She made no attempt to conceal the fact that some of her colleagues wanted to settle but that she was adamantly against it. She was clear-sighted about the danger of Scargill being able to claim a spurious victory. When the end came in March 1985, fifty-one weeks after the strike had started, it was the miners who disowned their leaders by streaming back to work with their funds running low and good men with their self-respect in tatters. But for the country as a whole it was essential for our self-confidence that intimidation and violence could be resisted without tear gas or mobilising the armed services. The police, with a few exceptions, did extremely well.

Meeting with the Prime Minister at Number 10 in 1983 I raised the question of SDP representation at the Cenotaph. I was barely halfway through my case than she intervened to reject it, declaring that she was adamantly opposed to widening representation. Suddenly the atmosphere was heated. I told her bluntly that I could see absolutely no reason why a party that had attracted three and a half million voters should not be entitled to lay a wreath at the Cenotaph. Eventually I rose to go and said that I hoped that, since the decision was formally the Home Secretary's, she would give the matter renewed thought, otherwise I would have to take my case before the bar of public opinion. She became incandescent, alternating between a prim 'How could you?' to a furious 'How dare you?' The *Daily Telegraph* reported that the issue sharply divided Ministers, that many senior members of the Government were unhappy and that one of the service chiefs had actually objected to our exclusion. Newspapers up and down the country took our side. It was a good example of the basic fairness and decency of the British people asserting itself. Eventually Whitehall produced a formula to save the Prime Minister's face. What the whole episode showed was that though she was still totally dominant, she did not have an absolute hold on public opinion or newspaper editors and was politically deeply partisan as she showed by taking the salute at the Falkland Victory parade instead of the Queen.

On the morning of 15 April 1986, Britain woke up to find that during the night the Americans had bombed terrorist targets in Libya using F-111 aircraft from bases in Britain. The Prime Minister was under immediate attack for authorising their use. Opposition leaders, like me, opposed the action as illegal. In government, however, decisions have to be made and the choice is often between two evils. The lesser evil in this case was to support President Reagan's request and try to pretend, as Margaret Thatcher did, that it was covered under Article 51 of the UN Charter and was an act of self-defence, whereas it was really retaliation forbidden under the UN Charter. Having been given crucial military support by President Reagan during the Falklands War, Margaret Thatcher knew that she owed him similar support. Given her personality, she would have found it impossible to refuse, and it is to her credit, in such trying circumstances, that she gave permission.

When history assesses whether Margaret Thatcher was a great Prime Minister, this decision deserves to be weighed in the balance. Her refusal would have done immense damage to our relations with the Reagan Administration. She showed courage and loyalty but she also demonstrated one of the distinguishing features of great leadership, the ability to turn a blind eye to instructions or to legal niceties and just to follow one's instincts.

After her 1987 election victory it was Margaret Thatcher in Number 10 on 7 July 1988 who proposed quite directly to me that I should join the Conservatives. She had given a dinner for Lord Carrington to mark his retirement from the post of NATO Secretary General and had quite deliberately taken both Debbie, my wife, and me aside as we were leaving. In her blunt way she said to Debbie, 'Your husband has a big choice to make and it can no longer be avoided. There are only two serious parties in British politics and we women understand these things; it is time he made up his mind'. Debbie bridled and I politely refused to join the Conservative Party then, as I had refused all others who had raised the issue with me.

Margaret Thatcher's downfall began on Tuesday 30 October 1990 when she came to the House of Commons to make a statement on the Rome Summit. I helped wind her up by my question supporting the use of the veto. It was already clear from her earlier press conference, when she came out with her series of 'No, no, no' statements that she was on an emotional high and the adrenalin was pumping around her system as she handbagged every federalist proposal. She was taking her stand against the single currency and even beginning to backtrack from the agreed Government position over the hard ecu. I watched Geoffrey Howe's face as she answered these questions; he looked miserable and unhappy. Truly, I thought, a dead sheep. How wrong I proved to be. On 1 November Howe resigned and his forthright resignation speech gave Michael Heseltine the opening he longed for to challenge her leadership. She had been brought down by hubris over the European Community, not the poll tax. Her excessive self-confidence was by then being flaunted day by day in the face of friend or foe alike. She had pitted herself against her own source of power, the Conservative MPs. She had reached a stage where she was not only not listening to her parliamentary colleagues but was contemptuous of their views. The Cabinet had been reduced in stature and in quality. Majority opinion was frequently flouted or manipulated. People of substance, who well knew that Cabinet government was a great constitutional safeguard, had allowed this to develop over the years to the detriment of us all. It was not just because she was a woman that the Cabinet had been so supine but it was a material factor. With the Cabinet too weak to act, the Conservative MPs had shown their power.

As leader of the SDP I identified with those parts of her modernising counter-revolution which would help reverse Britain's economic decline. In the late 1990s Tony Blair, as leader of New Labour, has continued courageously with much the same modernising programme as, in fairness, did John Major before him. In a real sense this is a middle-class counter-revolution. It has by the start of the twenty-first century not yet achieved all its objectives, and its gains are not yet permanent. But it has made much needed changes in Britain. Its driving force and its chief architect was Margaret Thatcher, but it has not solely been her revolution, nor that of the Conservative Party. Indeed, in terms of monetary discipline the revolution began with Denis Healey and James Callaghan in 1976. Many people in the country have supported this counter-revolution who do not consider themselves party political.

Essentially it has sought to reassert a national self-confidence, to redis-cover the commercial market-orientated prosperity of the Victorian era which had not just been the product of our Empire but owed much to British invention, design, entrepreneurship, and industrial skill. It has also been a movement to reassert the role of the individual and to roll back the frontiers of an intrusive state. Sadly, Margaret Thatcher did not draw sufficiently on those other middle-class aspirations to serve the common good, to contribute to society as a whole, and indeed at times, as over the NHS, she quite unnecessarily upset those who held those values.

For centuries the middle-class had been patronised by those with hereditary wealth but they had found they could escape from their backgrounds and by their own efforts create wealth. The crippling levels of personal taxation in the 1960s and 1970s, however, began to make it virtually impossible for the law-abiding, tax-paying, middle-class citizen to accumulate wealth. All that has changed. Now the middle-class are the wealth creators. Britain has become the fourth wealthiest country and we ought now to be able to progressively alleviate poverty and improve our health and education services.

Margaret Thatcher was one of the four radical Prime Ministers this century. As you walk through the door into the Members' Lobby in the House of Commons, you face statues of Winston Churchill and Lloyd George, guarding the entrance to the Chamber of the House of Commons. On the right of the door is a statue of Clement Attlee and on the left a place left empty for another statue. There is no doubt that eventually, as the first woman Prime Minister, she will occupy that position and deservedly so.

SIR MICHAEL SPICER

MP FOR WORCESTERSHIRE WEST

Sir Michael Spicer has served as the Member for South Worcestershire from 1974 until 1997 and as the Member for West Worcestershire since 1997. He has held ministerial positions in the Department of Transport, Department of Energy and Department of the Environment.

രാൾ

A heroine of Elizabethan proportions

For a brief period, during the 1983 General Election I acted as Parliamentary Private Secretary to Margaret Thatcher. I was already Deputy Chairman of the party. As I had coordinated most of the detailed planning for the election, it was decided that I was sufficiently under the skin of what was going on to stand in as the Prime Minister's bag carrier in place of Ian Gow, who somewhat understandably, felt he needed to spend a little more time in his constituency of Eastbourne.

For me personally this was an exciting time. Margaret Thatcher was at the height of her prowess and Conservative policies were rampant. It was also for me a dangerous time. Margaret was always wary of those who had seen her at very close quarters in moments of high intensity. A few events may help to explain why my career went into somewhat of a tale-spin after my spell as PPS to the PM.

In the run up to the election I went on a practice tour with the PM around East Anglia. The trip took us to the privatised Felixstowe docks. When we were shown the highest crane in Europe, Margaret

Thatcher expressed a desire to climb it. Not a single voter waited for us at the top, but the world's press stood slobbering with expectancy at the bottom; this was partly because she was dressed in a tight black skirt in which she intended to climb hundreds of feet of vertical iron laddering.

My job was to climb up so closely behind her that they never got the photo they were hoping for. Going up was a piece of cake. Coming down required me to guide the Prime Ministerial feet from rung to rung. The inevitably embarrassing (for me) picture did make the national press.

Then there was the occasion during the election itself when we were landing at Edinburgh Airport. I was chatting to Denis Thatcher in the seat behind me. Next to me was David Wolfson; beside him was the PM. Suddenly there came what were for me fatal words, 'See what Michael thinks of the last sentence of the speech'. I looked at it and said something banal like 'could do with some tightening up'. The PM exploded – she was hyping herself up for a mass rally of supporters waiting for her in the Scottish capital. 'Why am I always surrounded by so much negative unhelpfulness?'

When we landed I was put in a car with the Secretary of State for Scotland and his Deputy and told to come up with a 'last sentence' before we reached the city centre. I was still fairly relaxed and told the others that this was normal before a big speech. We came up quite easily with not one, but three 'last sentences' – each to be tossed back at us with contempt when through screaming crowds we finally reached the anti-room to the conference hall. The Press Secretary was going frantic. 'We've got to give something to the press'. It was Denis who found the answer. 'Don't have a last sentence', he said, and the PM went on to make one of her best speeches of the campaign. I don't think I was ever forgiven.

Then there was the time when, returning from a BBC programme chaired by Sue Lawley, on which someone called in to be rude to the

PM about the sinking of the Belgrano, I was asked to enquire of the chairman of the party (my old friend Cecil Parkinson) whether we could abolish the BBC after we had won the election. The PM was a few yards from me when I made the appropriate telephone call from her flat in Number 10. She could therefore clearly hear the Chairman's expletives, and laughingly turned to Denis with the words 'I don't think the Chairman likes our little idea'. It was a good joke.

Winning that election was never much in doubt, so much so that I was asked to leave the Prime Minister's aeroplane in the last week of the campaign while it waited for me on the tarmac. I found the nearest payphone in the airport terminal. My instructions were to ask Tim Bell to 'pull' a three-page advertisement from all national newspapers attacking our rivals; the last page of this was a complete blank and was meant to represent the Liberal manifesto. 'People will think that a total waste of paper,' the Prime Minister had pronounced, 'especially as we are going to win'. She was right. The 1983 election was the high water-mark of Conservative fortunes in the second half of the twentieth century.

She was the victor, a heroine of Elizabethan proportions. As at the court of the Fairy Queen, it was best to be a pace or two apart. No politician progressed very far after working intimately at her court.

LORD JENKIN OF RODING

CABINET MINISTER 1979–85

Patrick Jenkin served in Margaret Thatcher's cabinet from 1979 until 1985 initially as Secretary of State for Social Services moving to the Department for Industry in 1981 and the Department of the Environment in 1983. He was raised to the peerage by Margaret Thatcher in 1987.

ॐ

Always Margaret

Let me get one thing clear from the outset: never in all the 50 odd years that I have known Margaret Thatcher have I, or any of her colleagues in the Party in either House of Parliament, ever called her 'Maggie'. Indeed, we never used the word, either when speaking to each other, let alone when speaking to her. She was always 'Margaret', or, in Cabinet, 'Prime Minister'.

I mention this because it is a stark illustration of the gulf that exists between the world of politics as portrayed by the populist media and the real world in which the players actually operate. Apart from seeing the word in print, where I suppose journalists were after a snappy headline, 'Maggie Swings Her Handbag Again', one remembers the left wing demos where the marchers chanted 'Maggie, Maggie, Maggie, Out, Out, Out!' By giving a political leader a label like that, it becomes easier to build up a caricature that is further and further removed from the real person.

I once discussed this phenomenon with her, not because I myself ever had a media nickname (I was not important enough to merit that!), but I was experiencing what everyone in politics faces from time to time – a concerted press campaign of mockery and vilification which bears little or no relation to reality. Margaret's reaction was immediate and very clear: 'I never read the nasty things they write about me, because it would only upset me,' she said, 'and I strongly advise you to do the same!'

She was of course right; the press soon tire of pursuing one victim and go off to find another. I suppose that it sells newspapers but I wonder how many people who might make a real contribution to public life are put off, not because they fear becoming victims of what I recently heard described as 'tabloid crucifixion', but because of the endless denigration all politicians.

Yet there is another side, and this story illustrates it. I was ending an election walkabout with our candidate in Monmouth when, just as I was getting into the car, a man came up, and in that wonderful lilting Welsh accent, said: 'Excuse me, Mr Jenkin, can I have a word?'

'Of course,' I replied, 'if you can keep it short'.

'Oh, it won't take long. I just wanted to tell you' (and his voice became very bitter) ' I hate your Party, I hate your policies, I hate everything you stand for!'

I replied, with a smile, 'It doesn't sound as if we are going to get your vote!'

'Oh, yes you will!' he said; 'she's the only one who knows what she wants to do!'

The chattering classes have never understood that phenomenon. Margaret Thatcher's appeal, over the heads of the political establishment and the media, to millions of ordinary men and women in all walks of life was remarkable and was the foundation of her long spell as Conservative leader and Prime Minister. Mr Blair sees himself cast in the same mould, but spin is no substitute for character and focus groups are no substitutes for conviction. It was the force of Margaret's character and the conviction with which she pursued her goals that won her the huge support of the people, and ensured that she won every general election she fought.

I have known Margaret for nearly 50 years. We met in the early 1950s when she and I served on the Executive Committee of what was then the Inns of Court Conservative and Unionist Society. She had joined the same set of Chambers in the Temple as I had though we worked with different barristers. She came with a rising reputation as a formidable politician: her election campaigns in Dartford in 1950 and 1951 had attracted the attention of senior MPs, including Iain Macleod, who had spotted a winner very early on.

I remember an early argument with Margaret over the future of the steel industry. I had spent a week campaigning in South Wales and had witnessed, in Ebbw Vale, the early effects of nationalisation on investment in new plant, and was unsure whether it would be wise to try to denationalise the industry. Instead, I argued for giving the workers a stake in the businesses through some form of co-partnership. Margaret was scornful; only the full rigour of market disciplines would ensure the industry's success, and we should not shrink from the inevitable political row. But when the next Conservative Government did denationalise it, it was followed by re-nationalisation by the next Labour Government. Thirty years after that argument with Margaret, as Industry Secretary in her first administration, I prepared British Steel for privatisation which was finally achieved during her period in office. She was of course right – but it took over 30 years for her wisdom to prevail.

Despite our long acquaintance, I was not sure that she was the right person to lead the Party after Ted Heath had been defeated in the 1975 leadership election and I voted for Willie Whitelaw. She was well aware of that, and though I was in the Shadow Cabinet, she asked Denis Thatcher if she could rely on my loyalty. He gave me a clean bill, and I retained my job as Energy Shadow. In January 1976 she asked me to take over shadowing the Health and Social Security portfolio. 'You have been in the Treasury and understand public finance. You must now experience the pressures on a major spending department,' she told me. However, she went on to impress on me the overriding need to avoid any new spending commitments at all. Indeed, I was asked to ensure that the DHSS would find savings to contribute to the cuts in public spending needed to finance tax cuts – and thereby hangs a tale.

In the run-up to the 1979 election we had committed ourselves to just two specific pledges in my policy area: we promised that we would not cut NHS spending, and we promised to protect pensions and other long-term benefits against rising prices. On health, where we were to inherit the 3-year projection of modest increases in spending (at constant prices), I realised that during the campaign I would be challenged as to what our pledge meant: did we mean no cuts but no increases, or did we mean that we would maintain the modest increases planned by our predecessors? I was able to persuade Geoffrey Howe, the Shadow Chancellor, that I had to be allowed to say that it was the second of these, and I duly gave the pledge on a BBC Newsnight programme.

That did not stop the Treasury demanding cuts and in Cabinet, I came under pressure from other Ministers to find my share of the savings to which we were all committed. I read out the very specific pledge I had given on TV and Margaret at once, with no argument, agreed that that must be honoured – and of course it was.

We then came to Social Security. The Treasury demanded that we should allow no uprating of the short-term benefits in our first year, and uprate the pension and long-term benefits by less than inflation. I had earlier warned Margaret (in private) that I would feel obliged to remind colleagues of the words she herself had used in a radio interview. 'Of course, you must; we must have all the facts whatever we decide'. She had, of course, repeated the Manifesto pledge 'to protect pensioners against rising prices'. When

I read this out, one colleague said 'Well, that's it, isn't it? Next business" Margaret made it clear that she would be willing to face the music if the Cabinet agreed with the Treasury's proposal, but, very wisely, her colleagues demurred, and we held to the pledge that she had given.

It is far too soon for history to form a balanced judgement on her reign as Prime Minister. The legends and the myths abound – of her abuse of colleagues, of her taking sides against her own Government, of her trying to force decisions before even hearing the Minister in charge; there was an element of truth in all this but of course it would be wholly wrong to think that it was the whole truth. She often showed that she had a sharper brain than most of the rest of us, and if she got her way it was because she had an amazing eye for detail. I will end with an illustration.

As Industry Secretary, I faced pressure from Sir Ian Macgregor, Chairman of British Steel, to allow him to close the loss-making Ravenscraig plant at Motherwell. However, this works had become a touchstone of the Scots' conviction that Mrs Thatcher 'did not care about Scotland'. I made it clear to Sir Ian that closure was not politically possible, and asked him to explore other options.

He knew the American steel industry well. He asked me to meet one of the American steel bosses and the three of us met over dinner at the Waterside Restaurant at Bray, not far from Heathrow. There, they put to me a scheme which involved British Steel, then still in the public sector, buying a quoted American company, Kaiser Steel, with a big works near Los Angeles in California. Ravenscraig would manufacture steel 'semis' – large slabs of steel – for shipment to California for Kaiser to manufacture heavy pipes for the then burgeoning oil fields in Alaska. This would be a new UK export market, which was too far from the big US steel makers in Chicago and Pennsylvania for them to supply competitively. I asked them to work it up, making it clear that this would need Cabinet approval.

Although the negotiations to buy Kaiser were difficult and complex, involving as they did the technicalities of the rules of the New York Stock Exchange, a way forward was devised. I had the firm support of the Scottish Secretary, George Younger, and of several other Ministers. It all came to a head at a late night meeting in the cabinet room at which there were present, not only Treasury and Foreign Office officials, but also our New York investment bankers and lawyers. The Prime Minister questioned these Americans minutely, asking them to spell out exactly the several different stages in the acquisition process, concentrating on the issue of the precise point at which British Steel, and therefore the British Exchequer, would become committed. One of the answers caught me by surprise, and I did not immediately react as I could not see the way round it. It appeared that we would be bound at an earlier point than I had been advised, before we had had a sight of the full documentation on Kaiser.

This was a moment of truth. Margaret had spotted a weakness in the arguments, and from that moment the discussion could lead only to a decision that we could not go ahead on the basis proposed, and we broke up long after midnight, very disappointed at this outcome.

The next day I discussed the decision with her and indicated that it might be very difficult to revive the project in a way that would get round the difficulty she had identified. 'When you did not respond immediately to the lawyer's point,' she told me, 'I realised that your Department had not thought of it, and that it would be too risky to go ahead on the basis you and George were proposing.'

Significantly, she had refused to allow Sir Ian to attend that meeting: 'He will bamboozle us all into supporting his scheme and I need to be certain that it would be safe to commit the Exchequer to the guarantee it would have to give'. I have no doubt that, as so often, she was right!

Most people who decide to go into politics have the perfectly laudable ambition of serving in office. I was very fortunate that six of my ten years on the Government Front Bench were in Margaret

Thatcher's cabinets. Although she and I had several monumental rows during these years, I will always look back on those six years as the high point in my political career. When I retired to the backbenches in 1985, the *Guardian* chided me for an excess of loyalty to her. All I can say in response is that she earned it, and I have no regrets!

PATRICK NICHOLLS

MP FOR TEIGNBRIDGE

Patrick Nicholls has been the MP for Teignbridge since 1983. He served as a Parliamentary Under Secretary of State at the Department of Employment and later at the Department of the Environment. He is currently an opposition spokesman on Agriculture, Fisheries and Food.

࿐

Sadly missed

On the Monday following the General Election in 1987, the Under Secretaries were being appointed. Having been told I was to be responsible for Trades Union reform, apparently on the basis that I had been a successful divorce lawyer, I was invited to a drinks party that evening at Downing Street.

All the new Under Secretaries arrived and were standing ramrod straight with a glass of sherry waiting for the Prime Minister to come in. Uncharacteristically she was slightly late. She bustled in some ten minutes later and said: 'I have just had a meeting of the Cabinet. What a load of moaning minnies. They all said they were tired but I told them they weren't.'

A number of us saw the possibilities in this statement. Only I was rash enough to follow them up by asking: 'And when you told them they weren't tired, did they believe you Prime Minister?'

Without a trace of irony or humour she looked straight at me and said, 'Patrick, if I told them they are not tired, they are not tired.'

She was like that, Mrs Thatcher. She is sadly missed.

SIR PETER EMERY

MP FOR EAST DEVON

Sir Peter Emery was first elected as the MP for Reading in 1959 and served there until 1966. He was Member for Honiton from 1967 until 1997 and has been the Member for East Devon since 1997.

৵৵

Briefing Margaret

T here are, of course, many stories. One of the least known was when she was appointed by Edward Heath to be the front-bench spokesman on Power, taking over from Sir John Eden and being the first woman to be given this appointment. At the time I was Vice-Chairman of the backbench committee on Power, of which she, as the frontbench spokesman, was Chairman.

I went to brief her in her flat one morning soon after her appointment. We discussed all matters that were dealt with by the Ministry, including iron, steel, gas, electricity, nuclear power and the coal industry. Towards lunchtime Margaret had to leave for a luncheon appointment, and I said that the only outstanding matter was the oil industry. I was then a director of Philips Petroleum UK and I said that I could fill her in on this whenever it suited her.

She turned to me and said, with a twinkle in her eye, 'Peter, you don't have to bother. I sleep with the oil industry every night.' Of course Denis was then a Director of Burmah Oil.

LORD ARMSTRONG OF ILMINSTER

SECRETARY OF THE CABINET 1979–87

Robert Armstrong joined the civil service in 1950 serving in numerous senior positions both within the Treasury, Home Office and Cabinet Office, eventually rising to be Head of the Home Civil Service in 1981. He currently sits as a cross-bencher in the House of Lords.

જ⊷ⓢ

A call from the White House

One afternoon in May 1982, during the war in the Falkland Isles, the telephone rang on my desk. It was the National Security Adviser in Washington: would I please set up the 'hot line', as the President wanted to speak to the Prime Minister? I told the Prime Minister's Private Secretary that the President would be calling to speak to the Prime Minister, activated the 'hot line', and went through to Number 10 for the call.

The conversation began with the usual exchange of pleasantries about health and weather, customary even in such high level conversations, and then the President asked how things were going in the South Atlantic. This was something that the Prime Minister had at her fingertips, and she spoke well and fluently for about a quarter of an hour. Then the President began to speak. After two or three sentences he asked another question. The Prime Minister took the opportunity of dealing with a few points which she had not been able to cover in her first exposition and responded, once again speaking well and fluently for another fifteen minutes. She then thanked the President

71

for his call, expressed her gratitude to him and to the United States Government for their help and support, promised to keep him posted on future developments, said good–bye and replaced the receiver.

Not long afterwards I met the National Security Adviser, and I said that we had been a little mystified by the President's call and did not quite know what it was all about. He laughed, and said: 'We shan't try that again'. 'What do you mean?' I said. He said: 'Well, we had a message to convey which we thought that the Brits would find unhelpful, so we figured that it had better be conveyed by the President to the Prime Minister. The trouble was, the President couldn't get a word in edgeways.'

Many years later I happened to meet another American official who had been one of those who were in the Oval Office when this exchange took place. He told me that, during the Prime Minister's second exposition, the President had taken the receiver away from his ear and held it out in front of him so that they could all listen, saying as he did so: 'Isn't she marvellous?'

I think – though she never said as much – that the Prime Minister had a shrewd suspicion that the President was calling in order to convey some unpalatable message, and was not averse to the thought of making it difficult for him to do so.

SEBASTIAN COE

ATHLETE AND POLITICIAN

Sebastian Coe's athletics career saw him beat 12 world records, win two Olympic gold medals and receive numerous other awards. He became the MP for Falmouth and Camborne in 1992, serving until 1997. He is currently Private Secretary to the Conservative leader William Hague.

෭෧෧

Prime Minister, you're wrong

The enduring image of Margaret Thatcher is of an incredibly strong-minded woman with equally strongly held opinions. It was often written during her premiership that she had little time for those who disagreed with her. My own experience of her, long before I became a Member of Parliament or even entered active politics, was not altogether the same.

It was in 1988, in the run up to the Seoul Olympics. I was invited to a reception at 10 Downing Street at which there were many distinguished people drawn from all walks of British life, not just athletics. Mrs Thatcher was a consummate professional at such events, moving round the room and chatting to her guests. She came up to me and asked how my preparation for the forthcoming Olympics was going. She knew I was expecting to be defending my title for the second time and I told her I thought it was all going really well (little realising that, in the event, the selectors, had other intentions!). Her questioning then moved to how long in advance I would be going out to the region to acclimatise for the games and I realised I was getting in to a more detailed conversation than I had anticipated. Perhaps naïvely, I hadn't expected the Prime Minister to have thought about the preparations athletes make. Most people think you turn up, run, and come home. I explained I would be going out to Australia to train, on the same time zone as Seoul, and then fly directly to the Olympic holding-camp a few weeks beforehand.

'Oh, you don't need that length of time,' she said. 'Well, I think you do', I ventured in response.

And so our conversation continued, both of us convinced of our point of view. Our discussion became quite detailed with Lady Thatcher increasingly focused on winning me over to her point of view. The rest of the room was, for a while, denied her attention as she pinned me to these questions. For some minutes, there was no other issue that mattered to her. The best efforts of various private secretaries to guide her on to, the next person had no impact as our conversation became more and more animated.

Eventually the Prime Minister looked me in the eye and said, 'Mr Coe, I think you're wrong, and I am a research chemist.' To which I replied, 'Prime Minister, I think you're wrong – and I'm a double Olympic Champion.' For a moment, I thought my training would start sooner than I had planned but instead her natural, slightly stern, expression melted and she laughed. 'Right', she said, 'I am going to instruct our ambassador in Seoul to give you the complete run of the Embassy. You must have everything you need.'

ADMIRAL SIR JOHN WOODWARD

COMMANDER IN CHIEF, NAVAL HOME COMMAND

1987–9

*Admiral Sir John Woodward, known as Sandy, has had a long and distin-
guished career in the Royal Navy which he joined at the age of 14. He has
served on numerous ships and in numerous positions at the MOD eventually
rising to the rank of Admiral and the position of Commander in Chief of
Naval Home Command. He led the 1982 Task Force in its mission to recover
the Falklands. He is currently retired.*

࿇

Interrupting the Prime Minister

In 1985-86, I was just sufficiently senior in the Defence Ministry to
stand in for the Chief of the Defence Staff as professional military
adviser to the Secretary of State for Defence once or twice at a
cabinet meeting. The day after one such occasion, I was having lunch
with one of Mrs Thatcher's Civil Service secretaries (the row of
people who sit at the PM's right to record all that goes on) who said,
more or less out of the blue, 'You were very lucky yesterday'.

Being unaware of having had any particular stroke of good fortune
recently, I asked him what he was talking about. He replied: 'You interrupted the Chairman'.

'Chairman', I said, 'Chairman. What chairman?'

'The Prime Minister – Mrs Thatcher – you interrupted her in
mid-flow.'

'Oh, that Chairman – well, what's wrong with that? She was

giving her views on a professional military matter – and she was getting it wrong. Someone had to tell her'.

'Nothing's wrong with that as such, only . . .'

'But surely, if the Prime Minister is about to do something fairly crass as a result of less than full knowledge of the subject, someone has to interrupt, give her the additional facts, and let her make her political decision on the basis of a full and proper professional brief. And anyway, she stopped, let me say what needed to be said to keep her straight on military facts, took it in, and went on to arrive at a sensible course of action. What on earth is wrong with that? Where does the luck come in? Isn't this how business is ordinarily conducted, how it should be conducted?'

'Well, yes and no', he replied, 'the last junior minister to interrupt her like that was fired'.

'Serve him right,' I said. 'He can only have been giving her 'professional military advice' from a profound ignorance of the subject, or political advice which, after eight years as Prime Minister, she had already heard two or three times before. Hardly a valuable interruption, indeed a complete waste of her time most likely. He should have known better.'

My conclusion from this rather odd conversation was that we still had an excellent Chief Executive – provided only that she retained a few advisers who were prepared to say 'No, Prime Minister' from time to time. Luck didn't enter it.

I have to admit that the conversation is slightly embellished, mainly to make better sense. It is intended to bring out the point that in 1986 at least, she was still a good, if rather intimidating listener to sensible advice. I suspect that the cause of her later downfall was as much to do with running out of such advisers, as anything else.

SIR TEDDY TAYLOR

MP FOR ROCHFORD AND SOUTHEND EAST

Sir Teddy Taylor has been an MP since 1964, initially for Glasgow Cathcart then from 1980 for Southend and from 1997 for Rochford and Southend East. He served in Margaret Thatcher's Shadow Cabinet as Spokesman on Trade and then later as Spokesman on Scotland.

కతళ

The Thatcher Shadow Cabinet

One of my exciting times in Parliament was when Mrs Thatcher invited me to join her Shadow Cabinet in the post as Spokesman on Trade and Industry and then as the Spokesman on Scotland.

I have always had the feeling that one of the main reasons why I was appointed at all was because of my position to devolution in Scotland and, happily, the Party turned from its previous commitment to devolution under Mrs Thatcher's leadership. It has always been argued that devolution was the only way to undermine the growth of the Scottish National Party who believed in full independence for Scotland, and both Mrs Thatcher and I thought that far from undermining the nationalist devolution would simply provide them with an opportunity to grow. Happily, by taking the Nationalists head on without the devolution commitment we were able to virtually wipe them out in the 1979 Election. The only personal problem, of course, was that by wiping out the SNP vote I lost my own seat in Cathcart in Glasgow and returned to Parliament a few months later as MP for

Southend East in a by-election. I think I will never forget the fact that although Mrs Thatcher won the election and was on her way to Downing Street, she nevertheless found the time to phone me the morning after the election to offer her sympathy.

The discussions we had in the Shadow Cabinet when I was a Member were truly exciting because instead of endeavouring to make political propaganda we seemed to spend most of our time considering detailed and fundamental issues which were to be the basis of the Thatcher Administration. Amongst the most important issues we had to consider were the curbing of Trade Union abuses, the reduction of levels of taxation and the promotion of privatisation. Papers were constantly brought before the Shadow Cabinet and Mrs Thatcher always appeared to like having someone putting forward a contrary view which was subject to real discussion. If she won the argument she always expected everyone in the Shadow Cabinet to accept the decision and to go along with her, but if she lost the argument Willie Whitelaw had a habit of stepping in to suggest that the matter should be referred to a sub-committee and that was the end of the issue.

I will always remember Jim Prior who was one of those who was constantly putting forward strong arguments against some of the fundamental changes in policy, but was always amongst the most loyal and most co-operative Members of the Shadow Cabinet in giving full support for decisions once they were reached. I enjoyed taking part in all these discussions and expressing my opinions.

Mrs Thatcher ran the Shadow Cabinet like a teacher in a school and because of my strong views on the EU I was constantly endeavouring to persuade the Shadow Cabinet to adopt a more aggressive policy on the issue. I can well remember an occasion when she reached across the Shadow Cabinet table, smacked my hand and with a smile on her face said: 'Do not mention the EU again today Teddy', and there was laughter throughout the gathering.

I think the most impressive aspect of the Shadow Cabinet discussions for me was that under her leadership we looked with care and seriousness at problems which she felt had been neglected in Britain for far too long, and because these policies were implemented during her administration Britain was able to overcome many of the problems which other European nations still suffer from. I certainly think she was the greatest of all the politicians I have seen in Parliament in my long service here and she certainly did a great job for the country as a whole.

VÀCLAV KLAUS

PRIME MINISTER OF CZECH REPUBLIC 1992–7

Vàclav Klaus is one of the foremost politicians of post communist Eastern Europe. He became Prime Minister of the Czech Republic in 1992 after serving as the Minister for Finance. He has written numerous books on economic policy and has been the recipient of numerous awards for the cause of freedom.

ર&જ

An exceptional woman

Although Margaret Thatcher and I have met personally many times in the last decade, I would rather speak briefly of her opinions and attitudes than of personal issues. My view is the view of a politician from Central Europe and from a former communist country. That is probably what makes it somewhat specific.

There were certainly sufficient domestic reasons, motives and arguments, but we may say, with only a slight exaggeration, that the revolution in Central and Eastern Europe which brought about the end of communism was initiated in 1979 by the victory of the Conservative Party in the general election placing Margaret Thatcher at the head of the British government. She attacked the ever-expanding state – which represented the dominant tendency throughout the twentieth century. This was a century of socialism with all sorts of adjectives and with a highly varying degree of the humiliation and degradation of the individual – and her fight against socialism was the first example of success. She showed that it was possible to reverse this tendency and return to a liberal political, economic and social system.

Without wishing to be ideological, I cannot but recall that unlike many – more or less – conciliatory Western politicians, Margaret Thatcher understood the dangers of the communist doctrine and it was by her uncompromising attitudes that she contributed immensely to the end of communism.

She did not regard politics as a 'technology of power', but as an instrument for enforcing certain ideas and moral principles. This was the source of her uncompromising stance for which she earned the nickname the 'Iron Lady'. This had nothing in common with her personal characteristics in the way I got to know her. She was not the type of politician who makes compromises. Likewise, her allies either shared her ideas and moral principles or, if they did not, they could not be her allies.

She did not regard freedom as a way to greater efficiency and prosperity. It was a moral principle and the highest value. Therefore, a free society was not just an effective political slogan but a deeply rooted vision, which she continually endeavoured to carry out throughout her life. Those who accused her of being stubborn, persistent or obstinate were people who never really came to understand the real meaning of a 'free society'.

She entered politics at a time when the faith in a 'modern welfare state' and in a 'mixed economy' prevailed. *Laissez-faire* was considered a relic, belonging to the nineteenth century. Margaret Thatcher opposed these then-dominant opinions, which was, at the end of the 1970s and the beginning of the 1980s, unique. Fortunately, she found an ally in this 'campaign' for the restoration of old virtues on the other side of the Atlantic in Ronald Reagan.

Neither could she come to terms with the process of the unification of Europe. She always saw Europe as a community of free and sovereign states connected (or united) by free trade. However, the idea of creating some sort of a 'super state' or a federation of Europe began to prevail on the European continent. The bureaucratisation of European structures, the growing of the 'Eurocracy' and the abandonment of the principles of free trade on a global scale discouraged her and she entered the group of the so-called Euro-sceptics, to which I am honoured to belong as well.

Her attitudes in politics and her conduct in everyday life prove that she is one of the extraordinary figures of the last quarter of the twentieth century. I have met many giants of world politics but none have made such an impression on me as this exceptional woman.

ALEX AIKEN

CONSERVATIVE PARTY PRESS OFFICER

Alex Aiken was Chairman of the Conservative Students in 1989–90 and joined the staff of Conservative Central office in 1993 as a Press Officer.

৵৵৵

'Shut up', Prime Minister

The Conservative Student National Committee had an annual meeting with the Prime Minister. I attended the meetings in 1989 and 1990. I recall two points from the 1990 meeting.

First, we had a set agenda covering various higher education issues. These were always robust discussions which usually over-ran their allotted time. At the start of the meeting, followed the introductions Mrs Thatcher launched into an attack on 'socialism' in higher education As this continued, I feared that we would lose the later points on the agenda, so I intervened. I told the PM that though her views were correct we had to get through the agenda so we had better move on to the next issue. Slightly stunned to be stopped in mid-flow she said: 'Oh yes, OK – you tell us what's next'. Colleagues said afterwards that they were amazed that I had told the PM to 'shut-up'. However, we did get through the agenda.

Later in the meeting we were due to have an official photograph of the Committee and the PM. The arrangement of the furniture in her office made positioning difficult for the whole group. This didn't present a problem to the PM who simply lifted the large settee up and dragged it across the room to the astonishment of the Committee and officials.

During the two leadership elections of 1989 and 1990 the three chairmen of the youth sections of the Party – Young Conservatives, Students and National Association of Conservative Graduates – wrote joint letters in support of Mrs Thatcher during the Leadership elections of 1989 and 1990. We received personal replies on both occasions.

The day she resigned as Leader on 22 November 1990 the Conservative Student Office became a focal point for younger Conservatives. Around 30 came to the office in Artillery Row and simply sat and watched the events unfold in stunned silence. No one could believe it.

Mrs Thatcher caused panic in the Party's press office in May 1990 when she rang the press office in the early morning after the elections asking to know the results in the Borough of Barnet – covering her Finchley constituency. Neither the hapless duty press officer – it was about 7am – or any other staff knew the results. Naturally there was much recrimination and the following years saw the duty officers armed with comprehensive results for all seats.

ANGELA BROWNING

MP FOR TIVERTON AND HONITON

After serving as Chairman of Women into Business, Angela Browning became the MP for Tiverton and Honiton in 1992 and currently serves in the Shadow Cabinet.

꙰

Attention to detail

As an aspiring MP in the 1980s I was fortunate enough, as Chairman of Women Into Business, to host a reception at the Banqueting House in Whitehall. The Prime Minister spent the evening with us, presenting prizes and circulating among the guests, for over an hour. My husband had accompanied me and as the Prime Minister was about to leave I introduced her to him. She had never met either of us before but she immediately turned to him and said: 'Oh yes, you're an accountant, aren't you? Tell me, how are the businesses in Devon doing?'

I was quite stunned. Her attention to detail and the fact that she had done her homework for what must have really been a routine event was more than impressive.

CHERYL GILLAN

MP FOR CHESHAM AND AMERSHAM

Cheryl Gillan became the MP for Chesham and Amersham in 1992 after serving as Chairman of the Bow Group. She is currently an opposition spokesman on Foreign and Commonwealth Affairs.

ॐ

Encouraging women

So when are you going to try to become a Member of Parliament? We need more women in politics.*

These words were spoken to me at a formal dinner, just before the General Election of 1979 and readers might be surprised to hear, given some of the widely circulated mythologies about the lady involved, that those words were addressed to me by Margaret Thatcher.

At the dinner I sat next to Mrs Thatcher, who was then Leader of the Opposition. We chatted about how hard everyone was working to win the election and how she was about to become the first woman Prime Minister. She also shared reminiscences of what it was like to be a Cabinet Minister. When Mrs Thatcher asked whether I was interested in politics, I replied that I had always had a strong involvement. This is why I joined the Bow Group, which gave me a way to fulfil that interest in politics. Mrs Thatcher then asked her question, which set me off on a quest to become an MP and ultimately led to my election to the House of Commons in 1992.

Despite what many people have said about Margaret Thatcher, she really did encourage women to participate in politics – as I can testify.

LORD BELLWIN

LEADER OF LEEDS CITY COUNCIL 1975–9

Lord Bellwin became a councillor for Leeds in 1969 serving as the leader of Leeds City Council from 1975 until 1979 when he was raised to the peerage. He was Parliamentary Under Secretary of State at the Department of Environment from 1979 to 1983. He was the Minister of State for Local Government from 1983 until 1984.

৵৽

A True Leader

I first met Margaret Thatcher through my involvement in Local Government. This was in the late 1960s when I was Chairman of Housing on Leeds City Council. Together with Keith Joseph, she was co-chairing a small Party policy committee, looking into future housing possibilities.

I continued to meet her over the next few years, as a National/Local Government Leader and being the then Conservative Leader of the Council in Leeds. We had set up an informal liaison group which met with her three to four times a year.

The Ted Heath years did not produce good Local/National Government relationships. Heath was very remote and did not really want to listen to what his Party leaders throughout the country were saying.

As a contrast to this, Maggie, albeit not over enthusiastic about Local Government, was always thirsty for knowledge. Contrary to what is often said of her, in my experience she always listened, thoroughly questioned, and if convinced (not easy to do), she would take on board contrary views. She liked decisiveness and respected knowledge and practical experience, particularly if based on success.

She was invariably encouraging and whilst she expected loyalty, always gave it herself where she felt it was merited. She was, at all times, a serious, single minded and focused person, quite formidable really. I always found her to be kind and considerate and certainly caring. She was never one for small talk. Even when greeting visitors at the top of the stairs in Downing Street, she would quickly go straight to the point of the meeting in question.

She first spoke to me about the possibility of my joining her future Government a year or so before the event. She asked me if I would like to do this and go to the House of Lords when, not if, but when we won the next General Election.

It was never mentioned again for a year or so, but when forming the Government over that first weekend in May 1979, she telephoned to ask if I remembered our conversation. This consistency of thinking was absolutely typical of her.

As an amusing aside, when the call came, my late mother-in-law, a dear lady then in her eighties, first answered the telephone. The operator, having confirmed the number, asked her to hold on to take a call from the Prime Minister. 'The Prime Minister', said my mother in law, 'Just a moment I'll put my earrings on'. When I later told Maggie of this she said 'How charming'.

Looking back, an abiding impression is the remarkable hours Mrs Thatcher worked. She was always sprightly and immaculately turned out. Occasionally, whatever the lateness of the hour, she used to come into the Lords and sit on the steps to the Throne thereby giving support while listening to the debate. However tired she may have been, she never looked or acted it.

Unlike Tony Blair, she had a great respect for the House and its traditions. She always worked particularly hard in preparing for speaking in the Commons. Her in-depth briefing and preparation was thorough in the extreme. It was undoubtedly a major factor in the excellent performance she invariably gave at the Despatch Box.

One amusing incident I recall, albeit after I had left the Government, is when she stayed with us at our home in Leeds. She had a 6am start in the City the following morning and therefore had to stay overnight. It was quite an experience in many ways. I arranged for my grandson, Danny, to stay with us overnight – when would he otherwise get the chance to meet a Prime Minister! I suggested to him beforehand what questions she might put to him and I got almost all right – he was well prepared and did well – he was 14 at the time.

Although I had not seen her for some time prior to that overnight stay, on sitting down, her very first remarks were to ask what I had specifically meant by something I had said in the House of Lords a week or two beforehand – she had taken the trouble to read the Hansard.

A magic moment was when we had noted guards surrounding the house, part of the street blocked off, a bodyguard and secretary in the house and going to bed, my wife asked me if she should put the burglar alarm on!

Lunch on Sunday at Chequers was a memorable experience. It is a somewhat unusual place, not all that easy to find. We circled round looking for the entrance, eventually to be met at the door by the lady herself, on the steps, waiting to meet and greet visitors in her inimitable, dominantly cheerful way.

The morning was spent around the fire with the family, it being wintertime – all most congenial, pleasant, yet businesslike. When we walked into the dining room, the prepared table layout was completely rearranged and everyone reseated by her so that she could be close and most easily converse with whoever she felt could most contribute to such topics as she wished to discuss.

My decision to leave Government was something of a wrench. Had I lived in London I would certainly have wanted to continue. She was not happy that I wished to go, but once I pointed out that it was 'not fair to the family' she was most understanding and wrote a typically gracious and kind letter which was published in *The Times*.

I could tell many stories of situations, amusing and otherwise, but always it comes down to my memories of her being a true leader in every sense of the word. Her courage and determination are now legendary – in my experience they have never been more deserved. Critics and opponents may choose to forget the appalling shambles Margaret Thatcher inherited from Labour in 1979. History will remind them.

NICHOLAS RIDLEY

CABINET MINISTER 1983–90

Nicholas Ridley was amongst Margaret Thatcher's staunchest supporters and most trusted colleagues. He joined the Cabinet in 1983 as Secretary of State for Transport and went on to become Secretary of State for the Environment and finally for Trade and Industry. Nicholas Ridley died in 1992. This passage is taken from his book My Style of Government *published by Hutchinson in 1991.*

తు౪

Her Style of Government

Margaret Thatcher was always immaculately turned out herself. She dressed smartly, was well-groomed and expected other people to be so as well. During the 1987 election Nigel Lawson appeared on television with his hair in need of a trim; he got a complaint from next door. She wanted to set an example of high standards in all things, and for her example to be followed by others. She wanted 10 Downing Street to become renowned as a place of quality entertaining. She arranged for it to be redecorated in the mid-1980s with style and much gold leaf. It was transformed into a very grand and elegant house for entertaining the great and the good. It was adorned with good pictures from the national collections – one room contained a particularly lovely group of Turners. She entertained a lot. She saw to it that the food and wine, the flowers and. the service, were of the highest quality. Quality was the keynote – not extravagance. Whenever the programme of a visiting foreign dignitary allowed, she would give a dinner for him. These dinner parties were glittering occasions. Important and interesting people were asked; she also liked to have plenty of pretty and well-dressed women among the guests. She expected people to rise to the occasion, and they did. Her speech after the dinner was always a model of fluency, erudition and courtesy. She was a master of the impromptu speech. Some of her speeches when the East European leaders came to London were particularly moving. It seemed to cause her no nervousness or bother when she had to make a speech after dinner. This was not the case with some of her principal guests. I remember being fortunate enough to sit next to President Havel of Czechoslovakia when he dined there. Margaret Thatcher was on his left, and she talked to him for most of the meal. When my turn came, he hastily picked up his speech notes to make last-minute improvements. My attempts to engage him in conversation were dashed by Margaret Thatcher saying to me across him, 'Can't you see, Nick, he's trying to finish his speech.'

In addition to official dinners, she gave frequent receptions – for party workers, or a visiting overseas delegation, or for scientists, artists, musicians or entrepreneurs. She also held lunch and dinner parties at Chequers at weekends, particularly when an overseas visitor was staying there. I remember one particular lunch, given for Lech Walesa, the Polish Leader of *Solidarity*. He was very conscious of Poland's debt to her and of all her help and encouragement. But that didn't stop him calling for a lot more in his very effective after-luncheon speech. There was a strange affinity between the fiery Polish shipyard trade unionist and the high-principled British Tory Prime Minister – two people as different as they could be. It was because they both believed in freedom and in democracy with an equal passion that they were in alliance; not so much friendship, as a common cause to fight.

Sometimes groups of colleagues would be invited to lunch. It was after some such lunch that she resolved, after a long conversation with Nigel Lawson, Patrick Jenkin and myself, that another attempt must be made to replace the domestic rates. This was the day that she decided to start the studies which eventually led to the Community Charge.

She held a Boxing Day lunch every year to which family, friends and loyal supporters, both inside and outside politics, were bidden. It became a little too famous, and the press would find out who was there and who was not, trying to speculate as to who was 'in' and who was 'out'. It was difficult for her to keep any part of her life private. She always used to ask to this and other parties those acquaintances who had been widowed, or had been ill, or had suffered some misfortune, as well as her friends.

She was neither an egalitarian nor a puritan. From the way she entertained, it could hardly be said that she believed in a 'classless society'. She believed in equal opportunity for anyone to qualify to receive an invitation to one of her dinners; but once achieved, this was a distinction in a class of its own.

She liked to drink a little, although never too much. She preferred whisky and rarely did justice to the excellent wines that adorned the Number 10 dinner table. Government hospitality over the years had procured for Number 10 wines from the finest vineyards of France, and her predecessors cannot have done much damage to the stocks. The wine was always both excellent and adequate in quantity. She was entirely tolerant of those who had had one too many, unless they were proposing to drive themselves home. She often asked people before they had a drink whether or not they were driving and was very strict about this. One evening she unexpectedly visited the Whips Office in the Commons late at night. One of the Whips in the Lords happened to be there. He was considerably inebriated but thought he would go undetected if he stayed put where he was standing and hung onto the table firmly. 'Why don't you sit down,' she said. 'You look far too drunk to stand up.'

NICK HAWKINS

MP FOR SURREY HEATH

Nick Hawkins served as Member for Blackpool South from 1992 until 1997 when he became the MP for Surrey Heath. He is currently the Shadow Minister for the Lord Chancellor's Department and a Shadow Home Office Minister.

శ్రీ

Giving Britain back its pride

I am pretty confident that I am the only Member of Parliament who can accurately say 'My mother succeeded Margaret Thatcher in a job'. It is fairly well-known that Margaret Roberts – as she then was – studied Chemistry at Oxford. It is rather less well-known that she subsequently worked as a research chemist in the research laboratories of J Lyons & Co. When she moved on to pastures new, her successor was a London University graduate, a young research chemist originally from a Norfolk farming family – my mother. I first became aware of that family connection when Margaret was appointed Secretary of State for Education – my mother was by then a senior teacher in a girls' secondary school – and I was a Young Conservative, whilst at school myself in Bedford

After our General Election defeats in 1974, I spent a 'year out' prior to going up to Oxford – and whilst teaching and doing sports coaching at a prep school in North Yorkshire, I recall sitting in an otherwise deserted staff room cheering at the TV news that Margaret had been elected our new leader. I subsequently met Margaret for the first time whilst I was actively involved in Conservative politics at Oxford. Even though at that time she was often attacked in the media (the normal problem for all Opposition Leaders), her drive and determination to introduce real Conservative policies and stick to them – avoiding the U-turns of the previous abandonment of 'Selsdon Man' policies by Heath – was already evident.

Eight years later, I was fortunate enough to be one of Margaret's General Election candidates. Although Huddersfield was a safe Labour seat, we put up a good fight and my job was to try to divert Labour resources to ensure that the neighbouring marginals such as Colne Valley and Batley and Spen, could be won or held. In that, I hope we played some part. We had some splendid photo opportunities, including a visit by Margaret to nearby Dewsbury, and all the candidates who were not in reality likely to win were invited to the 'eve of poll' rally in Harrogate at which Margaret made her final superb campaign speech. (Those with a chance of winning were out 'on the trail' until the last moment.) At the end of a long campaign her tireless energy was, as always, in evidence. I always felt her stamina, as well as our firm and clear policies, was an extra 'secret weapon' as she always came over as so much stronger than the Welsh windbaggery of Neil Kinnock.

I was sad that I never served in the House under Margaret's leadership, but her place in history as a great Prime Minister who restored Britain to a position of strength (whereas in 1978–9 we had become an international joke, down at the bottom of the economic league with Turkey, the 'sick man of Europe', crippled by 'the British disease' of militant unions) is in my view secure. Those who are too young to remember the national shame of the Winter of Discontent and the years which preceded it, may be taken in by Blair's constant attempts to rewrite history and decry our achievements, but we who lived through it will always feel that Margaret Thatcher gave Britain back its pride as a country. This was especially evident during the Falklands

War. Her most important legacy internationally will be the part she played, with Ronald Reagan and George Bush, in leading the West in a tough stance which caused the collapse of the Warsaw Pact, European communism and the Iron Curtain. Britain was a world power again by 1990 and the lessons of the shambles of the 1970s, away from which she led us, should never be forgotten.

I was fortunate enough, in the 1997 Election, thanks to her campaign rally for Gerald Howarth MP and myself, to have my nomination paper signature witnessed by a rather significant figure – The Rt Hon Baroness Thatcher of Kesteven.

OLIVER LETWIN

MP FOR WEST DORSET

Oliver Letwin became the MP for West Dorset in 1997. He was a special advisor to Sir Keith Joseph from 1982 until he became a special advisor to the Prime Minister's Policy Unit in 1983, staying there until 1986.

လ◌∕

A little bit in love . . .

T he Prime Minister will see you now – terrifying words for a young man, especially one about to be subjected to a job interview by the Iron Lady. And there she was, the victor of the Falklands, sitting in a wing-chair in her study. The 'interview' lasted a few seconds: 'I gather you are joining us'. It was welcome news to my ears – and, as I subsequently discovered, typical of her approach to the mechanics of administration: clear, decisive, no precious time wasted.

Once on the staff, you were a member of the family – and there was pretty much the same plain-speaking as in a family. When coming to discuss a speech I had drafted on science, it was not immediately encouraging to be greeted in the drawing-room at Chequers by the PM standing by the fireplace, and saying to the Chief Scientific Adviser in that inimitable but much imitated voice 'yes, that speech was as much of a dead loss as this one'.

You had to know what you were talking about, and you had to stand your ground. We quickly discovered that when she was interrogating and criticising and opining, seemingly without taking the slightest account of what you were saying, she was in fact at her most attentive – ceaselessly testing, often enough to destruction, the weak points in the argument, the facts that contradicted the assertions, the claims that could not be substantiated. And when, in a certain domain, you had established that you knew, and that you could defend a position, her trust was almost frightening. The memoranda – always to be short and clear – came back, with signal points doubly and triply underlined. In Cabinet committees, a note passed to her would be read out, 'I have a note . . .' as if the truth had been delivered, not always to the pleasure of her colleagues.

In the end, as in any family, the strongest bonds were those of affection. We loved her – perhaps we were a little bit in love with her, not least because of the tremendous compliment she continuously paid of knowing and knowing that she knew – great as she was, and small as we were – who and what we were. In disaster, there would be flowers sent. In error, there would be support and acceptance. The worst case I can recall arose from the local government expenditure round. I had a little computer, and felt terribly proud to have installed a little programme of my own invention to determine the fiscal effects of certain decisions that fell to be made. Alas, in committee, the conversation took an unexpected turn, and it was only the next morning that I discovered my programme failed to work when a negative replaced a positive. Down to the study, to admit the error. Not a single word of reproach from the Lady: she was, despite all the appearances to the contrary, wholly able to absorb the idea that her staff were imperfect human beings.

They were turbulent times. It was something of a shock to be sent home one weekend, when the miners were out, and the dockers had just come out, to read the histories of the General Strike. But they were also times of seemingly boundless possibility. The impossible was being done – the rolling back of the socialist state – and she was hungry for more ideas. They might be devoured with delight or spat out in disgust: but the appetite for more was always there. It was as if we were living on the edge of a hurricane. We swept forward, blown and buffeted, but hugely exhilarated.

And at the eye of the hurricane, a still calm. She never rushed, never seemed to be aware of time. One Friday night, an urgent minute arrived from one of the members of the Cabinet: should we do something or not – yes or no by midnight? The Private Secretary and I rushed out a memorandum on the pros and cons and hastened to her flat. Up as always, and working on her boxes, she calmly read the minute and the memo. Then the fatal enquiry: *why* the need for a decision by midnight, or indeed before Monday? In our haste to answer the Minister's question, we had failed to question the question. For all her energy, she hastened slowly enough to see the point we had missed.

When the day came to announce departure, she was to be found in her room at the House of Commons. The response was theatrical. On hearing the news, she sat down, as if to steady herself. One knew, of course, that it was for effect – but how touching that she bothered to put on the effect. A politician to her fingertips, yes – but the Iron Lady had charm.

JOHN REDWOOD

MP FOR WOKINGHAM

After a successful career as an academic and then in banking, John Redwood became the head of Margaret Thatcher's policy unit in 1983 and remained there until 1985. In 1987 he became the MP for Wokingham, rising rapidly until he joined John Major's Cabinet as Secretary of State for Wales in 1993. He resigned in 1995 to fight for the leadership of the Conservative Party, a position he fought again for in 1997.

❧

Testing the argument

I always remember my first encounter with Margaret Thatcher. As Leader of the Opposition she had heard that I had set out a number of proposals to privatise Britain's unprofitable, unhelpful, unfriendly, lumbering nationalised industries. I was added to the guest list for one of her lunches in the Shadow Cabinet Room at the House of Commons. The main intellectual dish of the day was devolution. Margaret was about to go to the House to raise just this issue. I watched as a range of constitutional experts told her their thoughts, only to see her more than a match for them, well briefed, deadly in her questions. Now I realise she was fired up and a little nervous before appearing in the House. Then it was quite a spectacle to see such a powerful senior politician in full flight, clearly the mistress of her brief, able to deal with professors and advisers with forceful points and searching questions.

I steeled myself for the challenge. I knew my turn was to come soon. After what seemed like an age discussing devolution where I kept well out of the fray she turned to me to hear my thoughts on privatisation. I had soon grasped from watching and listening to the previous conversation that you had to be quick and make your best points while you still had the chance. Once you allowed your flow to be interrupted and the questions to begin you were going to be thrust on the defensive. I marshalled my best points. I was sure the position I had adopted was proof against the most forceful of counter-attacks. The questions soon came thick and fast and I held my ground. I was beginning to enjoy it, realising that if you could withstand the barrage you might even shift her position. As the nerves went and the deter-mination increased, Margaret Thatcher decided she had had enough as it was not the subject of the day. With a crushing 'That's all very well, Mr Redwood, but they'll never let me do that' I realised my time was up and we were on to the next question.

That first encounter fascinated me. Whilst I could see what many saw, that here was a strong minded lady who was powerful in argument and gave no quarter, it also struck me very forcefully that here was someone really interested in the issues who was learning by the clash of different opinions. It was, to adapt a phrase she made famous about someone else, 'someone I could do business with'.

I went away realising that if privatisation was to turn from the dream of a few of us to the reality of the many, we needed to create a climate of opinion in which Margaret Thatcher's political judgment sensed it was possible or safe to do it. Here was a canny, cautious, even defensive politician who could often judge the mood of the nation well and who was only going to lead them up to a point. Like all great leaders she knew that on many occasions she had to follow rather than lead. In a democracy the leader has to accept that there are limits to how far he or she can take the people, and there is an absolute prohi-bition on leading them in certain directions at all.

This first encounter had prepared me well for many meetings, arguments, debates, discussions and exchanges which I had with

Margaret Thatcher when I became her chief policy adviser after the 1983 General Election. It was satisfying to put to her a memorandum saying that in her second period as Prime Minister she now had the political strength and the financial and economic necessity to get on and privatise large chunks of the public industrial and service sector. It was a pleasure to find that now a lot of the caution and the worry had abated. Now the issue was not 'will the public buy it?' but 'how can we do it technically?' By 1983 Margaret Thatcher rightly sensed that the main problem was no longer public opinion, which was ready for some drastic changes to get Britain on the move again, but opinion in the City which was extremely cautious.

When I went round the City trawling opinion from my Number 10 base it was a disappointment to discover that many in the City strongly held the view that to sell something worth several billion pounds on the Stock Market was a technical impossibility. They believed that equity issues could not be larger than a few hundred million pounds and were strongly against selling shares in British Telecom. They preferred the idea of bonds to finance it in a different way. I proposed to Margaret Thatcher that we could overcome these difficulties with a new structure, selling shares direct to the public by mail order and newspaper advertisements, and selling to overseas interests at the same time as selling some of them through the conventional brokers and banks in the City. She saw the point and became excited by the possibilities and gave me the backing I needed at the Treasury and in the City.

The whole privatisation story illustrated Margaret Thatcher at her best. At first her caution was demonstrated by tough argument. She believed in testing people out, almost to destruction, to see if they could stand their ground. She knew that she would have to stand her ground in a very public way and wanted to make sure that those advising her really did believe in the idea and had thought it through.

It showed her brutal honesty in judging the public mood and judging what the obstacles were at the time. Finally, it showed that she was indeed prepared to change her mind as others helped her make the case and overcome the obstacles.

Throughout the years that I worked for Margaret Thatcher in one capacity or another, the thing that never ceased to amaze me, apart from her remarkable energy, was her constant striving for the truth and her constant willingness to change her mind. It could take months to get her to make a decision on a big issue. She would be argumentatively indecisive for long periods. It was because she knew that with her style of politics once she had committed herself to something and went public she had to fight it through all the way. She combined caution with radicalism in a quite remarkable way which enabled her to stay at the top of British politics for so long. It also meant that when people come to write the history of Britain in the twentieth century, with the benefit of some perspective they will see that, unlike many other prime ministers, she did have a general vision, a sense of direction, and she did find the measures and the men to help her carry it through in many important respects.

Privatisation may well go down as her greatest success. From modest beginnings it took off after the sale of BT. It spread around the world. The most unlikely people became converts, from the Labour governments of New Zealand and Australia, through the former communist states of Eastern Europe, to Fidel Castro's Cuba. It even eventually permeated the UK Labour Party, where a UK Labour government is now privatising Air Traffic Services, a bridge too far for the Conservative administration.

Margaret Thatcher came to see the connection between privatisation, wider ownership and every man a shareholder. She came to enthuse over it, as she had over her very successful campaigns to sell council houses to their tenants. It was a pleasure to take her such an idea, it was exhilarating to argue it through with her, and exciting to see it come to fruition.

SIR MALCOLM RIFKIND

CABINET MINISTER, 1986–97

Sir Malcolm Rifkind served as MP for Edinburgh Pentlands from 1974-97. He joined Margaret Thatcher's Cabinet in 1986 as Scottish Secretary. He was a Cabinet Minister throughout John Major's administration, latterly as Foreign Secretary.

❧

Having her way

Those who were privileged to serve in Margaret Thatcher's Cabinet will always be grateful for the experience. She had her own distinctive style of Cabinet Government.

For her a Cabinet discussion was a series of bilateral exchanges rather than a collective analysis of the issues of the day. Whereas John Major would keep his own views to himself until his Cabinet colleagues had expressed theirs, Mrs Thatcher would open the discussion by indicating the conclusion that she wished and expected.

On one occasion she sat down at a Cabinet Committee and began by saying 'I haven't much time, today. Only enough time to explode and have my way'. As each Minister expressed his view she would often engage him in battle before moving on to the next.

While this could be an alarming experience for a new member of the Cabinet it was neither as distressing nor as difficult for the Cabinet as a whole than this introduction might suggest. For all her bossiness and aversion to compromise, Margaret Thatcher was a constitutionalist and a believer in cabinet government to her fingertips.

Unlike an American President who is quite entitled to ignore his Cabinet, none of whom, except the Vice-President having been elected by the nation, a British Prime Minister is *primus inter pares* and often Mrs Thatcher found herself in the minority. This she accepted with varying degrees of enthusiasm but she never challenged the right of her colleagues to decline to accept her wishes. Indeed, when she went into battle she relished an adversary who was prepared to disagree with her as long as he knew what he was talking about. It was John Major's willingness as a mere junior Whip to tell her in front of his colleagues that she was wrong and misguided that first brought him to her attention and led to his ultimate coronation as her successor to the Tory Crown.

When Sir Anthony Parsons, our Ambassador at the UN during the Falklands War, was recalled to brief her she kept interrupting him. After the third interruption in so many minutes he remarked: 'Prime Minister, if you didn't interrupt me so often you might find that you didn't need to.' Some months later she appointed him her foreign policy adviser.

As long as she was Prime Minister her natural gut instincts were tempered by the need to carry her colleagues and ensure acceptable government. Since her retirement that has been less of a constraint. One recalls Gladstone's comment on Sir Robert Peel : 'Former Prime Ministers are like great rafts floating untethered in a harbour.'

SIR ROBIN BUTLER

PRINCIPAL PRIVATE SECRETARY TO MARGARET THATCHER
1982–5

Lord Butler of Brockwell served in numerous positions in the Home Civil Service from 1961 onwards but is best remembered as the Principal Private Secretary to Margaret Thatcher from 1982 until 1985, and as Cabinet Secretary and Head of the Home Civil Service from 1988 to 1998. He currently sits as a cross-bencher in the House of Lords.

ॐ

'It's what they would want'

My dominant recollection of working with Margaret Thatcher was the certainty of her instinctive reactions. When the IRA bomb exploded in the Grand Hotel Brighton at ten to three in the morning on the last day of the Conservative Party conference in 1984 I was with her in the sitting room of her suite at the Grand Hotel. She had just finished her conference speech and I had given her a paper on which a decision was needed by start of business next morning. Denis had gone to bed next door.

When the bomb went off, I thought it was a car bomb outside. I said to her 'we should move away from the windows'. As we went across the room we could hear the noise of collapsing masonry through the bedroom door.

Without hesitation she said, 'I must see if Denis is alright'. She opened the bedroom door, whereupon the noise of structural collapse became louder, and she disappeared into the darkness. I paused in the sitting-room, wondering what I should say to the tribunal of inquiry if she was killed by the collapsing building. To my relief she and Denis emerged almost immediately, Denis pulling on some clothes over his pyjamas.

We then moved into the corridor. Miraculously the lights had stayed on. (Thereafter Margaret Thatcher carried a torch in her handbag in case the same thing happened again – she always learned from experience). Some others joined us and we began to debate what we should do next. I suggested returning to London – only one hour away.

Margaret Thatcher said, 'I'm not leaving the area'. The decision was then taken out of our hands by the arrival of a fireman who – after one false start – led us down the main staircase and out of the back of the hotel, not without Margaret Thatcher breaking off to ask whether all the staff in the foyer were accounted for.

We were taken to the training accommodation at Lewes Police Station where the Thatchers were allocated bedrooms. At that stage I did not know that the bomb had been in the upper part of the building or that anyone was missing. I lay on the bench in the day room at 5 am. At 5.45 the telephone rang. It was John Gummer, then Chairman of the Party. He said, 'It's worse than we thought. The Tebbits, the Wakehams and others are trapped in the collapsed building.'

I decided not to wake Margaret Thatcher but turned on the television to watch the news, including Norman Tebbit being brought out. Margaret Thatcher appeared just after 8; she had seen the news on a television in her room. 'We must make sure the Conference re-starts on time', she said. I was appalled. I said, 'Surely you can't go on with the Conference when your colleagues and friends are being dug out of the rubble.' 'It's what they would want,' she said. 'We can't allow terrorism to defeat democracy.'

Another quality is that she never seemed to waste energy by looking back and worrying about whether she had done the right thing. What was done was done. The only thing worth using energy on was what to do next. I remember travelling back with her from a lunchtime engagement in the City during a bad moment in the coal miners' strike, when the dockers were for a short time also on strike and the prospects of importing the energy supplies needed were threatened. On this journey back we suffered another blow, learning that the Government had lost its case in the High Court over the banning of the GCHQ unions. Margaret Thatcher was faced with making a statement in Parliament in front of a jubilant Opposition. She was immediately clear about what she would do. 'I will make clear that we will appeal the GCHQ case to the House of Lords and, if we lose, we shall accept the judgement of the court. We cannot fight for the rule of law in one area if we don't accept it in another. Now back to the miners' strike'. The Government won its appeal in the House of Lords.

The legends about Margaret Thatcher's physical toughness and stamina are justified. In December 1984 she went to Beijing to sign the Hong Kong agreement and then went on to Hong Kong to reassure opinion there. Believing that Ronald Reagan was in the Western White House in California, the Foreign Office suggested that she should visit him on the way home following his re-election as President. Even if this information had been correct, the geography would have been dubious since it is a shorter distance from London to California than from Hong Kong. In fact, Ronald Reagan was in Washington and the visit involved a 24 hour flight from Hong Kong on the VC-10 but only a 12 hour time change. While the staff decided that we would get what sleep we could, Margaret Thatcher announced that she would stay awake and study the Anti-Ballistic Missile Treaty and Cap Weinberger's speeches in preparation for her talks with Ronald Reagan on the Strategic Defence Initiative.

She did this to such good effect that, faced with the President and the US defence establishment at Camp David, she persuaded them to accept the four principles which preserved the principle of nuclear deterrence. We returned home in time for Christmas Eve having flown right round the world. The full trip had lasted five and a half days or 130 hours, of which 55 hours had been spent in the air. I had occasion to telephone her on Christmas Day and asked whether she felt tired. 'Certainly not' she said. 'Why ever should I?'

On another occasion she had a dental appointment in the morning. On her return, I asked her whether she had had any trouble. 'I'm afraid the dentist said that I had to have my impacted wisdom teeth out' she said. Later that day, at the end of the usual round of meetings and engagements, I asked when she would like an appointment made with her dentist for the removal of the wisdom teeth. 'He did it this morning,' she said.

What was the secret of Margaret Thatcher's energy? Apart from the certainty of her instincts and her physical stamina, she seemed to have an inexhaustible supply of adrenalin. No occasion was too trivial for her not to take seriously, whether it was a school prize giving or a confidence debate in the Commons. All were the subject of intense and detailed preparation. As Principal Private Secretary, I regarded one of my many jobs as being the regulation of the adrenalin flow. For the most part this involved calming and reassurance. But just occasionally, after lunch, I felt that she was a bit too tranquil for a great performance at Prime Minister's questions in the House of Commons. On those occasions I would say 'Prime Minister, I think you are really vulnerable if the Opposition raise such and such a point.' That always did the trick. The eyes would light up and the thoroughbred would be pawing the ground before the off.

On the evening of the day when Margaret Thatcher left Downing Street, I invited her and Denis to a farewell party in my office with some of the civil servants I knew she regarded most highly. I said 'When we are very old the thing which our grandchildren and great grandchildren will think most interesting about us is that we worked with Margaret Thatcher.' I believe that still and I am glad that I said it to her at that moment.

ALAN CLARK

CONSERVATIVE MP 1974–92 AND 1997–9

Alan Clark, who died recently, was the MP for Plymouth Sutton from 1974 until 1992. He returned to Parliament in 1997 as the MP for Kensington and Chelsea. He served under Margaret Thatcher as Minister for Trade and then Minister of State at the MOD but he is best known for his notoriously indiscreet diaries. This extract is taken from his best-selling Diaries *(Weidenfeld & Nicolson, 1993).*

ॐॐ

Lovely and haughty

Monday, 19 November 1990

The whole house is in ferment. Little groups, conclaves everywhere. Only in the dining room does some convention seem to have grown up (I presume because no one trusts their dining companions) that we don't talk 'shop'.

'Made your Christmas plans yet?' All that balls. God, the dining room is boring these days, even worse than Pratts'. Big, slow, buffers 'measuring their words' oh-so-firmly; or creepy little narks talking straight out of Conservative News.

But in the corridors it is all furtive whispering and glancing over shoulders. The institutional confidence (seen at its most obvious in those who have served a prison term, and which I first noticed in my early days on Warren Street), that special grimacing style of speech out of the corner of the mouth, eyes focusing in another direction, is now it seems the only way of communicating.

Most people are interested – not so much in the result, as in knowing what the result will be in advance, in order to make their own 'dispositions'. To ingratiate oneself with the new regime – a new regime, I should say, because the outcome is by no means certain – even as little as a week before it is installed, looks better than joining the stampede afterwards. The issue which can be discussed semi-respectably, is who is most likely to deliver victory at the General Election? But it is packaging, conceals a great basket of bitterness, thwarted personal ambition, and vindictive glee. Talk of country, or loyalty, is dismissed as 'histrionics'.

And there is a strange feeling abroad. Even if the Lady wins – and here I am writing 'even if', pull yourself together Clark, say 'even after she's won' – there will be no escaping the fact that at least one hundred and fifty of her parliamentary colleagues will have rejected her leader-ship. That's a big chunk. Some people, particularly those who pose as Party Elders, like Tony Grant, are intimating that it might be 'better' if, faced with so blatant a show of No Confidence, she decided to 'heal' the Party by announcing her intention to stand down at a given date (i.e. become a lame duck which the Labour Party could taunt and torment on every occasion, and a busted flush internationally).

And as the savour of a Heseltine victory starts to pervade the crannies and cupboards and committee rooms, so more and more people are 'coming out'. 'Oh, I don't think he'd be so bad, really . . .' 'He's got such a wide appeal.' 'My people just love him, I must say . . .' 'I know what you mean, but he'd be so good at dealing with . . .' (fill in particular problem as appropriate).

Most conspicuous in canvassing are Hampson (loonily) Mates (gruffly) and Bill Powell (persuasively). Michael himself is quite shameless in offering all and sundry what they have always wanted. For example, he would probably have got Paul's support anyway, but 'sealed' it with an assurance that Paul would be Speaker in the next

House; Soames fell straight away for the 'your talents are long overdue for recognition' line, as did little Nelson and Rhodes James ('you've been treated abominably').

Michael stands in the centre of the Members' lobby, virtually challenging people to wish him good luck. He gives snap 'updates' to journalists, and greets supplicants who are brought along for a short audience by his team. The heavier targets he sees in his room. The Cabinet play their cards close to the chest, although Mellor apparently, speaks to Michael twice a day on the telephone. Some, like Kenneth Clarke, want her out so badly that they don't need even to blink. And I would guess that there are a fair coterie of Ministers of State and Parly Secs like Sainsbury and Trippier who feel uneasy with the Lady and like the idea of a change.

At the top of the ministerial staircase I ran into Garel Jones. He was bubbling with suppressed excitement. I don't think he actually wants 'Hezzy' as he (spastically) calls him, to win. It would be disruptive of the Blue Chip long-term plan. But he's high on the whole thing.

Tristan said, 'Of course every member of the Cabinet will vote for the Prime Minister in the first round.' Like hell they will.

I said to him, hoping he'd deny it, 'One cannot actually exclude the possibility that Heseltine will score more votes than her on the first ballot.'

'No, I'm afraid one can't.'

'Can one, even, be completely sure that he will not get both the largest total and the necessary margin to win without a second ballot?'

'No, I'm afraid one can't.'

This was really chilling. Apocalypse. Because time is horrendously tight if we have to organise an alternative candidate.

Four working days and a weekend. But if Michael scoops it in one gulp then that is the end of everything.

Maddeningly, I had to return to the Department. Meetings, and an official lunch. Scandinavians.

'I assume that there is no likelihood of Mrs Thatcher being defeated for the position of Prime Minister?'

'Oh no. None whatever. It's just one of these quaint traditions we have in the Conservative Party.'

But the encounter made me realise the enormity of what we're doing changing the Prime Minister – but without any electoral authority so to do. I thought I'd have a talk to Peter, although he doesn't encourage it, and I cancelled my early afternoon engagements and went back over to the House.

I listened outside the door. Silence. I knocked softly, then tried the handle. He was asleep, snoring lightly, in the leather armchair, with his feet resting on the desk.

Drake playing bowls before the Armada and all that, but I didn't like it. This was ten minutes past three in the afternoon of the most critical day of the whole election. I spoke sharply to him. 'Peter.'

He was bleary.

'I'm sorry to butt in, but I'm really getting a bit worried about the way things are going.'

'Quite all right, old boy, relax.'

'I'm just hearing bad reactions around the place from people where I wouldn't expect it.'

'Look, do you think I'd be like this if I wasn't entirely confident? 'What's the arithmetic look like?'

Tight-ish, but OK.'

'Well, what?'

'I've got Michael on 115. It could be 124, at the worst.'

'Look, Peter, I don't think people are being straight with you.'

'I have my ways of checking.'

'Paul?'

'I know about Paul.'

'The Wintertons?'

'The Wintertons, funnily enough, I've got down as 'Don't Know's.'

'What the fuck do you mean, 'Don't Know'? This isn't a fucking street canvas. It's a two-horse race, and each vote affects the relative score by two, unless it's an abstention.'

'Actually, I think there could be quite a few abstentions.'

'Don't you think we should be out there twisting arms?'

'No point. In fact it could be counter-productive. I've got a theory about this. I think some people may abstain on the first ballot in order to give Margaret a fright, then rally to her on the second.' (Balls, I thought, but didn't say.)

'What about the '92? They're completely rotten. They've got a meeting at six. Are you going?'

'No point. But I think you should.'

In deep gloom I walked back down Speaker's corridor. It can't really be as bad as this can it? I mean there is absolutely no oomph in her campaign whatsoever. Peter is useless, far worse than I thought. When he was pairing Whip he was unpopular, but at least he was crisp. Now he's sozzled. There isn't a single person working for her who cuts any ice at all. I know it's better to be feared than loved. But these people aren't either. And she's in Paris. 'Où est la masse de manoeuvre? – Aucune.'

I went into the members' tea room. The long table was crowded with Margaret supporters, all nonentities except for Tebbit who was cheering people up. Much shouting and laughter. Blustering reassurance. Norman was saying how unthinkable it was to consider dismissing a Prime Minister during a critical international conference. 'Like Potsdam in 1945,' I said. No one paid any attention. If they heard they didn't, or affected not to understand the allusion.

The crowd thinned out a little and when he got up Norman said that he wanted a word. We went into the Aye lobby and sat at that round table in the centre with all the stationery on it.

'Well . . . ?'

'It's filthy', I said.

'It could be close. Very close.'

I agreed, 'Fucking close.'

'If it's like that do you think she should stand in the second ballot?' I simply don't know the answer to this. Governing would be very difficult with half the Party against her. She might have to make concessions' to the left. I asked Norman if he thought she would have to, bring Heseltine into the Cabinet.

'She'd certainly be under a lot of pressure to do so.'

'Renton.'

'Yeah.'

I said that the key tactic was to get Chris Patten to stand, and draw off the left vote. At least the hard left vote, Charlie Morrison, Bob Hicks, all the wankers. Norman said, 'And Ken Clarke.' I told him no, if you have too many candidates people just get in a muddle and Heseltine walks through them, just as she did in 1975. Norman said that a lot of people now regarded Michael as a right-wing candidate anyway.

'Well, we know different.'

'Too true.'

Norman said, 'If it's open season, I'm dam' well going to put my name in. The right must have a candidate they can vote for.'

'You'd lose.'

'It's likely I would, but at least we'd know our strength. That could be useful in a changed situation.'

Look, Norman, we want to put additional names in to reduce his total, not ours. I don't think Heseltine has that big a personal vote. It's just an anti-Margaret coalition.'

I could see he was thoughtful. But he didn't want to prolong the conversation, which we were conducting in tones just above a whisper, though still arousing the curious attention of passers-by.

Raising his voice Norman said, 'Well, this time tomorrow every-thing will be settled,' and gave one of his graveyard cackles.

The '92 meeting was in one of those low-ceilinged rooms on the upper committee room corridor. The mood was tetchy, and apprehensive. There was a kind of fiction running from several (Jill Knight, for example, shockingly), just as Norman had foreseen, that 'Michael' – as defectors call him (supporters of the Prime Minister always refer to him as 'Heseltine'; and this is quite a useful subliminal indicator of how the speaker is going to vote when he or she is being deliberately or defensively opaque) – was 'really' on the right.

The trouble with this club, to which I was elected almost as soon as I arrived here, but with which I have never really felt comfortable, is that it personifies in extreme form two characteristics found in the majority of MPs – stupidity and egomania. It is only the shrewd and subtle guidance of George Gardiner that has prevented them becoming a laughing stock in recent years. But such integrity as they might originally have possessed has been eroded by the inclusion of many from marginal seats. None are quite as awful as Elizabeth Peacock, who spoke squatly and fatly against Margaret – why bother, she won't be here in the next Parliament anyway – but most are concerned solely with saving their own skins. I spoke loyally and, should have been movingly, of our debt to the PM. But there was a hint of what's-she-ever-done-for-us from the audience and with some justification, so few ministerial appointments having come out of the '92. I tried to make their flesh creep with what Michael would do, got only a subdued ritual cheer when I said Margaret is undefeated, and never will be defeated either in the Country or in this House of Commons. I'm not particularly popular with that lot. They think I'm 'snooty'. Perhaps my boredom threshold shows. But in the ballot tomorrow I'd say they will divide no better than 60/40.

After dinner I had a word with Norman Lamont. He'd just come back from somewhere-or-other. 'I don't like the smell,' he kept saying. 'There's a bad smell to the whole place.' He's right, of course. It's the smell of decay. It's affecting everything, the badge messengers, the police, the drivers. Something nasty is going to happen.

I write this very late, and I am very tired. Perhaps I'm just need-lessly depressed. I'd ring the Lady if I could, but she's at a banquet. She's not even coming back for the ballot. Lovely and haughty.

SIR ROBIN DAY

BROADCASTER AND JOURNALIST

Sir Robin Day, who died just before this book went to press, was among the most distinguished and best loved political journalists of our time. He started working as a political correspondent for the BBC in 1954, quickly establishing his reputation as a hard hitting interviewer. He is best known as the presenter of Question Time, *which he chaired from 1979 until 1989. His memoirs,* Grand Inquisitor, *were published by Weidenfeld & Nicolson in 1989 and his collected writings,* Speaking for Myself, *were published by Ebury in 1999.*

ॐ

1987 – The Beginning of the End

Of Thatcherism there will be many conflicting definitions. Here, in fairness, recorded for history, is her own exposition – the authorised version, as, it were, or the gospel according to Margaret. She gave it in answer to this question from me on television, three days before polling day in June 1987:

Q: *But you have stamped your image on the Tory Party like no other leader ever has before. We now hear of 'Thatcherism'. What is it that 'Thatcherism' means?*

A: *Sir Robin, it is not a name that I created in the sense of calling it an 'ism'. Let me tell you what it stands for. It stands for sound finance and government running the affairs of the nation in a sound financial way. It stands for honest money, not inflation; it stands for living within your means, it stands for incentives, because we know full well that the growth and economic strength of a nation comes from the efforts of its people, and its people need incentives to work as hard as they possibly can. All of that has produced economic growth. It stands for something else. It stands for the wider and wider spread of ownership of property, of houses, of shares, of savings. It stands for being strong in defence; a reliable ally and a trusted friend. People have called those things 'Thatcherism'. They are in fact fundamental commonsense and having faith in the enterprise and abilities of the people. It is my task to try and release those. They were always there. They've always been there in the British people, but they couldn't flourish under Socialism; they've now been released. That's all that 'Thatcherism' is.*

She may have learnt this off by heart. If so, she had learnt it well. She spoke it with a fierce and fluent vigour, with that rare political gift of making simple and familiar words sound new and compelling.

Margaret Thatcher was a political phenomenon. Not only was she the first woman to be Prime Minister of the United Kingdom. Not only did she lead the Tory Party for over fourteen years. What was also phenomenal about her was that she, a bourgeois Conservative, proved to be a radical Prime Minister. In adopting Thatcherism, she buried Socialism, or at least she buried 'Clause Four' Socialism. She was driven by conviction and instinct, rather than by intellect or reason. She was admired for her 'conviction' politics by that left-wing opponent of consensus, Tony Benn. And she is much admired by Tony Blair, who is apt, unless my ears deceive me, to echo these words of Margaret Thatcher:

'I decide with others the way we are going, then I bend every single effort to getting that through, overcoming all obstacles. It is not arrogant in my view. It is determination and resolve.'

From the poor Tory performances in the 1989 Euro-elections it looked as if the Thatcherite ascendancy was coming to an end. What with rising inflation and industrial stoppages, an American TV reporter quipped: 'The Iron Lady is showing signs of metal fatigue.'

There was the acrimonious resignation of her Chancellor, Nigel Lawson. And after the messy Cabinet reshuffle, in which she booted the long-suffering Sir Geoffrey Howe out of the Foreign Office, the Thatchocracy ended sooner than expected.

In her 1988 Bruges speech, she signalled her determination to prevent the EC from becoming a super-state: 'We have not successfully rolled back the frontiers of the state in Britain,' she declared, 'only to see them reimposed at a European level.' This appalled the pro-European establishment.

Did she set out to whip up Euroscepticism? Or was she responding realistically to a cooling of Euro-enthusiasm among the British people? Who can say? But there are no prizes for guessing how she will urge us to vote in the Euro referendum.

But, until the end came, Mrs. Thatcher dominated her Cabinet like no other recent Prime Minister. There was no obvious successor to her. She achieved all this – and here was a strange feature of the Thatcher phenomenon – without being a great parliamentarian, without being a brilliant orator, without having a gift for words or memorable phrases, and without displaying a notable sense of humour. Probably more than any Prime Minister in my lifetime, she was anathema to many intellectuals, such as the petty-minded Oxonians who shamefully voted to refuse her an honorary degree.

But her style of leadership, however domineering or strident, did not prevent her from winning another huge majority (102) in 1987. She thus became the first British Prime Minister to have been elected to three consecutive terms of office since Lord Liverpool over 160 years ago.

At that 1987 election, strong claims could be made for Margaret Thatcher's leadership. Had she not rolled back the state, curbed the trade unions, defeated Scargill, Galtieri and Ken Livingstone, and defied terrorism? Had not her Chancellors, Howe and Lawson, reduced the top rate of income tax from a monstrous 83% to 40%? The pound was strong. Inflation had stayed in the 4–5% range. The economy was growing.

But the second Thatcher government had seen some rough weather. There was no shortage of ammunition for critics of Thatcherism. There was the violence during the prolonged miners' strike, and in the printers' dispute at Wapping. There was the Westland helicopter affair, when normal Cabinet government disintegrated. Michael Heseltine stalked out of the Cabinet, and Thatcher came perilously near to falling from power. As she herself said to someone in Downing Street as she left for the Westland debate: 'I may not be Prime Minister by six o'clock this evening.' Thus for about three hours on the afternoon of Monday 28 January 1986 did Sir Geoffrey Howe seriously think that he might become Prime Minister that day.

Labour, with its media skills, including a brilliant film boosting its new Leader, Neil Kinnock, was widely held by the chattering classes to have won the 1987 campaign. But Labour lost the election.

So that election was a triumph for what had come to be called Thatcherism. Few people, if any (certainly not I), then thought that this three-times victor, this invincible vote-getter, this woman so admired around the world, would soon be forced out of office. Yet only three years later, in 1990, that is what happened to Margaret Thatcher. For the first time ever in peacetime a British Prime Minister in good health, commanding a majority in the Commons was kicked out of office.

This was not only the end of an epoch, but the extraordinary end of an extraordinary epoch. Whether you were glad or sad to see her go, she was the only Prime Minister whose name has been given to an 'ism'. No one ever talked about Disraeli-ism, Macmillanism, Heathism, or even Churchillism. As Margaret Thatcher herself tearfully remarked at her very last Cabinet Meeting, 'It's a funny old world.'

My favourite memory of her will always be that 1987 election interview. She was on her top form, in full flow, almost unstoppable. In content and style, this was vintage Thatcher. My attempts to interject were frequently cut short. At one point I was driven to suggest that we were 'not having a party political broadcast, but an interview which must depend on me asking some questions occasionally.' The Prime Minister replied 'Yes indeed, *Mister* Day', and went on exactly as before. According to Richard Last, the admirable TV critic of the Daily Telegraph, 'Sir Robin was crushed with the effortlessness of a beautifully coiffured steamroller flattening a blancmange.'

I do not remember her as 'Maggie', or ever hearing anyone call her 'Maggie'. To me she was 'Prime Minister' or 'Mrs Thatcher'. If I spoke of her, it would be as 'Mrs Thatcher' or 'Margaret'. But never 'Maggie'.

RONALD REAGAN

PRESIDENT OF THE USA 1981–9

After his career as a film actor and as Governor of California Ronald Reagan became President of the USA in 1981 and held the office for two terms until 1989. His great friendship with Margaret Thatcher and their shared political priorities cemented relations between Britain and the USA throughout the 1980s. This extract is taken from his memoirs An American Life, *published by Hutchinson in 1990.*

৵৹

Moral Duty

On a trip to England in 1978 I bumped into Jason Dart, one of the Californians who'd been in my Kitchen Cabinet, and he said he wanted me to meet a friend of his who had recently been elected the first woman to head the British Conservative Party.

I'd been planning on spending only a few minutes with Margaret Thatcher but we ended up talking for almost two hours. I liked her immediately. She was warm, feminine, gracious and intelligent and it was evident from our first words that we were soul mates when it came to reducing government and expanding economic freedom. At a reception that evening, an Englishman who had heard about our meeting asked me:'What do you think of our Mrs Thatcher?'

I said I'd been deeply impressed.'I think she'll make a magnificent Prime Minister.'

He looked at me out of the comers of his eyes with a kind of mocking disdain that seemed to suggest the idea was unthinkable:'My dear fellow, a woman Prime Minister?'

'England once had a queen named Victoria who did rather well,' I said.

'By jove', he said. 'I'd quite forgotten about that.'

↾⇛

Throughout the eight years of my presidency, no alliance we had was stronger than the one between the United States and the United Kingdom. Not only did Margaret Thatcher and I become personal friends and share a similar philosophy about government, the alliance was strengthened by the long special relationship between our countries. The depth of this special relationship made it impossible for us to remain neutral during Britain's war with Argentina over the Falkland Islands, although it was a conflict in which I had to walk a fine line. After the landing on South Georgia island, Margaret Thatcher called me and said that Britain would never submit to a takeover of one of its crown colonies. She asked me to telephone Leopoldo Galtieri, President of the military junta that ruled Argentina, to urge him not to proceed with the invasion and to say that Britain would use whatever force was necessary to keep her colony. I spoke to Galtieri but couldn't budge him.

The junta misjudged not only Margaret Thatcher's will but the strength of our ties to England. We assured Margaret Thatcher that we were fully behind Britain. Margaret Thatcher, I think, had no choice but to stand up to the generals who cynically squandered the lives of young Argentinians solely to protect the life of a corrupt and iron fisted totalitarian government. She did so, I believe, not because, as was speculated in Britain, her government might fall if she did not, but because she believed absolutely in the moral rightness of what she was doing and in her nation's obligation to guarantee the handful of people living in the Falklands the right of self-determination.

SIR RONALD MILLAR

MARGARET THATCHER'S SPEECH WRITER

Sir Ronald Millar was an accomplished playwright and film-script author. He began writing speeches for Prime Minister Edward Heath in the early 1970s. He was then invited to continue as speech writer firstly to Margaret Thatcher and then John Major. He was the author of a phrase that has entered our language – 'The Lady's Not for Turning'. Sir Ronald died recently and this extract is taken from his autobiography A View from the Wings, *published by Weidenfeld & Nicolson in 1993.*

ৡৎ

Lincoln's Address

Margaret Thatcher was elected Leader on 11 February 1975 but stubborn loyalty to her predecessor was still with me when, six days later, I was summoned to meet her in the House of Commons. At this first meeting her attitude to me was guarded as was mine to her. I had the feeling she was thinking: What sort of writer is this who worked for Ted? Not one of us, that's for sure. I was thinking: she must have something special or they wouldn't have made a woman Party Leader, but I wasn't clear what it was and in any case not at all sure that I wanted to be further involved politically.

I had heard that she was intent on change and fine, I thought, change is not only inevitable, it's desirable, but let's not wipe out yesterday like a wet sponge cleaning a blackboard. No one had said she intended this but the word was that she was a force to be reckoned with, a woman with all the determination of a man and therefore, in all probability, up to no good. However, seeing her in daylight for the first time, and suppressing one of those cliché assessments that were to dog her throughout her political life, there was a kind of senior girl-scout freshness about her that was rather appealing, as though she had stepped straight out of the *Sound of Music*, though I doubt if 'soft woollen mittens and whiskers on kittens' were ever her favourite things.

She offered me a chair and a coffee and said she had inherited a five minute Party Political Broadcast that was to have been given by Mr Heath and she understood that I helped with these broadcasts, was that right? 'Helped' was an understatement, but I nodded. Well now, would I consider doing this one for her? I explained that my play was opening in a few days time and I was completely taken up with final rehearsals. She said she understood but that the broadcast only required a five minute text. Couldn't I find time to squeeze it in?

I pointed out that a five minute text took rather more than five minutes to write and in any case I'd no idea what she wanted to say. 'Just set out my stall in general terms. There won't be any time for more than that. My politics aren't quite the same as Mr Heath's, you know.' Yes, I did know that. I also knew that as well as strong views she had a sense of mission and people with missions could be difficult to work with.

'Well?'

Assuming I could find the time, exactly when did she want it?

Could I manage a draft by tomorrow morning say, about eleven? This really was rather tiresome. Reluctantly I said I would see what I could do.

'Thank you. Till tomorrow, then.'

A polite smile, which I returned. There had been no instant meeting of minds, rather on my part, a feeling of irritation at being diverted from something more important to me, if not to the charismatic new Leader of the Conservative Party. I too could be stubborn on occasion. I really shouldn't have agreed so easily. I hurried away from the Palace of Westminster and sat at the back of the stalls in the Haymarket, my eyes on the stage and the actors and my mind concentrated nine-tenths on the play. During the lunch break I scribbled a few thoughts in my Rymans notebook but couldn't think of an ending. If stuck, 'go for a quote' is a cliché but it's not a bad fall-back position. I managed to remember some lines from a speech attributed to Abraham Lincoln, his most memorable after Gettysburg, which I had learnt once for an audition.

Next morning at eleven I returned to the new leader's office.' May I have it?' she held out her hand. On a sudden impulse I said, 'May I read it to you?' She seemed surprised but indicated a chair some way from her across the room. Then she sat down and half covered her eyes with her left hand. Was the light troubling her or did she fear the worst? 'It helps me concentrate,' she said. 'Go ahead. I'm listening.'

When I had done there was a total silence. I thought, well, that went down like a sack of potatoes. I'm off the hook. Glory hallelujah! But then she took her hand from her eyes and reached into one of these large holdalls in which nowadays women carry everything but the microwave. From this receptacle she produced a handbag. Out of the handbag came a wallet and from the wallet a piece of yellowing newsprint. All this was done very slowly and methodically without a word being uttered. Finally she got up and came across the room to me and handed me the piece of newsprint. 'It goes wherever I go,' she said. It was the Lincoln quotation.

There are moments in life when something goes 'click' in what one assumes to be the brain and you find yourself without warning on the same wavelength with a total stranger. This appeared to be just such a moment. I started to explain that I'd turned to Lincoln because I hadn't really had time for a peroration, my mind had been up there on stage with the actors. She said: 'If that's what you can do when you're not really trying, what will it be like when you are?' And this time the smile was more than polite. It was a dazzler.

SIR JOHN JUNOR

FORMER EDITOR OF THE SUNDAY EXPRESS

Sir John Junor was editor of the Sunday Express *for the first eleven years of Margaret Thatcher's leadership of the Conservative Party. This extract is taken from Sir John Junor's autobiography* Listening for a Midnight Train, *published by Chapmans in 1990.*

༺⚬༻

Acts of Kindness

My first impressions of Margaret Thatcher were mixed. She did not seem quite as attractive as the pictures suggested. Indeed she gave me at my first meeting with her the impression of being entirely asexual. Nor was I over-impressed with her as an intellectual.

If I had thought Margaret Thatcher lacked sex appeal that first time I met her, my views were to change in time. So were those of many others. Of course there were some who had always found her sexy. Douglas Clark, when Political Editor of the Sunday Express, attended a Tory Conference at Blackpool when she was Minister of Education in Heath's government. After a night of drinking with delegates in the various hotel bars and reception rooms he retired to his bedroom in jolly mood and still not ready for his sleep. Suddenly he found himself thinking of Margaret Thatcher and in a mad impulse picked up his bedside telephone and asked to be connected to her room. When a sleepy and utterly virtuous Margaret Thatcher answered she gave a very dusty answer indeed to his suggestion that she might care to come to his room for a nightcap.

As the years pass Margaret Thatcher's sex appeal has actually increased. Jim Prior told me once how one or two ministers had, as he inelegantly put it, tried unsuccessfully to get a leg over. Which proves, I suppose, the truth of the old adage that power is the greatest aphrodisiac of all.

Margaret came to the dinner given by Victor Matthews at the Ritz to celebrate my 25th anniversary as editor of the Sunday Express in November 1979. Ted Heath had shared our table. Not long afterwards I asked Margaret why she would not have him in the Cabinet. I pointed out that it might lessen her difficulties enormously. She looked at me and replied: 'I couldn't. He wouldn't want to sit there as a member of the team. All the time he would be trying to take over. I have to tell you this, John. When I look at him and he looks at me I don't feel that it is a man looking at a woman. More like a woman looking at another woman.' Poor Ted.

In 1981 I was asked to broadcast a six minute talk on any subject I pleased. I chose Margaret Thatcher. I related a few stories.

One concerned her driver George Newell, who had died from a heart attack at the age of 62. His funeral was in Eltham on a Friday in a week that had been a crisis week for the Prime Minister. The easiest thing in the world would have been for her to send a representative. But no. She went herself. She sat in a pew comforting the widow. And she tried her darndest to prevent the story of her kind act getting any publicity at all.

Another concerned a young member of her staff whose wife had left him, taking their children with her. It was three days before Christmas. He was in the depths of despair at the thought of having to spend Christmas on his own. Then the telephone rang. It was the Prime Minister. 'Are you doing anything for Christmas?' she asked. 'If not, why don't you come and spend it with Denis, Carol, Mark and myself.' For she had known the desperation of his loneliness. And cared.

After making the broadcast Margaret was good enough to write and thank me. 'Bless you for all the nice things you say and they came just at the right time.' It was a warm gesture to make. But then that is the kind of gesture Margaret Thatcher always makes.

LORD HOWE OF ABERAVON

CABINET MINISTER 1979–90

Geoffrey Howe was Margaret Thatcher's first Chancellor of the Exchequer (1979–83). He went on to become Foreign Secretary (1983–9) and Deputy Prime Minister (1989–90). His resignation in 1990 over European policy and his savage resignation speech in the House of Commons were key factors in Margaret Thatcher's eventual downfall. These reminscences are drawn from Lord Howe's memoirs, Conflict of Loyalty, *published by Macmillan in 1994.*

ॐॐ

1969

Arthur Seldon sought my view of Margaret Thatcher, as a possible target for the Institute of Economic Affairs. My response was cautiously encouraging: 'I am not at all sure about Margaret. Many of her economic prejudices are certainly sound. But she is inclined to be rather too dogmatic for my liking on sensitive issues like education and might actually retard the cause by over-simplification. We should certainly be able to hope for something better from her – but I suspect that she will need to be exposed to the humanising side of your character as much as to the pure welfare-market-monger. There is much scope for her to be influenced between triumph and disaster.'

February 1975

Two days after her election as Leader of the party, Margaret Thatcher came to address the regular Thursday meeting of the 1922 Committee.

The room was packed. Unusually, Shadow Cabinet members were present as well. The new leader, escorted by the chairman, Edward du Cann, entered the Committee room through the door opening onto the platform. She was flanked only by the all-male officers of the Committee. Suddenly she looked very beautiful – and very frail, as the half-dozen knights of the shires towered over her. It was a moving, almost feudal, occasion. Tears came to my eyes. The Conservative Party had elected its first woman Leader. And this over-whelmingly male gathering dedicated themselves enthusiastically to the service of this remarkable woman. By her almost reckless courage she had won their support, if not yet their hearts. A new bond of loyalty had been forged.

June 1979, Tokyo

The real star of the Summit was Margaret Thatcher, making her first appearance on the world stage as Prime Minister. In those days it was still the custom for each head of government to make a separate closing statement to the final press conference – a fearful recipe for competitive tedium. As the newest member, Margaret was the last head to perform. The 'press corps' assembled at the new Otani Hotel contained a startlingly large clutch of Japanese women – some journalists, no doubt, but many more diplomatic and political wives, secretaries and the like, all fired with curiosity by this female phenomenon. Margaret did not disappoint them. Speaking without a note (but far from extempore) she sparkled alongside the soberly scripted statesmen who had gone before. For the first time I realised just how powerful an international champion Britain now had.

Spring 1982

One colleague had concluded that: 'the way in which Margaret operates, the way her time is consumed, the lack of a methodical mode of working and of orderly discussion and communication on key issues with other colleagues, mean that our chance of implementing a carefully worked out strategy is very low indeed ...'. There never was any real improvement in Margaret's working methods of the kind that he would have liked. Yet the important agenda items were being tackled, albeit in a less systematic way than he or I might have wished. This was happening, above all, as a result of Margaret's input, authority and, sometimes, judgment. The difference from our more analytical approach was that her influence was deployed much more opportunistically and instinctively than we should have planned. But throughout Whitehall and Westminster her instinct, her thinking, her authority, was almost always present, making itself felt pervasively, tenaciously and effectively. It came gradually to feel, as the months went by, as though the Prime Minister was present, unseen and unspeaking, at almost every meeting. The questions were always being asked, even if unspoken: how will this play at Number 10? What's the best way of getting the Prime Minister on side for that? And so on.

February 1984

It was her unflattering perception of union loyalty that caused Len Murray and his colleagues such distress. For them the charge of disloyalty to the Crown, which Margaret implied was a consequence of union membership, was equivalent to a charge of treason. It was that insult, as they saw it, which made them angry. But this was a case where Margaret was at the end driven by her 'all or nothing' absolutist instinct. She could not find room in her thinking for acceptance of the parallel legitimacy of someone else's loyalty. It was probably the clearest example I had seen so far of one of Margaret's most tragic failings: an inability to appreciate, still less accommodate, somebody else's patriotism. A great patriot herself, with an enormous instinctive loyalty, she found it hard to respect or sympathise with the sense of loyalty of others, or even with the idea of a wider or different loyalty for herself. Even Welshness, I sometimes felt, she regarded as somehow beyond some unspoken pale – still more Irishness. A citizen, she seemed to feel, could never safely be allowed to carry more than one card in his or her pocket, and at GCHQ that could only be Her Majesty's card.

October 1985: Commonwealth Heads of Governments, Nassau

Before the world's television cameras, Margaret set out to present not the successful achievement of a concerted Commonwealth policy for change in South Africa but only the triumphant insignificance of the concessions *she* had had to make to achieve it. With forefinger and thumb only a few millimetres apart and contemptuously presented to the cameras, Margaret proclaimed that she had moved only 'a tiny little bit.' With four little words she had at one and the same time humiliated three dozen other heads of government, devalued the policy on which they had just agreed – and demeaned herself. She had certainly ensured that things would be a good deal less easy at any future such meeting. Even I could scarcely believe my eyes.

May 1983: Williamsburg Summit

Ronald Reagan was a splendidly natural host, with a straightforward and engaging tenacity on points that mattered. There was a spontaneity about his mutually supportive attitude towards Margaret. She likewise blossomed with admiring, almost affectionate, directness towards him. It was for both of them a personally satisfying and politically supportive relationship.

March 1985: Funeral of General Secretary Chernenko

The style of Margaret's second meeting with Mikhail Gorbachev, late-evening at the Kremlin, was to the point and friendly. Scheduled for only fifteen minutes, we were there for almost an hour. Margaret enthused over Gorbachev's recent London visit ('one of the most successful ever'). 'We must,' replied Gorbachev, 'continue to meet and talk to one another.' 'People in Britain,' concluded Margaret, 'took great pleasure in Gorbachev's appointment and would be pleased to see Gromyko in London.' Gorbachev chuckled. 'Mr Gromyko,' he said, 'is waiting for the London fog to clear.' Certainly the two leaders were attracted to each other, relished each other's company. But neither Margaret nor Mikhail ever completely lowered their guard.

September 1983: Foreign Policy Seminar at Chequers

I explained to Margaret that her own unique relationship with President Reagan, and her standing in Europe and elsewhere, could give Britain a voice in the Alliance which it badly needed at a time when the Soviet campaign against our deployment of intermediate range nuclear forces was obviously entering its peak period. 'One notable success,' said one official, 'had been to convince the PM that there was very little scope for destabilising the Soviet Union or Eastern Europe.' This important advance in understanding was probably to prove crucial to the successful outcome of Margaret's first encounter, still more than twelve months ahead, with Mikhail Gorbachev. The force with which Margaret later expounded this and argued the case for dialogue with Moscow was no less crucial in turning President Reagan away from the 'evil empire' rhetoric and encouraging him towards a similar relationship with Gorbachev. I sometimes think this may be seen by historians as her greatest achievement in foreign affairs.

March 1987: Russia

It was marvellous to behold the impact which Margaret herself had on ordinary Russians whose path she happened to cross. The three Soviet television journalists, who interviewed her for the long, uncensored interview which they broadcast, had never encountered anything like the whirlwind that swept them aside. The nationwide television audience loved it. This was indeed reflected in the reaction of Russians in the streets of Moscow and, even more, of Georgians in the streets of Tbilisi. When Margaret decided, as she did on more than one occasion, to make an unconventional exit from her Zil limousine to greet passing pedestrians, she was instantly overwhelmed by enthusiastic recognition and acclaim. 'Her driving personality', said the *Mail on Sunday*, 'puts her head and shoulders above anyone else on the world stage.'

September 1988

I was driven finally to conclude that for Margaret the Bruges speech represented, subconsciously at least, her escape from the collective responsibility of her days in the Heath Cabinet – when European policy had arrived, as it were, with the rations. Margaret had waited almost fifteen years to display her own distaste for the policies which she had accepted as a member of that government. I began to see her – and I do so even more clearly now – as a natural member of the gallant but misguided back-bench group of Enoch Powells, Robin Turtons and Derek Walker-Smiths, who had fought so long and hard against the European Communities Bill in 1971. Yet her deeds from day to day generally continued to belie that analysis. For she went on acting, for the moment at least, as though she was indeed the Prime Minister of a Member State of the European Community. And we had to continue conducting business on that basis. It was, I imagined, a little like being married to a clergyman who had suddenly proclaimed his disbelief in God. I can see now that this was probably the moment at which there began to crystallise the conflict of loyalty, with which I was to 'struggle for perhaps too long.'

Conclusion

And so came the years of triumph that ended in tragedy. Margaret Thatcher's eleven years as Prime Minister still stand as a period of remarkable achievement, albeit marred by decisive errors in her final term in office. She was beyond argument a great Prime Minister. Her tragedy is that she may be remembered less for the brilliance of her many achievements than for the recklessness with which she later sought to impose her own increasingly uncompromising views. For Margaret Thatcher in her final years, there was no distinction to be drawn between person, government, party and nation. They merged in her mind as one seamless whole. Her interests were axiomatically those of Britain. Any criticism of her was an unpatriotic act. The insistence on the undivided sovereignty of her own opinion dressed up as the nation's sovereignty was her own undoing.

LORD CRICKHOWELL

SECRETARY OF STATE FOR WALES 1979–87

Lord Crickhowell, then Nicholas Edwards, served in Margaret Thatcher's Cabinet as Secretary of State for Wales from 1979 until 1987 when he was raised to the peerage. He became chairman of the National Rivers Authority in 1989, a position he held until 1996. The following piece is a shorter version of an essay about Margaret Thatcher and the work of the Cabinet in his book, Westminster, Wales and Water *published by the University of Wales Press in 1999.*

❧

She loved an argument

Meeting in the Prime Minister's room in the House of Commons, we were discussing education policy. Keith Joseph, who she liked and admired and to whom she owed an immense debt of gratitude, but who she sometimes treated badly, was interrupted with increasing frequency as he attempted to present his case. At first these astringent interjections came every few sentences and then with the staccato bark of an automatic weapon they ripped every sentence into increasingly minute fragments,. Most of us examined our papers in silence with increasing irritation and embarrassment; but Nigel Lawson, deciding that enough was enough suddenly leant across the table and snapped, 'Shut up, Prime Minster, just occasionally let someone get a word in edgeways.' There was a stunned silence: we all looked up waiting to see what would happen. For the first and last time I saw Margaret Thatcher blush and then for twenty minutes she was silent, and during this extraordinary lull Keith presented his Paper and we went on to have one of the most constructive discussions that I ever remember in a Cabinet Committee chaired by the Prime Minister. I don't remember any other occasion when a cabinet colleague was quite so blunt; but it is nonetheless a myth that we were all always supine and subservient. The techniques for standing up to the Prime Minister's extremely combative conduct of business varied; but they were more effective than has been generally acknowledged. In reality she seldom behaved quite so badly as on that occasion with Keith Joseph and there is much to be said for the technique of testing the strength of a case by vigorous argument, though there were a few members of the Cabinet who found it unendurable.

Margaret Thatcher loved an argument and respected those who stood up to her when they had command of their subject. She invited contributions from around the table, sometimes from those of us who would have preferred at that particular moment to stay silent. The system of testing a case to destruction had the great advantage that it frequently exposed a flaw and prevented a disaster; but the drawback was that it sometimes destroyed perfectly good policy and prevented it being pressed further. As time went on, the runners in the race also found that the challenge had been made more severe by the simple manoeuvre of packing the committees with hostile critics. After the Industry Committee had produced a series of decisions and recommendations with which the Prime Minister disagreed, she regained control by assuming the chair herself. Committees that were not considered sufficiently robust found that the membership was changed, or decisions were taken by *ad hoc* groups of Ministers, frequently without the circulation of papers or adequate interdepartmental consultation. There was nothing very new in this but the Prime Minister carried the process further than most of her predecessors. Despite these manoeuvres there were frequent occasions when the Prime Minister did not get her way and when she accepted, sometimes with visible irritation, the majority decision.

She always came to the table impeccably well briefed. The Treasury commentary would be to hand; she would have underlined key passages in the papers before her with a yellow marking pen; her extraordinary memory provided a further challenge. On occasions she positively overwhelmed the opposition. This was always relatively easy if the unfortunate minister's colleagues simply did not believe that this was a policy for which they were prepared to fight and risk injury or worse. For most ministers the injury they feared most was the loss of some treasured policy of their own: if your own paper was next on the agenda, you would not prejudice its progress by stirring up advance hostility. Having said that, it is also true that in the great majority of cases when the minister sought approval for a policy he considered important and was prepared to fight, he would get his way, although sometimes it did not feel like it at the time.

An account that concentrates on arguments round the cabinet table inevitably gives a partial and distorted picture of the Prime Minister's character and conduct. The aggressive and dominating characteristics which she used to such effect in cabinet discussions were frequently matched by acts of great personal kindness. She always seemed to know a great deal about her colleagues and their troubles, and a Member of Parliament would be surprised to be stopped in a corridor with an inquiry about a recent sickness or a family problem. It was because of actions of that kind that she was so much loved by her staff at Chequers and Number 10, and by all those who worked closely with her.

She paid numerous visits to Wales and for nearly eight years gave me all the support I could have wished, even though my instruments were government agencies and regional policies that she did not much favour. As in so many other cases, she was more pragmatic and flexible in achieving her objectives than many of her critics have understood or acknowledged. She seemed most at home with the people of Wales in the period before tight security restricted her movements and cut her off from contact with ordinary people. On the last Christmas in opposition before she became Prime Minister, we arrived in Wrexham late one evening when the streets were packed with shoppers. She went from stall to stall in the market buying groceries and talking to stallholders and customers and then we emerged into the main street just at the moment that a huge float bearing Father Christmas appeared round the corner. The crowd surged forward and in a moment of inspiration, and perhaps because there was almost nowhere else to go, we pulled her up onto the float beside Father Christmas and there through the packed crowd they travelled together to a surging, warm, enthusiastic welcome that was unique in all my experience of political life. During the last election campaign in which I took part in the Summer of 1987, things were very different – every move was carefully scheduled. Security was tight, contact with crowds was minimal. I took her down to Cardiff Bay, and as we drove away, a small but noisy group booed and one man raised his fingers in an obscene gesture. The Prime Minister visibly froze, obviously offended, and turned to me saying, 'Oh what dreadful people, we are really wasting our time – what is the point of all your efforts if they appreciate them so little.' One felt that she was not at her best and this was alien territory, far from the England that she knew and understood. In a way it was the Scottish story all over again. Her efforts to help were not rewarded; the support that she gave for her Secretaries of State was not appreciated; there was a barrier that somehow she was not able to surmount.

My formal responsibilities as Secretary of State finally came to an end on Election Day and that weekend, as I sat in my Welsh home with Ann, I was surprised to receive a telephone call from Number Ten.

'The Prime Minister would like to speak to you.' There were a few words said about the way that the election had gone, sadness at seats that had been lost, and then she said, 'I have decided to appoint a very senior member of my Cabinet as Secretary of State for Wales.' 'Oh, yes, Prime Minister,' I said, 'And who is that?'

'Oh, I can't tell you', she replied, 'Because I have not yet told him'.

'In that case I cannot really comment,' I responded.

By this time Ann was in a fever of excitement, all agog to know who it was to be – we had been speculating long and hard. 'Well I will tell you if you promise not to tell anyone,' she said.

'Of course,' I replied.

'I have decided to ask Peter Walker to take on the job,' she told me.

'Peter Walker,' I repeated clearly, at least in part for Ann's benefit, 'I am sure he will do it excellently, what a brilliant idea.'

After she had rung off, I wondered why she had telephoned. It cannot be that if my reaction had been hostile she would have changed her mind. In any event I was rather touched and I appreciated the fact that she had taken the trouble to tell me, particularly as Peter Walker was apparently still totally ignorant of his fate.

'Will he accept it?' said Ann doubtfully. 'Oh, yes, I am sure he will,' I said. 'After all, he knows the difference between being in and out, and in the circumstances he will have an almost free hand to do anything he likes.'

BARONESS TRUMPINGTON

MINISTER OF STATE AT THE MINISTRY OF AGRICULTURE FISHERIES AND FOOD 1989–92

Raised to the peerage in 1980, Baroness Trumpington of Sandwich served as a junior minister from 1985 until 1992. Initially a Parliamentary Under Secretary of State at the DHSS, she took up the same position at the Ministry of Agriculture, becoming the Minister of State for that department in 1989.

෬ᚪᚷ

Terrified

I owe Margaret Thatcher everything since she made me a Life Peer in her first Honours List as Prime Minister. That was a huge surprise and I shall never cease to be grateful to her.

Having said that I am and always shall be terrified of her.

I well remember the first occasion I attended a full Cabinet Meeting in the place of John MacGregor. I was a brand new MAFF Minister and I had been instructed to press for a particular Professor to be appointed for a job. My only briefing was given at the last moment and consisted of the bare words that the Department for Education agreed with this appointment.

When it appeared that my great moment had arrived all I could do was to repeat the above words, several times, with less and less conviction.

Feeling a total prat and surrounded by the great and the good I subsided in much sweat.

As the Prime Minister left the Cabinet Room she patted me affectionately on the shoulder and said 'Don't worry dear, we will see your professor gets the job.'

The reason I think I am so frightened of her is because I never feel I can say the sort of thing I would say to my women friends, but always feel I have to ask her something meaningful about the state of the world. I am sure it's my fault, and I have never been afraid of sticking to my guns when I felt deeply over any issue. She never held that against me.

LORD JOPLING

CHIEF WHIP, 1979-83

A Member of Parliament from 1959 until 1997, Michael Jopling served in Margaret Thatcher's Cabinet from 1983 until 1987. He was Chief Whip in the first Thatcher government and served as Minister of Agriculture from 1983 to 1987. He was raised to the peerage in 1997.

☙❧

Handbagging

Much has been written and spoken about Margaret Thatcher's affection for Ronald Reagan and the way their partnership played a major part in bringing about the collapse of the Warsaw Pact and the Soviet Union.

Much has been written and spoken about her capacity to 'handbag' those who crossed her.

But I never saw her more incandescent than the occasion when I was Chief Whip, when one of her officials told her about President Reagan's so-called deal with President Gorbachev at Reykjavík.

Apparently the two of them had gone into a private session with interpreters only. Gorbachev had persuaded Reagan that it would be a good thing for the two of them to agree to the total elimination of nuclear weapons. Reagan had agreed to this, seemingly oblivious that it would leave the Soviet Union with a massive imbalance, in their favour, of conventional weaponry.

I cannot remember her exact words but the phrase was used by someone in the room that the idiot had no idea of the power balance between NATO and the Warsaw Pact. I recall someone else pointing out that Reagan had sold the shop, the contents and the goodwill as well.

The last sight I recall of her that morning was of her marching off to telephone Reagan.

I do not know what was said, but the verbal deal between the two Presidents was quietly dropped.

BARONESS FOOKES

DEPUTY SPEAKER OF THE HOUSE OF COMMONS, 1992–7

Janet Fookes served as the Member of Parliament for Merton and Morden from 1970 until 1974 and for Plymouth Drake from 1974 until 1997. She became a Dame of the British Empire in 1989 and was raised to the peerage as Baroness Fookes of Plymouth in 1997.

છો∕ઉ

Art of the Possible

More years ago than I now care to remember, I was confiding my own political ambitions to my boyfriend of the time, a Dental Surgeon. He rather poured cold water on the idea saying that his father, who was a leading Conservative Agent, had seen a very able young woman turned down by the Selection Committee in his constituency and both father and son thought that women were never going to get very far in politics. The able young woman concerned was none other than Margaret Thatcher. I was therefore delighted when she finally obtained her seat in Finchley and soon after her election came down to speak in my own constituency. Although I heard her speak many times thereafter, this first one will always remain in my mind as typical of her single-minded energy in pressing a point home. The theme on this occasion was that 'politics is the art of the possible'.

LORD LAMONT OF LERWICK

CHANCELLOR OF THE EXCHEQUER 1990–93

The MP for Kingston-upon-Thames from 1972 until 1997, Norman Lamont served as a junior minister in the Department of Energy, the Department of Trade and Industry, the Ministry of Defence and the Treasury between 1979 and 1989. In 1989 he became Chief Secretary to the Treasury in Margaret Thatcher's Cabinet and in 1990 he became Chancellor of the Exchequer, a position he held until 1993. He was raised to the peerage as Lord Lamont of Lerwick in 1997.

❦

Winning an argument

M argaret Thatcher was one of the greatest ever peace-time Prime Ministers. I was very happy to be in her Government for all eleven years. But Margaret Thatcher was generally thought to be a somewhat fearsome colleague and demanding Prime Minister. However, she liked people to stand up to her and whatever her manner she respected those who put a good case against her. It was important also not to take everything she said literally.

I only once got the better of Mrs Thatcher in an argument. She had returned from a visit to the United States and had been sitting on the airplane next to a well-known American movie mogul. This person had somehow convinced Mrs Thatcher that Britain ought to create its own Hollywood and ought to use government money to create a whole lot of new film studios. Mrs Thatcher, in an informal meeting, announced this to me and a group of astounded Ministers. She solemnly proposed that Government money should be used to subsidise these film studios which would be situated in Rainham Marshes in Essex.

I and other Ministers vainly pointed out that the whole thrust of her Government had been to remove subsidies from industry. There was no case for subsidising employment in Essex where there was little unemployment. Furthermore, the film industry was a curious one to subsidise. And lastly, Rainham Marshes was a strange site which would require massive investment in infrastructure to make the project practicable.

I remember vividly Mrs Thatcher turned on me, in front of colleagues, when I voiced my objections and said very sharply: 'You are hopeless. You are thoroughly negative. All you know is how to say 'no'. You do not have any imagination or any constructive ideas. If you had been in my government since 1979 I would have achieved nothing!'

I was a little taken aback by this but managed to pull myself together and to reply: 'Well, Prime Minister you are invariably right on most matters, but there is one point on which you are wrong. I have been in your government ever since 1979.'

Mrs Thatcher momentarily looked a little abashed but stuck to her argument. We ended the meeting by saying that if this was what she wanted to do of course we would put it into practice, although we all disagreed.

Forty-eight hours later I received a telephone call from her private office saying that she had changed her mind and that we should not proceed with the idea. It was often the case that if one put objections to her they might be overruled at the time but nonetheless they were absorbed. Contrary to what critics said she both listened and was flexible.

Another characteristic of Margaret Thatcher was that she was always extremely thoughtful about all those who worked for her. She really did mind about them and their families. I was once told by the manager of Smythson, the Stationers in Bond Street, that their largest buyer of notelets was Mrs Thatcher. Certainly she was very adept at sending little handwritten notes commiserating with people or congratulating them on this or that. I have several such notes from her. I am quite sure that Mrs Thatcher has carried out many private acts of kindness that are unknown to the wider world because she simply has not told anyone about them and only the individuals know.

Mrs Thatcher had a very strong sense of the need to honour one's obligations. One year my Conservative Association in Kingston decided to ask the Prime Minister's husband, Denis, to speak at a function which was being held in the Banqueting Suite at Twickenham Rugby Ground. On the Saturday afternoon I was sitting at home reading a newspaper in an armchair when the telephone rang and a voice said 'The Prime Minister for you'. Mrs Thatcher then came on the line and said 'Denis has strained his back and can't be with you tonight at Kingston.'

I replied 'Well, Prime Minister thank you very much for ringing, it is very good of you to tell me and I know everybody will understand.'

The PM went on, 'No no, you don't understand what I'm saying. I'm coming instead.'

I replied 'Prime Minister that is extremely kind of you but it isn't really necessary because everybody will understand that Denis is not at all well.' I was rather worried as I didn't think it was a grand enough occasion for a Prime Minister. Some people would be annoyed they didn't know she was coming. I was also concerned about the short time available to lay on the necessary security and all the other complications that would follow from a unexpected visit by the PM. But Margaret was insistent. 'We always keep our promises, and I am coming,' she said. She did. She stood in for Denis at the dinner, and of course the evening was a huge success.

SIR CHRISTOPHER LAWSON

DIRECTOR OF MARKETING,
CONSERVATIVE CENTRAL OFFICE 1981–7

Sir Christopher Lawson is a management consultant. After a career in marketing with Mars plc he joined the staff of Central Office to introduce modern direct marketing techniques into the party's campaigning methods.

જ્જી

Concern for others

It is not difficult to understand that many people think of one of our greatest Prime Ministers as merely a single-minded hard politician, for that was through her total dedication to her task. I have a very different memory of her. I saw many occasions when she was concerned for others at times when it would have been better to have that concern for herself. I think especially of her worry for others after the Brighton bomb.

I also remember that on the day after the 1983 election results and also the day after those of 1987, both a Saturday morning, I received a letter from her thanking me for my help in the campaigns. She must have been up all night writing her 'thank you' letters!

After each of the 1983 and 1987 elections the Prime Minister gave a celebration party at Number 10 for the new Members of Parliament. At each of these her 'staff' were expected to enthuse the new members and remind them that now was the time to prepare for the next election.

She had the great ability to enthuse others and did so in many ways through her uncanny depth of understanding of the problems of ordinary people.

At Downing Street parties she would circulate freely, guiding, thanking, encouraging, sometimes demanding of those attending these functions. After the guests left she would often kick off her shoes, have her first drink and relax completely. This was a Margaret Thatcher that most never saw!

I remember being at Chequers in early 1990 when I warned the PM that she was in danger from within the party and that she was likely to be challenged. She walked me around the garden and said that she was not worried. She was undoubtedly misled by her staff, who had told her that she had no problems. History proved differently!

Margaret Thatcher to me showed the world that Britain could and would cure itself of being the laughing stock of the western world. In this she succeeded and the country owes her a great debt.

Those of us who can remember the 'Seventies' will never forget the changes that developed during ' The Thatcher Years', when once again one became proud to be called 'British'.

LORD BAKER OF DORKING

CABINET MINISTER 1985–92

A junior minister in the Conservative government of 1970-74 and in the early years of the Thatcher administration, Kenneth Baker joined the Cabinet in 1985 as Secretary of State for the Environment. He went on to become Secretary of State for Education and Science, Chancellor of the Duchy of Lancaster and ended his ministerial career in 1992 as Home Secretary. He was raised to the peerage as Lord Baker of Dorking in 1997.

࿏

Contents of the handbag

In popular memory Prime Ministers are remembered for a characteristic feature. For Disraeli it was the monocle and the small wisp of a beard; for Gladstone, the great shock of white hair; for Chamberlain, the umbrella; for Churchill, the cigar; for Harold Wilson, the Gannex mac; but for Maggie, it would have to be the handbag: she was never without it and it became a formidable weapon. When she joined the Lords there was a cartoon which depicted the Peers cringing away from an empty Front Bench on which was deposited just one handbag.

I have attended meetings where Maggie would 'handbag' a colleague. But in all fairness that colleague usually deserved it. She liked a good argument and she always respected people who would argue strongly and stand-up for their corner, as long as they knew their facts and had researched their argument. Woe betide the Minister who was casual or careless – those are the ones who would get the full blaze of her contempt.

But Maggie had another use for the handbag. It contained not only all the things that women carry in their handbags, but also little scraps of paper. At a Cabinet Meeting she would have a brief prepared by the Cabinet Office under the guidance of the Cabinet Secretary. This, you could be assured, was well-read, underlined and marked even to the last page. Then she would have a second brief prepared by her political advisers from the Number Ten Policy Unit and this, too, would be carefully marked. That brief came to her in a separate box which the Civil Servants did not see. These were to arm her for the debate which would take place on the issue under discussion.

The Minister leading the discussion would have no idea what was in either brief but you knew from an early stage what her view was. Her style was not to go around the table like John Major collecting the voices and then coming down upon the side which had the majority. Maggie knew what she wanted but on several occasions she did not get her way.

When Maggie was really up against it and the argument was running against her, she would then pick up her handbag, put it on the Cabinet table and, opening it carefully and slowly, she would take out a piece of well crumpled and thumbed paper. This was the brief that came from no one knows whom – a friend, or someone who had rung her up who had a particular view about the matter in hand. It was unpredictable, sometimes illuminating, at others weird, sometimes an interesting new light, at others a worthless piece of gossip. Whenever she drew out a piece of paper like this the Cabinet Secretary would pale, and the Minister would raise his eyes to the ceiling knowing full well that he was about to be grounded.

When I was Education Secretary, I did discover one of Maggie's private briefers – her hairdresser. He had a child in one of the inner London comprehensive schools and when he was doing the Prime Minister's hair she would hear about his child's poor experiences. The

Prime Minister would then tell me and her colleagues that something more had to be done.

Discussions at Cabinet are never predictable. Many are the Ministers who have cursed the contents of that wretched blue handbag.

❧

The following passage is an extract from Kenneth Baker's memoirs The Turbulent Years, *published by Faber & Faber in 1993.*

Early on the morning of 22 November 1990 I was telephoned by Andrew Turnbull from Number 10 and told that the Prime Minister had decided to resign. A great leader of our country, a very great Prime Minister, had been struck down by a collective loss of nerve among her colleagues. It was the end of an era and of a very great Prime Minister.

When I arrived at Number 10 I found my fellow cabinet colleagues waiting outside the Cabinet Room in a funereal and uneasy silence, not at all keen to catch each other's eye. The Prime Minister came down the stairs a little after nine o'clock, and with head lowered went alone into the Cabinet Room. After a few minutes we were sent in to take our places. Margaret looked very red-eyed and under considerable strain. She began by saying that before the formal business of the Cabinet she wanted to make her position known. She started to read from the paper in front of her, but when she reached the part which said, 'having consulted widely among colleagues', she broke clown and could not continue. The words choked in her throat and she wiped away tears from her eyes. She started again falteringly and said, 'I am so sorry.' Cecil Parkinson, sitting next but one to her, suggested that the Lord Chancellor should read the statement. Margaret blew her nose, shook her head and continued, 'I have concluded that the unity of the

Party and the prospects of victory in the General Election' – here she paused again and choked on the words, but went on – 'will be better served if I stood down to enable Cabinet colleagues to enter the ballot for the Leadership. I should like to thank all those in Cabinet and outside who have given me such dedicated support.'

David Waddington was dabbing his eyes at this stage, and others were close to tears. Some, while remaining expressionless, must have been relieved. But nobody around that Cabinet table had ever thought they would witness such a scene. Margaret went on, 'It is vital that we stand together. The unity of the Party is crucial and that's why I am giving up. I couldn't bear all the things I have stood for over the past eleven years being rejected. The Cabinet must unite to stop Michael Heseltine.'

Slowly Margaret recovered her composure. It had been a moving scene. Never before had she broken down in front of her colleagues. But at the end she was a real person of flesh and blood, not the cold, unfeeling automaton she was so often portrayed as. Then the Lord Chancellor, James Mackay, read the passage which Robin Butler the Cabinet Secretary had prepared for him, recording the Cabinet's tribute to Margaret's leadership of the country.

'As Party Chairman', I said, 'you have and will always continue to have the love and loyalty of the Party. You have a special place in the heart of the Party. You have led us to victory three times and you would have done so again. Speaking as one of the longest-serving Cabinet Ministers', I added, 'those who have served you recognise that they have been in touch with greatness.' Then Douglas Hurd said he wanted to place on record the superb way in which Margaret had carried herself at the Paris Conference over the last three days, especially with the pressures of the leadership election upon her.

We then turned to other matters, the business of the House and so on. When it came to Foreign Affairs, Margaret gave a spirited, very detailed and long report on her talks with Gorbachev and Bush. She was clearly getting back into her stride. But towards the end of the meeting I could see she was close to tears again.

We were all asked to stay on for coffee, which we then had sitting around the Cabinet table. We talked about the future. Margaret was very keen and insistent that it should be a member of the Cabinet who was elected to succeed her. 'I think the Cabinet will have to do everything it can to ensure this. You will have to work very hard,' she said.

During this meeting I passed a note to Douglas Hurd asking whether he had come to any agreement with John about the candidacy. I had assumed that some time over the last twenty-four hours they must have talked together about this and come to an arrangement. Douglas sent back a note saying they were going to issue a joint statement declaring that they had worked very closely together and would continue to do so but, in all the circumstances, the best way of uniting the Party would be for both to go forward in the next ballot. It would be a friendly contest. Douglas drafted this statement then and there, and passed it to me. It was perfect, a masterly composition. One of Douglas' great gifts is his capacity to draft elegant statements at the drop of a pen. Norman Lamont, who had been promoting John's cause for some time – he had actually canvassed Cecil Parkinson twenty-four hours earlier – could now openly become John's Campaign manager. It was clear to me that despite the disavowals of the two protagonists a good deal of preparatory work had already been done by the two camps to marshal their campaign teams.

Cecil was quite scathing about the whole situation. He said both campaigns would be negative if the contestants were going to be friendly. 'If they are going to be friendly, why bother to turn up and vote for them?'

As the meeting broke up I told Cecil and Douglas that as Chairman of the Party I would make a statement to the cameras outside Number 10 on behalf of the Cabinet. I jotted something down outside the Cabinet Room, and then went out to the massed cameras opposite the front door of Number 10 and said, 'This is a typically brave and selfless decision by the Prime Minister. Once again Margaret Thatcher has put her country and the Party's interests before personal considerations. This will allow the Party to elect a new leader to unite the Party and build upon her immense successes. If I could add just a personal note, I am very saddened that our greatest peace-time Prime Minister has left Government. She is an outstanding leader, not only of our country but also of the world – I do not believe we will see her like again.'

I was deeply moved by the events which I had just witnessed. I was very close to tears myself in the Cabinet Room. I had started by being cool about Margaret Thatcher, but over the years I had come to admire her. She has traits of character which can make her not particularly endearing. As Prime Minister she was personally dominant, supremely self confident, infuriatingly stubborn and held a strange mixture of broad views and narrow prejudices. But Margaret also had a strength of character that made her a natural leader. She was a patriot, always putting the interests of Britain first. She also realised that Britain had to be saved from economic and institutional collapse. No Prime Minister I have known since the War would have seen through that tough Budget of 1981 which deepened the recession we were then going through but proved to be the foundation of the prosperity of the middle and late 1980s. No Prime Minister I have known would have had the courage to launch a sea and land offensive 8,000 miles away to secure the independence of a small group of colonial islands. No Prime Minister since the War would have withstood a miners' strike for over a year. And no Prime Minister since the War would have reduced the power of organised labour in the way that Margaret did.

ALEXANDER HAIG

NATO SUPREME ALLIED COMMANDER IN EUROPE 1974–9

General Alexander M Haig Jr is Chairman of his own international advisory firm, Worldwide Associates Inc, based in Washington DC. He was White House Chief of Staff for President Richard Nixon, Supreme Allied Commander in Europe (NATO) and President Ronald Reagan's first Secretary of State.

಄ೲ

Giant among leaders

Margaret Thatcher is a giant among contemporary world leaders. She is a woman of conviction, courage, and principle.

I first met her in the mid-seventies while I was serving as the Supreme Allied Commander in Europe (SACEUR). I recall being urged by one of Great Britain's leading conservative political leaders to meet with an upstart conservative lady who believed she could be the next prime minister of Great Britain. He urged me to meet her in Brussels and brief her on the European security situation, adding that her intellectual well was somewhat dry on such things. Because of the position of the caller, I agreed and after spending approximately one hour with this attractive, bright, and enthusiastic political hopeful, left with the impression that my contact's assessment had been an accurate one as it applied to European security issues.

I saw Margaret Thatcher six or eight months later at a point when she had become the nominee of the Conservative Party. In the brief intervening period between our two meetings, she had acquired a level of military knowledge that was both remarkable in scope and the match for a professional with years of European security background. During the remainder of my time as SACEUR I met frequently with the then Prime Minister, and remained in awe of her military and geopolitical acumen.

Some years later, as America's 59th Secretary of State, I came to know Margaret Thatcher in an environment where the vital interests of both of our respective nations were at stake on several important occasions. Perhaps the most difficult of those occurred at the end of my service in the Reagan Cabinet during the Falklands War. In my first book entitled *Caveat: Realism, Reagan, and Foreign Policy* I described this remarkable woman in the following brief paragraph:

In the Falklands, the West was given a great victory by Great Britain. I do not mean the defeat of Argentinian soldiers by British soldiers. Every man who fell on either side represented a loss to the free world. British arms prevailed, but principle triumphed. The will of the West was tested and found to be equal to the task. The rule of law was upheld. The freedom of a faraway people was preserved. For this, the free world may thank the men of the British task force and Mrs Thatcher, who was by far the strongest, the shrewdest, and the most clear-sighted player in the game. In times of acute national crisis, a leader will always hear advice that clashes with his inner convictions. Easier courses than the right course will be thrust upon him. It is the leader, who knowing where the true interest of the nation lies, resists such counsel and perseveres in his principles, who deserves the name of statesman. Margaret Thatcher belongs in that company.

SIR DAVID STEEL

LEADER OF THE LIBERAL PARTY 1976–87

Sir David Steel was leader of the Liberal Party for almost all of Margaret Thatcher's period as Prime Minister. He led the Party into an Alliance and later a merger with the SDP becoming a founding father of the Liberal Democrat Party. Sir David Steel is currently the Presiding Officer of the Scottish Parliament.

৵৽

Contradictory memories

I have two contradictory memories of Margaret Thatcher. The first is the public one – her strident uncompromising battling at House of Commons question time, especially her memorable (but rather flattering) put-downs of me: 'Let me tell this young man . . .'

The second is a private one. On one of the many occasions when she felt obliged to invite me as leader of the Liberal Party to dinner at Number 10 for a distinguished foreign guest (we always parade our multi-party democracy on such occasions) my wife was struck down with 'flu and could not travel from Scotland. She greeted me 'So sorry to hear Judy is ill. I didn't want you to be alone so I've arranged for Carol to join us and partner you into dinner.' A genuinely thoughtful and kind touch.

EDWARD PEARCE

AUTHOR AND JOURNALIST

Until recently, a columnist for the Scotsman *and former Commons sketch writer for the* Daily Telegraph, *Edward Pearce has published nine books including* Machiavelli's Children, The Lost Leaders *and* Lines of Most Resistence. *He is currently working on the official biography of Denis Healey.*

⌒∾⌒

Personal kindness & public outburst

Personally, unlike most contributors to this book, I am not a fan of the Lady – too rigid, too narrow, too full of animus, a sort of Protestant ethic gone rogue. Oddly, she was so much better with what we inadequately call 'ordinary people' than with coadjutors. There is a nice story about custard. At a cabinet dinner, a very inexperienced and frightened young waitress spilt a great dish of custard all over Geoffrey Howe. Instead of berating her, or going all steely silent, Margaret threw her arms round the girl and said 'My dear, you mustn't cry. Anyone could have an accident,' and to Geoffrey Howe who was ineffectively sponging away at his suit, 'Geoffrey! Stop making such a fuss.'

It could be of course that the victim being Geoffrey, between whom and herself there was something of a sympathy deficit, charitable feeling came very easily. But it shows her very nicest side and wasn't the only example.

When her chauffeur died, she didn't send a card, she went to the funeral in person. Contrast, under the present Tory regime, the death of Giles Shaw earlier this year. He was a Minister of State, a former serious candidate for the Speaker's chair and very widely liked. The only sitting MP at his funeral in Yorkshire was Tam Dalyell!

I saw most of Margaret Thatcher in opposition and really rather liked her. Pity about the politics. Actually I mean that seriously. She did behave well enough and pretty nicely away from politics. The excesses came with the party struggle. After all, Neil Kinnock isn't a Communist, but Maggie thought he was and said so in the Commons. 'He is a Marxist, a crypto-Communist.' It was an unbelievable remark, but instructive. The good nature and manners of ordinary life would regularly be swept away in the political context, but so was all sense, sophistication and judgment.

The same is true of that outburst on TV, instantly recalled and apologised for – 'drooling and drivelling about the poor'. It is one thing to be hard-headed, but that spoke a partisan rage beyond party, directed rather at a class. Would she ever have embarked on the Poll Tax which fell so heavily on the claimant, canned beer-drinking, football-watching, undeserving part of mankind if the 'drooling and drivelling' outlook hadn't been an underground stream in her nature? Like I said, a Protestant ethic gone rogue.

Class was central with her and I'm not alone in noticing. At a seminar at Durham about five years ago I set out before lunch the notion of Margaret Thatcher, class warrior. Alan Clark, her great fan, breezed in on time for what he would have called 'pudding', and afterwards launched himself onto the thesis 'It's all absolute crap of course to talk about liberal market theory. What Margaret is on about is the Class War.'

I don't mind the fierceness. Where Blair cringes, she bops and when she does, sometimes you find yourself at the other end of the telescope approving!

I was at a dinner for her in 1985 where Charles Moore was attacking the new Anglo-Irish agreement, 'Robert Armstrong's revenge' as some of us called it. 'What about the Protestants?' he asked in the odd Orange way of so many English Catholics. She leaned into the table and in her best, taut, intense, Puff the Magic Dragon way, said 'Yes, Charles and what about the Catholics?' She had heard John Hume's great speech not long before she was actually listening to people like Armstrong. Consequently all the fierceness which she would misuse in hating the Germans and despising the unemployed, was turned towards getting a decent equity for the minority. It was wonderful.

'Am I no a bonny fighter?' asks Alan Breck. Yes indeed but too much so in Margaret Thatcher's case. For she started fighting her own side. When a leader of a party creates factionalism as she did in her last two years — and during the term of her successor when she called in backbenchers to bully them into voting against the Tory whip — it is simply ruinous. For a head of government to summon a seminar to collectively analyse the character faults of a notably friendly neighbour, Germany, was to do something against reason. And in politics, whatever the joys of raging conviction, reason has its uses.

She was 'the little girl with a curl, right in the middle of her forehead'. And you know how that ends.

NEIL HAMILTON

MP FOR TATTON 1983–97

Neil Hamilton served as MP for Tatton from 1983 until the 1997 general election. He was a member of the No Turning Back Group of MPs. Neil Hamilton currently works as a writer and broadcaster.

ॐॐ

Getting the joke

Contrary to popular mythology, Margaret is not at all stuffy or narrow-minded and has a good sense of humour. She likes raising a chuckle by acting up to her caricature handbagging image – a joke all the more amusing to observe when played on someone who thinks she is being serious.

But I have to admit that getting her to see the point of someone else's jokes is sometimes no laughing matter – as I occasionally discovered to my cost. After *The Spectator* awarded me the title 'Parliamentary Wit of the Year' in 1988 she engaged me as a resident jokesmith to add some souffle lightness to the bread-and-butter pudding of a Prime Ministerial speech.

It was no easy task. For example, in October 1989 I was at Chequers helping with her speech for the debate on the Queen's Speech. This annual debate concerns the Government's programme for the year ahead but technically arises on a motion to present a Loyal Address to the Monarch, thanking her for 'her gracious Speech'. The Government chooses two of its own backbenchers for the honour of proposing and seconding the motion – the first, usually an amiable old buffer long past his sell-by date, and the second, usually some oily young man on the make. They are followed immediately by the Prime Minister, who has to shower compliments upon them before getting on with the serious business.

The seconder in 1989 was an amiable young buffer, Jeremy Hanley, then Tory MP for Richmond-upon-Thames. A chartered accountant by training, he was also a member of MENSA, the club for the very brainy. But his roots were more theatrical – his mother being star of stage and screen, Dinah Sheridan; his father, the well-known comedian, Jimmy Hanley. Jeremy was an excellent and amusing raconteur in his own right and could be relied on to rise to the occasion.

What could Margaret say about him? I suggested a mild witticism, combining a reference to his intelligence and amiability: 'He is very clever and amusing but he never allows his brains to go to his head.' The joke seemed pretty obvious to me, but not alas to Margaret, who exploded: 'I can't say that! If his brains aren't in his head, where will people think they are?' We grappled with the abstruse metaphysics of the humour for some time but, try as I might, I could not get her to see the punchline – she was convinced everyone would think she was suggesting his brains were in his backside!

CHRISTINE HAMILTON

WRITER AND BROADCASTER & BATTLEAXE

The wife of former Conservative MP Neil Hamilton, Christine Hamilton first came to public attention for her vigorous defence of her husband during the 1997 General Election. She capitalised on her image by writing the Bumper Book of British Battleaxes *for Robson Books and now works as a presenter on radio and television.*

ༀ

Love of chocolate

During the 1992 General Election Margaret came to speak at a rally for Neil in Knutsford, arriving at our home for supper beforehand. It had been an exciting day. That afternoon she had done a walkabout in Stockport for Tony Favell and had been attacked – fortunately only with a bunch of daffodils. Margaret, of course, carried on with supreme sang-froid but her minders were understandably alarmed by the breach of security.

On arrival with us, all memory of daffodils had been expunged and she beetled in through the front door, reluctantly stepping on the pristine red carpet we had rolled out for the occasion, demanding to know 'What are the trade figures? What are the trade figures?'

She marched into the drawing-room where Neil steered her to an armchair. Adjacent to this we had carefully placed the cardboard cut-out figure of Margaret which I had bought in Carnaby Street back in the mid-70s which normally sat in our hall to frighten off burglars (very successfully). It was exhilarating to have the real three-dimensional Margaret sitting next to her two-dimensional replica but she affected not to notice, perhaps thinking there was nothing unusual about this and that every home should have one!

Into the dining-room for supper and, amongst a multitude of goodies normally classed in our household as 'forbidden or controlled substances' was a magnificent rich, dark chocolate torte which I had lovingly made. I knew that, although chocolate was one of Margaret's favourite foods, she had given it up for Lent. I assumed, therefore, that she would refuse the proffered delicacy and accept the fruit salad alternative. Not a bit of it! She took a particularly large wedge and rapidly demolished it with gusto. When I gingerly expressed my surprise, she replied in a magisterial tone of mock stern rebuke: 'I have given up chocolate BARS – this is quite different!'

The torte had the desired effect – at the rally, she gave a breathtakingly spectacular tour de force, speaking for over an hour without a single note.

SIR MARK LENNOX-BOYD

PPS TO MARGARET THATCHER 1988–90

The MP for Morecambe and Lunesdale from 1979 until 1997, Sir Mark Lennox-Boyd was the Parliamentary Private Secretary to the Prime Minister from 1988 until 1990. He went on to become the Parliamentary Under-Secretary of State at the Foreign and Commonwealth Office.

ঔৎৎ

Cooking for Denis

No-one who knows Margaret will ever underestimate the extraordinary trouble she took for those who worked for her, for her friends and of course for her family.

Notwithstanding her reputation for hard work, Margaret used to get extremely tired and one of the responsibilities of her PPS was to protect her from unnecessary demands on her energy. I well remember one incident which initially caused me bafflement. She had an engagement on a Friday afternoon with the Thames Valley Police and another late morning meeting on the Saturday at Chequers. The obvious plan was to drive from the police meeting to Chequers for the night, but earlier in the week in question, she announced that she intended to return to Number 10 on the Friday evening for a quiet supper and work and to be driven to Chequers on the Saturday morning. She was as usual clear and firm, but provided no explanation as to why she wished to subject herself to an extra two or more unneeded hours in a car, some of it in rush hour traffic. I pressed her and she realised that she must give an explanation if she was not to lose credibility with the several people who were present. 'You see Denis has a dinner in London on Friday and I wish to return to be at Number 10 with him because he likes eggs and bacon for breakfast on Saturday, and there will be nobody in the flat but me to cook.' I cannot remember if we managed to get Denis driven to Chequers after his Friday dinner, but I very much hope we did.

MICHAEL DOBBS

NOVELIST AND BROADCASTER

A former Chief of Staff and Deputy Chairman of the Conservative Party,
Michael Dobbs is most famous as the author of the House of Cards *trilogy*
of political novels. His latest novel is Whispers of Betrayal, *published by*
HarperCollins..

ॐ

The fall & rise of the House of Cards

They sow the seeds of their own destruction, even the greatest. And so it was with Margaret.

The date was the fourth of June, 1987, exactly one week before the election triumph that returned her to Downing Street for a record third time. Her victory was unprecedented, and it was to be her last.

I was Chief of Staff of the Conservative Party and on that fateful day was sitting in my claustrophobic room in Conservative Central Office. When I had been appointed to the position I had been told by Norman Tebbit, the Chairman of the Party, what to expect. 'There comes a point in every war when the generals require that someone be taken out into a courtyard, put up against a wall and shot. Your job is to find the body. Or to be the body.' I had thought he was joking.

A Gallup poll the night before had shown an alarming reduction in the size of the Tory lead. On the basis of the poll we were headed for trouble, but every other piece of information suggested we were going to win, and win big.

It was a rogue poll.

It didn't, however, stop the panic. Margaret was holding a morning summit in the room next door to mine with Norman, David Young, Willie Whitelaw and Stephen Sherbourne. Suddenly John Wakeham burst into my room and asked for the press advertising that was proposed for the following day. I was not responsible for the advertising but it had been left in my room for security. I handed the layouts to John, but he shook his head. 'I'm not going back into that room without you.'

So I took the layouts and walked into the room. If John had been kind he would have offered me a blindfold. It was time to be stood up against the wall.

The next few minutes of what became known as 'Wobbly Thursday' remain distinct in my mind, but I won't report the gory and distasteful details here, except to say that although the confrontation that took place was ostensibly about advertising, it had far more to do with power, access and intrigue. For the Court of Queen Margaret had turned into a Byzantine maze of crossed wires and conniving acolytes. Margaret was at the height of her powers, and it seemed that everyone wanted their own individual piece of it.

And that is the point of this story. She was at the height of her powers. She could rant and rage to the point of incoherence (and did during those minutes); I felt as though the handbag had been buried deep in the back of my skull. Willie Whitelaw rolled his oyster eyes at me in sympathy, but only Norman Tebbit tried to stand up to her, to restrain her, to direct her onto safer ground. It was to no purpose. In more than a decade of working for her I had seen her in pain, in tears, in triumph, but never had I seen her in such a condition.

She was the Leader, one of the greatest leaders of the century, and about to score another historic victory. Except she seemed to doubt that herself.

As we left the meeting we were all shaking. I walked next to Willie

Whitelaw, that wise and often underrated old bird, who said something that was to change my life. 'That is a woman who will never fight another election,' he muttered.

It seemed a preposterous suggestion. She bestrode the world. Yet three weeks later, as I sat beside a swimming pool in Gozo, the thought was still bothering me. I worked it over. They never know when to go, the great leaders. They all have to be pushed, shoved, hacked from office. Lloyd George. Churchill. And Thatcher, too. I realised that Willie was right.

She had lost the sensitivity and patience that had guided her so successfully through the difficult years when she had rebuilt a party in tatters and set it upon a course that transformed the country. It wasn't so much a matter of principle or policy but of personal style that, in the end, forced away from her even many of her closest allies. She became a political Chernobyl from whom so many were to distance themselves.

That realisation transformed my life. I sat down beside the swimming-pool and began work on a novel about the destruction of a Prime Minister. It was called *House of Cards*.

Like so many of the ancient gods, she could not be brought down by mere mortals. She could only be brought down by herself. Oh, but while it was good, wasn't she magnificent!

SIR RICHARD NEEDHAM

CONSERVATIVE MP, 1979–97

Richard Needham joined the Thatcher government as a junior minister in the Northern Ireland Office, where he remained until 1992. Between 1992 and 1995 he was Trade Minister at the DTI. This extract is taken from his memoirs Battling for Peace, *published by Blackstaff in 1998.*

❧

Summoned

During the seven years that I held a government post under Margaret Thatcher there were only two occasions when I was summoned in attendance. The first was a general meeting of all parliamentary private secretaries in the Downing Street whip's office. Everyone fell over themselves to be ever more syco-phantic in an often vain effort to impress on the PM, within the thirty seconds allotted, why they possessed more shining talents than their colleagues. The whips stood around the back of the room making mental notes and smirking. The second happening was an invitation to lunch at Number 10 in early 1988 when I had been two and a half years a Minister. There were eight of us including Lord Young, Willie Whitelaw, Ian Stewart, Colin Moynihan and Edwina Currie. The PM started to savage Ian Stewart. 'What are you doing to tighten up spending in the Defence Department?' she demanded. His attempts at explanation were cut off in mid sentence when the guns were turned on Edwina. Edwina was made of stern stuff and fought her corner. The PM then turned on little Colin Moynihan. 'Why do we need a

Minister for Sport?' she demanded. 'To deal with drugs,' he replied. This nonplussed her. 'Explain,' she rasped. 'Well as you know Prime Minister, drugs are endemic in sport. When there are governing bodies which need government money or subsidy we can insist on internal rules and procedures that can eliminate drug taking. We are being successful, particularly in sports such as athletics, but the biggest problem is snooker.' 'Snooker?' she asked incredulously. 'That dreadful game where everyone smokes and drinks and which Denis watches late at night in the flat? What drugs do they take?' 'Beta-blockers Prime Minister. They slow down the heartbeat so the player does not jerk as he plays his shot.' 'I've never heard of them,' she reflected. 'Then none of us round this table would ever have any need of them, would we Willie?' Willie blinked and as he pushed his little pillbox under his napkin, boomed out: 'Certainly not, Prime Minister!'

SALLY PIPES

PRESIDENT, PACIFIC RIM INSTITUTE FOR PUBLIC POLICY,
SAN FRANSISCO

Sally Pipes is president and chief executive officer of the The Pacific Research Institute. Prior to working for PRI, she was assistant director of the Fraser Institute, based in Vancouver, Canada.

ලංග

Turning the Tide

Stand Back Buenos Aires. That was the headline of the *Los Angeles Times*, plucked from 'Evita,' when Margaret Thatcher sent the fleet to recover the Falklands from the Argentine despots who thought the islands were theirs for the taking. That bemedalled junta based its gamble on the probability that Britain's leader, a woman, would be even more inclined to appeasement and surrender in the face of aggression than her male predecessors. As they say here in America, they bet wrong. They didn't know with whom they were dealing. But they soon found out it was no Evita Peron.

Mrs Thatcher's forces quickly forced surrender and recovered the territory. The victory not only boosted her international standing, sending a message to bullies far and wide, but it helped topple Argentina's military rulers and opened that nation to free elections. Had she caved in to them, as the surrender lobby urged her to do, they would still be in power and the Falklands would now be the Malvinas. But Margaret Thatcher was not fond of caving, and the same resolve that led Mikhail Gorbachev to dub her the 'Iron Lady,' would serve her well on the home front, where the opposition, though not armed with Exocet missiles, was no less daunting.

Despite ample warning from F A Hayek, Milton Friedman, and others, Britain, following World War II, was travelling the road to serfdom at more than the usual speed. By the time Mrs Thatcher took the reins, the British welfare state had bloated to grotesque proportions, choking initiative, killing jobs, and turning what was once a great nation into an international laughing stock. Union bosses, seething with class hatred, ran amok like medieval bandit kings.

Faced with this situation, the most serious for Britain since World War II, Margaret Thatcher was not content to, in the words of William F Buckley, stand athwart history yelling 'stop'! Like C S Lewis, she knew that if one is on the wrong road, it is not 'progressive' to keep on driving. One must turn around. Mrs Thatcher knew that the welfare state had to be dismantled and that something had to be offered in its place. That something could not be rhetoric, though taking a cue from Orwell, she recognised the duty of stating the obvious.

Many of the tasks performed by the government could be done better and cheaper by private enterprise. Mrs Thatcher's genius was to that this was the truly progressive course, which the British public was soon to confirm. When she took office in 1979, Britain taxed savings income at 98 per cent and earned income at 83 per cent. By the end of her tenure, the rate had been reduced to 40 per cent and the Prices and Incomes Board had been abolished. The nation, as she put it 'began to hum,' rising from the dregs to fifth in the world in prosperity, a remarkable comeback.

As one raised in Canada, where the nanny state still reigns virtually unchallenged, I admire her tenacity, especially in the face of a hostile and partisan press, whom she handed with an ease seldom seen in our time. Margaret Thatcher never accepted the still common notion that those less than worshipful of socialism lack compassion. She had no use for the politics of sentiment and never played the game, common in America, of trying to show that she cared more than the opposition. She knew that what matters most is results, not rhetoric, and that the policies of an ordered liberty would improve the lot of everyone. In the face of furious opposition, she stayed the course.

It bothered her not at all that, despite her huge accomplishments, achieved despite humble beginnings, feminists refused to admit her to their honour roll of heroes. They thus revealed what Lady Thatcher also knew, that feminism is the women's auxiliary of socialism. Though she came from humble beginnings, she didn't need feminism to achieve, and her victories exploded the feminist dogma that Western democracies are oppressive patriarchies that keep women down. But Mrs Thatcher's feminist critics also revealed that they didn't speak for all women.

The ideas Margaret Thatcher championed, ordered liberty, the rule of law, and privatisation, carry on in the marketplace of ideas. The Pacific Research Institute is one of those institutions still carrying that banner. Most world leaders would decline the invitation of a San Francisco-based think tank, but Lady Thatcher showed she was not like other world leaders.

She accepted an invitation to speak at our 20th anniversary dinner, and said it was an honour to address an institute promoting the idea of law-governed liberty. But we all knew that the honor was ours. Lady Thatcher's wit and wisdom dispelled the media caricatures, and she showed she had not lost a step. In a marathon question period she covered everything from taxes to missile defence, with deft, detailed answers. 'I have never been lethargic on missile defence,' she said, showing the familiar aplomb she demonstrated in the Commons. She easily outlasted the audience and when asked if, on the current world scene, she saw a pair similar to herself and Mr Reagan, supplied a ringing curtain line.

'There is not a comparable pair today,' she said, 'but hope springs eternal.'

LORD WAKEHAM

CHIEF WHIP 1983–87

John Wakeham was Conservative MP for Maldon & Colchester South from 1974 to 1992. He joined the whips office in 1979 and was appointed Chief Whip in 1983. In 1987 he became Leader of the House of Commons and was appointed Energy Secretary in 1989. He was elevated to the peerage in 1992 and became Leader of the House of Lords, a position he relinquished in 1994.

ॐ

Remembering the achievements

I entered the House of Commons in 1974 – one year before Mrs Thatcher became Leader of the Conservative Party. I left it for the House of Lords barely eighteen months after she left Number 10. My time as an MP was therefore dominated by this giant figure – one of the greatest Prime Ministers this country has ever seen, and probably will ever see.

Tributes elsewhere in this timely volume testify eloquently to the dramatic changes she wrought in British politics – permanently transforming an economy in decline into the powerhouse we have today, and turning us into a nation of owners with stakes for the first time in our businesses, our major industries and, for many, many more in our own property. Few dispute that success, and the permanent legacy, even among Margaret's detractors.

I do not want to add to this catalogue – but rather to add my own personal memories of the saddest point of Margaret's premiership, her resignation in November 1990.

Those of us who were closest to her knew that a challenge to her leadership from Michael Heseltine was almost inevitable from the moment Geoffrey Howe made his famous speech in the House of Commons. It seemed then a question not of if, but of when.

I had little part in her campaign during the first ballot, because it fell during the climax of the electricity privatisation for which I was responsible. One thing I knew was that the result could never be certain: far too many of my colleagues in the Parliamentary Conservative Party would be telling Margaret's Campaign Managers what they wanted to hear, not how they were really intending to vote.

The result when it came was a great body blow – so near yet so far, with the outcome of a second ballot far from certain.

It was at that point that Margaret asked me to run her campaign for the second ballot. Before we could make any plans, I knew there was one central issue we had to confront. In a Parliamentary system such as ours, no Prime Minister can long remain in office if he or she does not have the support of the Cabinet – and, in this case, that support was regrettably far from clear.

I knew, therefore, that Margaret had to see all the members of the Cabinet to ascertain where they stood. If they were all behind her, there was a very good chance of victory in the second ballot; if they weren't then that victory was far from clear.

On the afternoon of Wednesday 21st November, Margaret gave an accomplished performance in the House of Commons during a statement on the Paris summit. After that, she agreed rather reluctantly to see her Cabinet colleagues one by one in her office overlooking Parliament Square. She asked each of them their views.

Many Cabinet colleagues said they would stick by her to the end. Some reaffirmed the view expressed by Cranley Onslow, the Chairman of the 1922 Committee, that she should permit the contest to be widened to allow in figures like John Major and Douglas Hurd. At least three warned her that they were prepared to resign if she stayed on. A large number added that they thought, whatever their own decisions, support in Parliament was crumbling away – and that standing again may risk handing victory to Michael Heseltine.

To those who told her they could not see her winning the second ballot, or who themselves refused to support her, she mused that politics was a funny old world. She had won a record three elections; she maintained the overwhelming support of the Conservative Party in the country; she had never lost a motion of confidence in the House of Commons; and the first leadership ballot had shown she still commanded the support of a substantial majority of Conservative MPs – although not quite enough to win through the antiquated and eccentric electoral system that then existed.

Two quite amusing incidents occurred during this round. The first was when Peter Brooke went in to see her and give his support. He was dressed in White Tie and Tails on his way to a City Dinner and he remarked to me that there was a time in his days at Oxford when White Tie and Tails was the only appropriate dress in which to make important decisions.

The second came when the late Alan Clark also rushed in without an appointment and said 'Prime Minister, you must fight on – of course you will lose but what a glorious defeat!'

That round of meeting finished at about 8.30pm and Margaret told me she was going back to Number 10 to think things over. She was clearly very depressed – and had to face hours of work on her speech for a Confidence Motion, moved by Neil Kinnock, the next day.

To try and prevent the formation of cabals among Cabinet Ministers and others, it was made clear to colleagues that Margaret was going to sleep on things. The Cabinet meeting was brought forward to 9am to allow decisions to be reached before the formal business began.

By morning – and after consultation with the most important person in her life, Denis – she had decided that it was impossible to carry on and she said so to the Cabinet. It was, understandably, an emotional moment, but composure was soon regained and the meeting ended quite quickly.

The rest, as they say – including her bravura final appearance at the Dispatch Box – is history.

I look back many times at that awful week and ponder whether anything different could have been done. Each time, I come up with the same conclusion – that, against the background of the first ballot, we did everything we possibly could.

Ten years on, the manner of Margaret's departure has, I hope, faded from memory. After all, she deserves to be remembered for all that she achieved for the British people in eleven magnificent years – not for the way it all ended. Those achievements live on, and always will, because she changed Britain for ever. Even so, she would be the first to acknowledge there is still a great deal more to do!

BERNARD JENKIN

MP FOR NORTH ESSEX

Bernard Jenkin is the Conservative MP for Colchester North and is the son of Lord Jenkin of Roding who served in Margaret Thatcher's Cabinet. He is a merchant banker by profession and is a member of William Hague's Shadow Cabinet.

ॐঔ

A true friend

Afriend of mine was wandering past a bookshop on Piccadilly a few years ago, where he spied Lady Thatcher engaged in one of her marathon booksigning sessions. He wandered in to observe the growing mêlée which surrounded her, as she rattled off one signature after another. Everyone who approached her seemed to have a little tale to tell. One chap explained that he was a friend of Cecil Parkinson. 'A true friend', said Lady T. My friend, who had by this time joined the queue, held out his book for her to sign and said: 'I'm a friend of Bernard Jenkin.' 'Bernard,' she exclaimed, 'is a true believer.' 'Yes,' said my friend, 'a good Eurosceptic.' Lady Thatcher looked up at him and said. 'I prefer to describe him as a defender of Britain.' With that, she handed the duly signed book over and looked towards a teenage girl who was next in the queue. 'I'm not a friend of anybody's,' announced the girl. Lady Thatcher apparently dissolved into fits of laughter!

PETER LILLEY

CABINET MINISTER 1989–97

Peter Lilley entered Parliament in 1983 as MP for St Albans. He was a founder member of the No Turning Back Group of Thatcherite MPs. After a succession of junior ministerial jobs he was appointed to Margaret Thatcher's Cabinet in 1989 as Secretary of State for Trade & Industry. He remained in the Cabinet until the general election defeat in May 1997. He was a candidate in the ensuing Conservative Party leadership election and was appointed Deputy Leader of the Party in June 1997.

᐀

Listening

One of the greatest myths about Mrs Thatcher is that she didn't listen. People jumped to that conclusion because she did not respond to their ideas with some bland remarks like 'how very interesting.' Instead she argued with people to test their ideas to destruction. But if the ideas could withstand her assault she took them on board. I remember the Thatcherite No Turning Back Group of MPs inviting her to discuss our draft plans for schools. She tore them to pieces; we counter-argued and she lay into those arguments too. When she left, even some of her strongest devotees were saying 'It is true, she doesn't listen. Our arguments were much more convincing than hers.' Those of us who knew her said, 'Don't worry, we won the argument. She knows we won so she will be giving hell to whoever briefed her.' Sure enough, she took most of our proposals on board in the manifesto and implemented them. She had listened.

BOB HAWKE

PRIME MINISTER OF AUSTRALIA 1983–91

The trades unionist and Labour politician Bob Hawke is amongst the most influential figures in Australian politics. He became Prime Minister of Australia in 1983 remaining in that position until 1991. This passage is taken from his book The Hawke Memoirs, *published by William Heinemann in 1994.*

క్≈

Sneaking admiration

On Saturday afternoon at Lyford Cay the forty-nine Commonwealth heads met without officials. The meeting followed a plenary on that morning where heated argument had erupted over Margaret Thatcher's lone opposition to sanctions. Debate was at times bitter and the atmosphere spilled over into the afternoon. Margaret was implacable as she fought back against attacks by a number of the speakers. She had a terribly rough time, and although I repudiated her stance, I sympathised with her for the enormous physical and emotional strain she was under.

The afternoon session delegated to a committee of seven (Prime Minister Lyndon Pindling of the Bahamas, Margaret Thatcher, Rajiv Gandhi, Brian Mulroney and myself, with Presidents Robert Mugabe of Zimbabwe and Kenneth Kaunda of Zambia) the Herculean task of trying to reach some common ground on the sanctions issue. The seven of us met that evening, with Robert and Kenneth preferring, literally, to sit on the sidelines. We were to witness a vintage Thatcher performance, Margaret at her best and worst.

Margaret Thatcher was the hardest working head of government I ever met. Her application was prodigious and she was always extraordinarily well briefed for every meeting. Whatever the subject, she could press her sometimes jarring and belligerent viewpoints with great authority, and for that I deeply respected her. But while she had first-class application, she did not always display a first-class mind. In argument she often seemed to be playing catch-up. She sought to buy time while exchanging views so that she could more easily absorb contrary positions and give herself room to marshal her thoughts and responses.

In my experience she had two techniques for stalling debate. First she was an inveterate interrupter. I never dealt with a leader who interrupted other speakers so often. It was a cause for irritation among many of those with whom she dealt. Her other technique for slowing the pace of discussion was what I called her delay-by-parenthesis approach. If a leader was unwise enough to attach a parenthetical observation to the main thrust of his argument, Margaret was away. She would grab hold of the parenthesis like a terrier with a bone, tearing into it and worrying it to a degree that often made her interlocutor and the rest of us wild with impatience.

A bizarre example of this technique surfaced in the Lyford Cay committee meeting. We were discussing the Eminent Persons Group and the stage-by-stage concept of sanctions. Brian Mulroney was developing his main argument in support of Rajiv's and my attempt to persuade Margaret to come in behind the idea. Brian was unwise enough to refer to an aside she had made during the afternoon's discussions: 'Margaret, when you said that, I thought that the fat was really in the fire.'

At that her eyes blazed and she pulled herself erect in the chair. 'What do you mean the fat was really in the fire? Just what do you mean? What fat? What fire?' she asked imperiously. 'Brian, I was brought up to mean what I say, and to say what I mean. What do you mean, the fat was really in the fire?'

'My God!' I thought. I couldn't refrain from jumping in: 'Margaret! for Christ's sake! Forget the bloody fat and the bloody fire, it's got nothing to do with anything. Just listen to what Brian's saying, will you.' Margaret looked at me in some astonishment but, to her great credit, she copped it. Then I turned to my friend Mulroney and said: 'Brian, get on with it, and leave the fat out of the fire.'

Margaret could also, I thought, be a little less than straightforward at times. There was one occasion when she seemed to me, to almost deliberately misunderstand a proposition. One of the proposed sanctions included the proposition that governments would agree not to enter into contracts with majority-owned South African companies. In our private discussion Margaret said she couldn't agree to that because in South Africa there were so many companies with whom Britain had to deal. 'Margaret, we're not talking about in South Africa, we're talking about in our countries. The Australian Government won't have a contract with a majority-owned South African company, you there in the United Kingdom shouldn't deal with such a majority-owned company, I explained to her. 'Oh, I see,' she replied.

But the very next day she did not see and in our discussion she went off on the same thing again. I thought she was being a little slippery. I do not intend these comments to disguise the fact that I have a certain admiration for Margaret Thatcher. There is so much of her philosophical approach to domestic and international politics that I cannot share, but she is a formidable and remarkable person – applied, committed, dogged, dogmatic, determined and certainly courageous.

TERRY MAJOR-BALL

JOHN MAJOR'S BROTHER

Best known as the brother of John Major, Terry Major-Ball has held numerous jobs including, famously, a garden gnome maker. He wrote his life story in Major Major *published by Duckworth in 1994 from which this memory of Maggie is extracted.*

చీళ్

A great and remarkable lady

I am often asked what I think of Mrs Thatcher, and I have to say I have always admired her, even when her policies led to Philips making redundancies and me losing my job in 1989. I have met the lady only twice, once at Number 11, and once in the Chancellor's office in the House. She was very polite to me, only correcting me when I referred to the 'Poll Tax'. She told me 'Community Charge' was the correct term but appeared not to take any offence.

The question I hate being asked is why Lady Thatcher has been saying less than helpful things recently. For many years I was one of her most enthusiastic supporters and I remained one even towards the end of her time, when with many others I began to think she was losing her touch and was disregarding the people who voted for her. Many of the people I worked with were beginning to say that she had to go, that we needed someone more in tune with our way of thinking. After John was made Chancellor the stick I had to take about her increased. I became an obvious target for remarks by many people in the office where I worked who were fed up with her ways.

Whenever they said she must go, I stuck to my ground, saying: 'Look at all the great things she has done.' When they said she was arrogant and didn't care about ordinary people I had a stock reply. 'Oh yes, she does,' I would say with some authority, 'John tells me so.' I would relate little tales I had been told to demonstrate the other, less cold side to her nature – like the time a young lady serving dinner at Chequers tripped and deposited meat and gravy all over a minister and she went to comfort the girl, not the minister. I continued to support her, even after I was certain a change was needed, because I felt that if an expert like John was prepared to support her, I should too. I just hoped she would stop looking for fights and get on with the job.

After my firm closed and I found myself redundant, people would ask me: 'How can you support Thatcher when you're out of a job and can't get another?' 'Look abroad,' I would say – it was always the same answer. 'We're better off than a lot of countries. Things will come round in time. We've had all this before, and come out stronger.' I was saying this right up to the time of the leadership challenge, despite my private thoughts. Why? Because I knew John was prepared to vote for her right up to the wire. How? Because of our conversations. As far as I'm aware, John only agreed to stand himself after he knew there was no hope for her. I have to admit I was hurt and mystified whenever I read of the criticism Margaret was reported to be making of John, the man we are told by the media whom she had chosen and supported as her successor and who had been so loyal to her.

I was especially hurt when I remembered how she complained about the treatment she received from her predecessor. Apparently she thinks her case is different because she never lost an election, whereas Ted Heath did. I find this reasoning odd. It is strange too that she has savaged former colleagues whom she chose for the Cabinet herself. What happened to her judgment then? Recently I heard her say on television that it was better to have them in the Cabinet then on the back benches making trouble. Why did I have a feeling of *dèja vu*?

Now that her memoirs have been published and she has had her say, perhaps her sadness at leaving office is passing and peace can reign. I hope those historians who were planning to say, as a footnote to her achievements, that she didn't know how to retire from office gracefully will return their pens to their stands unused. I and many others can remember her great deeds while forgetting her miscalculations.

I'll even be prepared to say sorry for using the vulgar expression 'Poll Tax' to her face on that occasion when we met. She is a great and remarkable lady.

MIKHAIL GORBACHEV

PRESIDENT OF THE SOVIET UNION 1985–91

Mikhail Gorbachev was the last President of the Soviet Union. He presided over a period of intense change in his country and is credited with the introduction of the modernising policies of perestroika and glasnost. He famously attempted to foster peace between the superpowers and received the Nobel Peace Prize in 1990. This extract is taken from his memoirs, published by Doubleday in 1996.

☙◆❧

A woman I could do business with

At my first meeting with Mrs Thatcher in late 1984, we had established what proved to be a good and lasting relationship. We both appreciated the contact and got on very well. This first meeting might be the reason why the Soviet-British dialogue made such a good start on my taking the helm of the Soviet Union in 1985 – although British policy towards us during the first years of perestroika was not exactly what you would call friendly. Great Britain was the first Western country to support the American Strategic Defense Initiative and to participate officially in its development. Margaret Thatcher viewed the Reykjavik meeting as a failure and fully supported Ronald Reagan's position, blaming the Soviet Union for the lack of an agreement. The British Government made a big show of expelling a group of Soviet officials, accusing them all of being agents of the KGB.

But at the same time the British spoke out in favour of a

'constructive long-term dialogue' with the Soviet Union. It is revealing that Margaret Thatcher took the initiative in visiting the Soviet Union after my election as General Secretary. She was a frequent guest in Washington, and it seemed as if she intended to represent Western European interests in the dialogue between the superpowers.

Mrs Thatcher came to Moscow in late March 1987. Our talks took place in the Kremlin, in the presence only of our personal assistants and interpreters. Stressing the significance of her visit, I remarked that the last high-level visit to the Soviet Union by a British Prime Minister had taken place more than twelve years earlier. She corrected me immediately, saying that the last British Conservative Prime Minister had visited the Soviet Union more than twenty years before.

Before getting down to business, I expressed my astonishment at a speech she had made in Torquay only a week before leaving for Moscow, delivered in the spirit of Reagan's anti-Communist crusade. I said that we even had the impression that she might cancel her visit.

Mrs Thatcher had maintained that the Soviet Union aspired to 'establish Communism and domination worldwide' and that 'Moscow's hand' could be seen in virtually every conflict in the world. Obviously I could not leave it at that and replied that much of her speech in Torquay as well as most of the accusations she had made were conservative stereotypes going back to the 1940s and 1950s. But Mrs Thatcher stood her ground: 'You are supplying weapons to the Third World countries,' she rejoined, 'while the West supplies the food and aid in addition to helping establish democratic institutions.' The discussion became very heated.

Looking back I must admit (and it seems to me that I have already done so) that our policy towards developing countries had been highly ideological and that, to a certain extent, Mrs Thatcher had been right in her criticisms. However, it was well-known that the West had always been the prime supplier of weapons to the Third World and thus supported authoritarian and even totalitarian regimes, working on the principle that 'that dictator is a son of a bitch, but he is our son of a bitch.'

Our discussion had reached a point where I considered it necessary to say: 'We have frankly expressed our respective views on the world in which we live. But we have not succeeded in bringing our standpoints any closer. It seems to me that our disagreements have not become less after this conversation.'

My partner struck a more conciliatory note. Suddenly changing the course of our conversation, she said: 'We follow your activity with great interest and we fully appreciate your attempts to improve the life of your people. I acknowledge your right to have your own system and security, just as we have the right to ours, and we suggest taking this as a basis for our debate. In spite of all the differences between our systems,' she added, 'we can still exchange some useful experiences. We are deeply impressed by the vigorous policy of reform you are trying to implement. We have a common problem here – how to manage change.'

We went on to discuss our main topic, arms control. At the time Soviet–American talks on strategic arms were being held in Geneva. I went on the offensive, asking Mrs Thatcher directly: 'Is the West ready for real disarmament or have you been forced into negotiations under pressure from public opinion in your countries? I would appreciate it if you could clarify your position.'

Mrs Thatcher advanced the familiar argument that nuclear weapons represented the best guarantee for peace and that there could be no other guarantee in present conditions. 'We believe in nuclear deterrence,' she continued, 'and we do not consider the elimination of nuclear weapons practicable.'

In reply I delivered quite a long harangue, the gist of which was that the West did not want a solution, but was only interested in complicating the issue. I concluded: 'Today, we are closer than ever before to making a first step towards genuine disarmament. But the moment we were given this opportunity, you hit the panic button. Is the Tory policy exclusively aimed at hindering disarmament and the reduction of the level of confrontation in the world? It is amazing that Great Britain should feel comfortable in such a position.'

Mrs Thatcher seemed somewhat taken aback by my tirade. 'That's what I call a speech!' She exclaimed. 'I don't even know where to start.' And she assured me that the West did not in any way intend to make life difficult for us or complicate reform in the Soviet Union by rejecting disarmament.

Again and again, Margaret Thatcher repeated her main argument: nuclear weapons are the only means to ensure the security of Great Britain in the event of a conventional war in Europe. For this reason, Britain did not intend to commit itself to limiting in any way its nuclear arsenal. In short, our conversation was going round in circles. In an attempt to ease the tension, Margaret Thatcher told me about a 'funny occurrence', as she put it, which happened during a meeting with Hua Guofen. The meeting was scheduled to last one hour. The Chinese leader spoke for forty-five minutes, and when Mrs Thatcher asked one single question, he continued his monologue for another twenty minutes. Seeing this, Lord Carrington (the British Foreign Secretary) handed the Prime Minister a written note: 'Madam, you tend to speak too much.'

Mrs Thatcher came to Moscow in June 1990. I had returned from my trip to the United States and Canada on 5 June, a few days before her arrival. She seemed greatly impressed by the results of the visit and complimented me on the 'extraordinarily successful meeting' with George Bush. Indeed the talks with the American President had dispelled a number of mutual concern, including issues we had often discussed with Margaret Thatcher.

During our first conversation, she remarked that she believed it was essential to emphasise the positive aspects in our relations and to point out our convergent views on a number of issues at our joint press conference. 'Journalists tend to highlight negative aspects,' she said, 'and we must therefore concentrate on the positive achievements. It seems to me that many people, including many of the press, have not yet fully grasped how far we have come and how much the summit meetings contributed to this.'

'In 1986 my idea of a nuclear-free world was perceived as wishful thinking,' I reminded Mrs Thatcher. 'Today we are about to conclude an agreement with the Americans on a fifty-per-cent cut in strategic nuclear arms, and we have agreed on the elimination of our chemical weapons stockpiles. We have made much headway in only three years! Or, to take another example, the idea of a political settlement of regional conflicts was seen as another utopia. Today, the process has begun. And I must say that you personally have greatly contributed to this.'

My last meeting with Margaret Thatcher in her capacity as Prime Minister took place in Paris on 20 November, on the occasion of the European conference. We concentrated on the situation in the Gulf. I had discussed the issue with Mr Bush on the eve of our meeting, and Margaret Thatcher 'OK'd' our exchange of ideas. However, she admitted that she did not believe that a political settlement was possible and thought the use of force was inevitable. Hence she proposed that the next UN Security Council resolution (we had discussed it with George Bush) should be formulated in more severe terms, complaining that the Americans seemed to be 'somewhat over-cautious.' Needless to say, we also talked about the situation in the Soviet Union. The British Prime Minister did not hide her concern – she was an experienced politician and she perceived the dangers. We bid farewell at the entrance to my residence. 'God bless you!' she said in a soft voice.

The elections to the leadership of the British Conservative Party took place in Mrs Thatcher's absence. She failed to obtain the necessary majority on first ballot. She had told me that she had enemies – in eleven and a half years at the helm, this is virtually unavoidable. Yet she seemed to have no intention of capitulating. In Paris, when she was informed of the result of the election, she declared to the waiting press that she was 'going to show them' back home. Upon her return to London, however, she announced that she would resign. It was a noble act. Nonetheless, I regretted it.

Margaret Thatcher did much to support our perestroika. Needless to say she had her own views on the reforms, perceiving them as winning the Soviet Union over to Western positions, as a Soviet version of 'Thatcherism'. Nonetheless, she genuinely wanted to help us and to mobilise the efforts of the Western countries in support of our policies. During the August 1991 coup, she spoke out in defence of the Soviet President and his family.

One must give her credit for her services to her country. Mrs Thatcher took over at a time when the United Kingdom was lagging behind the other Western nations, and she succeeded in radically changing both the domestic and international situation of Great Britain. However Mrs Thatcher's tough methods and her inherent authoritarianism soured even her closest supporters, not to speak of the opposition, and eventually led to conflict situations. I had the impression that, in order to work with her, you had to accept her style and character unconditionally. Her authoritarianism and her penchant for forceful methods were manifest in British foreign policy. In crisis situations, she spoke out in favour of military sanctions. Even after her resignation as Prime Minister, we would occasionally receive information that 'Mrs Thatcher is suggesting air raids'. She was particularly tough in her approach to the Gulf crisis.

Margaret Thatcher was not an easy partner for us, and her fierce anti-Communism would often hinder her from taking a more realistic view on various issues. Still, one must admit that in a number of cases, she was able to substantiate her charges with facts, which eventually led us to review and criticise some of our own approaches. All in all, she was a strong advocate of Western interests and values indeed.

Margaret Thatcher had much of what I would call the 'Old English Spirit', at least as we Russians usually imagine it, which shows in her commitment to traditions and 'tried and tested' values. During our official meetings she was always very considerate and courteous. We eventually came to know each other better and she showed genuine warmth towards me and Raisa Maksimovna – despite the differences in our views and our political arguments.

HARVEY THOMAS

INTERNATIONAL PUBLIC RELATIONS CONSULTANT

Harvey Thomas was the Director of Press and Communications at Conservative Central Office from 1985 until 1987. He continued to serve as Director of Presentation to the Conservative Party until 1991.

৵৽৻

Selling Maggie

I suppose I am one of the original people accused of being a 'Spin Doctor. It amazes me now how little 'spin' we needed to do with Mrs T compared with today's requirement for constant spin on everything and everybody in politics, in an apparent desperate attempt to make it look as though they know where they are going.

Agree with her or not, Maggie knew where she was going and for the most part, the media was so busy keeping up, that 'news management' was pretty straight forward.

But that never really included too much on the personal side. Behind the unavoidable 'public personae', Denis and Margaret Thatcher were, and are, pleasantly private people. So, perhaps the memories that are most appropriate for me are those that illustrate her personal touch – and her concern for, and loyalty to, friends.

The phrase that I recall hearing more than others, was 'Because it's right.' People would suggest political direction or action and Mrs T would say time and again, 'No, we've got to do it this way, because it's *Right!*'

In many ways, her thinking was quite simplistic – even though she has considerable capacity to master detail as well. But, 'because it's right', has always been the driving motive in her private as well as her public life.

In 1985 I had gone to New York to prepare for her speech to the United Nations 40th Anniversary Celebration.

She had been out of the country for more than two weeks – I believe at the Commonwealth Heads of Government Meeting in the Bahamas. While she had been away, a number of critical comments about me had appeared in the *Times* Diary, the Peterborough Column in the *Telegraph*, and one or two other political gossip columns. Nothing in the mainstream news passed on to the Prime Minister in the Bahamas – but enough to be personally hurtful.

When the Prime Minister arrived at the Hotel in New York, she came full steam into the Suite, and the first thing she said was, 'I hear there have been some nasty comments in the papers, Harvey – don't worry about it. I know where they are coming from and I'll make sure they stop.' I would never have brought it up – and I have no idea who did – but she certainly made my day!

And in private, she has a dry sense of humour. Four of us were sitting with her having a sandwich lunch in the Finchley Constituency Office during the 1987 election. It had been a frantic morning and we had afternoon and evening visits ahead of us.

After two weeks of campaigning, we were all struggling to keep going and as we shovelled the sandwiches down, I said, 'Boy, I am ready for a siesta now.'

The other three nodded and agreed and I looked at Mrs Thatcher at the other end of the table and said, not very hopefully, 'Well that makes it almost unanimous.'

'It's certainly not unanimous,' she said, 'it's a majority of one against!'

I'm not sure that Maggie ever really understood that it was simplicity and integrity that gained her so much support, especially inside the Conservative Party.

The media consistently speculated on whether we deliberately kept applause going at the big rallies in the eighties. And if so, how we did it! We did, and it wasn't hard. I would zoom the cameras projecting her picture onto the Giant Screens, into a tight close-up shot of her face.

I first used this approach with Billy Graham fifteen years earlier. When the audience sees a Speaker's face occupying a whole 20 feet screen, the eyes are about two feet wide – and they give away all the Speaker's emotional feelings.

Integrity shines through, and, perhaps surprising to some, Mrs T's eyes at the end of a speech always had the message, 'Wow, you're all being a bit overgenerous with the applause – but thank you!'

It was as though those words were printed across the screen – and as long as we kept the cameras close-up, the applause would continue – once in a while helped by a six inch tear appearing out of the corner of an eye!

For her, she was simply 'telling it like it is' and for all of us who saw our role as 'a ministry of helps', that just made it easy for people to get the 'Maggie Message'.

SIR REX HUNT

GOVERNOR OF THE FALKLAND ISLANDS 1980–85

After an eventful colonial and diplomatic career, Sir Rex Hunt became the Governor of the Falkland Islands. He was present at the Argentinian invasion in 1982, removed by them and returned after liberation. This extract is taken from his book My Falkland Days *published by David and Charles in 1992.*

৵৵

A Welcome visit

The last of the Service chiefs to visit us in 1982 had been the Chief of Air Staff, Air Chief Marshal Sir Keith Williamson. He stayed in Government House and, on the first morning, asked to see me alone in my office. There he disclosed that the Prime Minister intended to visit the Islands from 8 to 12 January and handed me a letter from Sir Robert Armstrong, then Secretary of the Cabinet and Head of the Civil Service. Written in his own hand, with paragraphs and lines thoughtfully lettered and numbered to ease reply, Sir Robert stressed that security must be maintained and that the only person with whom I should discuss the programme was the Military Commissioner, Major General David Thorne. If news of the visit leaked out, it would be cancelled. He sketched a possible outline for a four-day visit, finishing with a postscript: 'The PM does not like much spare time on visits like this.' David and I mapped out a provisional programme and I sent it back in a handwritten letter to Sir Robert. He wrote again with a few further comments and told me to reply only if we disagreed. That was that. It was the easiest VIP programme

I had ever arranged. Normally, and particularly where the military were concerned, such visits entailed weeks of preparation and discussion, with voluminous programmes and numerous printed revisions. For the Prime Minister, three handwritten letters sufficed.

It was not, of course, quite as simple as that for David, who was responsible for the Prime Minister's protection. On a strict need-to-know basis, he and his staff prepared a contingency plan 'for the visit of a VIP to the Falkland Islands.' No names or dates were mentioned, but it was planned for a Saturday arrival and Wednesday departure. The give-away was that one of the party was shown as 'VIP's wife/husband'.

As no announcement about the visit could be made beforehand, the journalists who would normally have accompanied the Prime Minister were to follow twenty-four hours later. There was a BBC television team in the Islands, led by Nicholas Witchell, but it had been there since before Christmas and was due to leave on 5 January, three days before the Prime Minister's arrival. That morning, I received a call from Bernard Ingham, the Prime Minister's press secretary, telling me to keep the team on the Islands but not to disclose the reason. I rang Nicholas at the Upland Goose, where he and his colleagues were happily packing, and asked him to come to my office. There I explained that something was likely to happen over the next week that he might wish he had stayed for and my advice was for him to postpone his departure. He said that must mean that we were expecting someone we wanted to see or someone we did not want to see; either way, he would stay (at the time, there were rumours that an Argentine intended to bring some next-of-kin to the Islands to pay homage to their dead). I think he guessed that the Prime Minister was coming but, to his credit, he kept it to himself.

I told Mavis, of course, about our forthcoming guests, but we had to pretend to the staff that they were preparing for a party of journalists who could not be accommodated at the Upland Goose. In the village atmosphere of the Falklands, the slightest hint of an impending visit by the Prime Minister would have been flashed round the Islands by 'diddle-dee radio' within minutes and Don, for all his excellent virtues, would have been one of the first on the air. I hoped that he would forgive me for denting his reputation as a reliable newsmonger. I warned Patrick Watts and other local journalists to be at the airport by 4.30pm on Saturday, 8 January, but did not tell them who was coming.

As soon as Mrs Thatcher stepped off the Hercules, Patrick telephoned the FIBS studio, which interrupted its normal programme to announce her arrival. In the twenty minutes that it took Don to drive along the four miles of pot-holed airport road, the Stanley townsfolk flocked out of their houses and gathered along the route to welcome the Prime Minister. At her request, Don stopped at various points and she and Mr Thatcher got out and shook hands with scores of people. She said to one group, 'You were all marvellous,' to which Mike Bleaney, who was standing with young Daniel on his shoulders, replied 'You didn't do too badly yourself, Ma'am!' As we passed near Harold Bennett's house, he came to the taxi window and handed Mrs Thatcher a single rose. His eyes were moist and he was too choked to speak. He turned away but the Prime Minister told Don to stop, jumped out of the taxi and hurried after him. I followed and introduced him. He still could not speak and I could see that Mrs Thatcher, too, was deeply moved as she thanked him for the rose. All along the route, the crowds had gathered. It seemed that the whole of Stanley had come out to greet her. For a normally undemonstrative community, it was a remarkable display of affection – spontaneous, sincere and from the heart.

The Prime Minister's party consisted of the Chief of Naval Staff, Admiral Sir John Fieldhouse, who had been the commander of the Task Force operations from April to June, 1982, based at Northwood; her Principal Private Secretary, Robin Butler, who was later to take Sir

Robert Armstrong's place as Secretary of the Cabinet and Head of the Home Civil Service; a Private Secretary, John Coles, who was seconded from the Diplomatic Service, Press Secretary Bernard Ingham and a duty clerk, Alan Logan. There was no security officer or personal detective. I showed Mr and Mrs Thatcher to their room and pointed out the Argentine bullet-holes in the ceiling. The Prime Minister elected to sleep in the bed beneath them. As she tidied up, Mr Thatcher came down to the small drawing room and stood warming himself in front of the peat fire. Our first engagement was a briefing at HQ BFFI and I was surprised to see that he made no move to get ready. 'Oh, I can't come,' he said, 'I've not been security cleared.'

I ran through the programme with him and the secretaries who had now joined us, and pointed to one or two items that might be omitted if they thought that we had given the Prime Minister too much to do. I got a few rueful smiles in response and an assurance that she would fulfil every bit of the programme, and probably more. At the briefing, it was interesting to see the close rapport between the Prime Minister and Sir John Fieldhouse and the detailed grasp that she had of military matters. Afterwards, we had a small dinner party at Government House with a few of the leading Islanders. There were only seventeen in all, but even this was a bit of a crowd for the small drawing-room. Nevertheless, that was where we stayed because the Prime Minister decided that she preferred it (as we did) to the main drawing-room. After the other guests had gone, she naturally gravitated to Mavis's chair beside the peat fire, kicked off her shoes and relaxed with a whisky and soda – a practice she was to follow each evening.

Sunday started with a visit to Stanley airport to see the RAF units and to visit the engineering works at the nearby quarry. The Royal Engineers were producing thousands of tons of crushed stone to build roads from the airport to the coastel sites along the Canache. The first coastel had arrived from Sweden in December on the *Ferncarrier*, a semi-submersible heavy-lift vessel, and we had hoped to have it in position in time for the Prime Minister to open, but the wind and tides had to be exactly right and the correct combination did not occur until the evening of her departure.

In the latter part of the morning, the Prime Minister attended a joint meeting of Executive and Legislative Councils, followed by lunch at Government House with councillors. They each expressed their thanks and undying gratitude to Mrs Thatcher for sending the Task Force and reiterated their loyalty to the Queen. Looking to the future, they emphasised that Islanders had no wish to resume negotiations with the Argentines for as long as the Argentines equated negotiations with the transfer of sovereignty. They were grateful to Britain for providing the necessary security and for responding generously to Lord Shackleton's recommendations: they recognised that it was now up to Islanders to make the most of the opportunities thus created. Councillor Tony Blake urged the break-up of more of the larger farms and Councillor Tim Blake pressed for the development of the Islands' deep-sea fisheries by using the 150-mile protection zone in which to license fishing. Tim also explained the work of the Select Committee, of which he was chairman, on revising the constitution and the electoral procedure for the Islands and expressed the hope that proposals would be forwarded to HMG by July.

After lunch, the Prime Minister visited the Rookery Bay minefield and the Camber, where the Gurkha engineers, RAF Search and Rescue and several Royal Navy units were based, and then flew back across the harbour to see the Port Squadron of the Royal Corps of Transport, finishing a busy afternoon with a visit to the Field Post Office and the bakery. The latter was, literally, a museum piece. Used in the First World War, it had been taken out of an army museum and transported to the Falklands, where it performed magnificently until the troops moved to the Canache, after which it was returned to the museum. Parked under canvas between two FIC warehouses, it was a popular place to visit not only because of the appetising smell of freshly baked bread but also because it was the warmest place in town.

Before evensong in the cathedral, the Prime Minister laid a wreath at the cross of sacrifice for those Falkland Islanders who had lost their lives in the two World Wars. She had brought a number of wreaths from England, all beautifully made with flowers rarely seen in the Falklands. David was host for dinner that night in Britannia House.

Monday was, if anything, busier than Sunday. We visited four settlements in East Falkland and two in the West. At each place the Prime Minister gave speeches to the Islanders and to the troops and spoke to a large number of them individually. In order that she might meet as many Islanders as possible, David had kindly arranged for helicopters to bring them in from outlying settlements, so there was a large crowd (by Falklands' standards) wherever we went. Local journalists and the BBC team were joined by others from Britain who had flown in on the Sunday. Microphones and cameras were thrust in front of the Prime Minister at every opportunity and she sustained the barrage with unfailing good humour and patience. We travelled in a Sea King, with a Chinook for the Press and the infantry escort. Mrs Thatcher was welcomed with tremendous warmth wherever we landed, but none more so than at Goose Green, where the men, women and children who had been incarcerated in the community hall gave her three resounding cheers and gathered round to shake her hand and offer their personal thanks.

Brook Hardcastle and Eric Goss took us to the grave of Lieutenant Nick Taylor RN, where Mrs Thatcher laid one of her wreaths and Eric assured her that the people of the settlement would tend the grave with loving care for evermore. We then visited 'Y' Company of the 1st Battalion, the Royal Hampshire Regiment, accompanied by the battalion commander, Lieutenant-Colonel Hastings Neville. Sited near the remains of the old schoolhouse between Goose Green and Darwin, theirs was the first camp to be provided with Portakabins and was well on the way to completion. The Prime Minister was concerned about the welfare of the garrison and hoped that David's objective of having most of them out of tented accommodation by the onset of winter would be achieved.

From Goose Green we flew to Port San Carlos, where Alan Miller and his small band were sharing the settlement with the RAF Chinook detachment, the Harrier forward operating base and a platoon of the Royal Hampshires, and thence to San Carlos to lay a wreath at Blue Beach cemetery. Pat and Isabel Short provided lunch for the Prime Minister's party: after so many VIP visits they were becoming expert hosts. Indeed, I never ceased to admire Isabel for the seeming ease with which she adapted to the changed circumstances. Before the war, she had been extremely shy and retiring, but now she chatted easily to all and sundry, from the Prime Minister down. This I noted was a heartening characteristic of Islanders in general: they rose to the occasion, whether at home, like Isabel, or the UN, like John Cheek, or in London, like Lewis Clifton.

San Carlos Water was still protected by Rapiers, the crews of which lived in dug-outs reminiscent of the trenches in the first World War, but their morale could not have been higher, as the Prime Minister discovered. At Kelly's Garden, across the bay from San Carlos, the Royal Engineers were busily constructing a camp, which was intended to house the Chinook detachment and the headquarters of the ground air defence battery. Like most of the camps under construction, the biggest enemy was mud. We wore wellingtons as we splashed from hut to helicopter.

The Prime Minister refused to wear wellingtons for our next port of call, which was Port Howard cemetery. In fact, she was quite indignant when I suggested on the aircraft that she should put them on. 'I am not wearing wellingtons to Captain Hamilton's grave,' she said firmly, and promptly donned her best shoes. A Gurkha guard of honour presented arms as she walked through the mud to lay a wreath on Captain Hamilton's grave. I followed in my wellies, wondering whether a male Prime Minister would have been so sensitive.

After chatting to the people in the settlement, we flew from Port Howard to Fox Bay East, where Islanders from Fox Bay West, Port Stephens and Chartres had assembled. It was also the base for 'A' Company, the Royal Hampshires, whose camp was taking shape a little way up-river, at Doctor's Creek. Returning to the triangle after so many take-offs and landings, and so long in a noisy helicopter, I think that we were all feeling tired; within half-an-hour, however, we were changed and heading for a public reception at the Town Hall. On the short journey from Government House, I warned the Prime Minister that we had a surprise in store. Councillors had decided to confer upon her the freedom of the Falkland Islands, a unique honour in that only the freedom of Stanley had been awarded before (and that only to the Royal Marines and the West Yorkshire Regiment, which had been based there in the Second World War). Harold Rowlands, as the most senior kelper in the FIG, had been chosen to present the scroll; I would introduce him and we would both speak for no more than two minutes. She would be expected to say a few words in reply, but not to make a long speech.

The Town Hall was packed. There must have been 600 or more there, in a room normally considered crowded with 200 (indeed, the Director of Public Works was concerned that the floor might not take the weight). The atmosphere was electric and the Prime Minister perked up as soon as she entered: she was engulfed in a sea of grateful well-wishers and it took the best part of an hour to guide her through the crowd to the stage at the other end of the hall. I introduced Harold and stuck to my allotted two minutes. Harold was equally brief: describing the occasion as the greatest moment in his life, he said that he was echoing the sentiments of all Falkland Islanders in expressing his pleasure at being able to thank Mrs Thatcher in person for their liberation and pledged Islanders to build a better future to ensure that the war had been worth-while and that British lives had not been lost in vain. He read out the formal proclamation, presented the scroll and then brought the house down by kissing the Prime Minister. Clearly elated, Mrs Thatcher made what many of the audience told me afterwards was the best speech they had ever heard. It lasted for twenty minutes, without notes or briefing (none of us had prepared any material for her), and touched exactly the right chord. She received the most enthusiastic reception ever witnessed in the Falkland Islands. The biggest cheer came when she said 'Today again the Union Jack flies over Port Stanley, and may it ever fly there.' This had of course particular significance for me, for it was here in the Town Hall that General Garcia had told me that the Argentines would stay 'forever'. It was an intensely moving experience for us all, including the Prime Minister's party. Bernard Ingham came up afterwards and smothered me in a huge bear-hug. Dinner that evening was a lively affair, with all the day's fatigue banished. Indeed, though well past midnight, Mr. Thatcher had difficulty in persuading the Prime Minister to go to bed.

Tuesday was largely a nautical day but, before flying to HM *Antrim,* the Prime Minister visited the junior and senior schools, the hospital, the post office, the power station, PWD, the Brewster houses and the FIGAS hangar, where the Beaver was being reassembled. At sea, she went from HMS *Antrim* to the RFA *Fort Grange,* the *Stena Inspector* and HMS *Charybdis,* returning in the evening to give interviews to the Penguin News and the local radio. David was host at a tri-service dinner that night, which lasted until after midnight. Relaxing in front of the peat fire before going to bed, the Prime Minister suddenly said, 'I haven't seen a penguin, I must see a penguin before we leave.' As she was due to depart at 8am that morning, there was not much time to arrange a visit to a penguin colony. Then she added, 'And I should like to walk over Tumbledown.' I groaned inwardly. 'It will mean getting up at five Prime Minister,' I said. 'That's fine,' she replied. After she and Mr Thatcher had retired, David organised a helicopter and I got hold of Ian

Strange. We agreed that we should be able to fit in both Tumbledown and Seal Point before breakfast.

It was a miserable morning, blowing and raining. Undeterred, the Prime Minister jumped into the Sea King and we landed in the wet on Tumbledown. Mr Thatcher urged her to put a scarf over her head, but she would have none of it. Although the dangerous ordnance had been removed, there was still plenty of evidence of the battle, sangars and foxholes festooned with bits of webbing, tattered clothes and the inevitable tubes of toothpaste. Surveying the difficult terrain in the wind and the rain, the Prime Minister marvelled that the Scots Guards had been able to storm the Argentine positions. From Tumbledown, we flew down to Seal Point, on the tip of Port Harriet, and the jackass penguins obliged the Prime Minister by coming out of their burrows and eyeing her curiously. Thanks to the helicopter, we were back at Government House and having breakfast by 7.15am.

Everything had gone without a hitch up till now; we had even managed to keep the Prime Minister's departure a secret. To convince the Press that she would not be leaving until the following day, one of the crew of her Hercules had been told to stay up late drinking with the journalists (who were sharing the Upland Goose with them). He played his part so well that, when the rest of the crew climbed out of their bedroom windows at 4.30am, he failed to surface and had to be quietly spirited away by his colleagues. Most of the Press had accepted an invitation to be flown on a wildlife tour for the day and were on their way to a penguin colony when we escorted the Prime Minister to the airport. We bade our farewells and the Hercules door closed at precisely 8am. As it was raining hard, David and I sought shelter in the helicopter and sat waiting for the Hercules to take off. We were congratulating ourselves that everything had gone well when the intercom crackled and our pilot reported that the Hercules was taxiing back. Apparently all four engines had lost power as the pilot opened the throttles. There was no danger because he had scarcely started his take-off run; but it was worrying. David and I dashed out of the helicopter and across the apron to be at the foot of the steps again as the Prime Minister and her party disembarked. We waited in the Station Commander's Portakabin while the RAF decided what to do. The Prime Minister was naturally perturbed about losing precious time; her programme was as full as ever, with a big reception at Ascension on her way home (she had passed through unknown on the way down) and she wanted to be back in London for question time in the House of Commons the following afternoon. The choice lay between checking the faulty engines, which might have taken several hours, transferring the special caravan, which had been fitted into the Prime Minister's aircraft, into the Press Hercules, or taking the Press Hercules as it stood. As switching the caravan would also have taken several hours, the Prime Minister elected to go in the Press Hercules, without trimmings. After almost an hour's delay, we said farewell a second time and breathed sighs of relief as the heavily laden Hercules lumbered off the runway and disappeared into the overcast skies. We had thoroughly enjoyed the visit, but another day at that pace would have been hard to bear. 'Early night, tonight, David,' I said, as we flew back to the triangle, with which, he heartily concurred.

Before she left, Mrs Thatcher said that she had been deeply touched by the warmth and kindness of the welcome she had received everywhere she went and from everyone she had met. She knew that what was being expressed to her was the loyalty of the Falkland Islanders to Britain and their gratitude for the professionalism and gallantry of the Task Force in freeing them from the domination of a military invader. But that was only part of the story. What in truth the Islanders were expressing was their gratitude to Mrs Thatcher for sending the Task Force and never wavering in her determination to liberate the Islands. They believed that, had she not been the Prime Minister at the time, the Task Force would never have sailed and they would have been under Argentine domination 'forever'.

In coming 8,000 miles to meet the Islanders, the Prime Minister boosted morale as nothing else could. The citizens of shabby, shell-shocked Stanley needed a tonic and the Prime Minister's visit was the perfect medicine. It was fitting that she should come in the month that marked the 150th anniversary of continuous British settlement, the date by which the Argentines had determined that they would achieve sovereignty over the Islands. Her clear, unequivocal commitment to the Islanders both reassured them and instilled confidence in the future. Whatever other politicians or the Foreign Office might do or say, Islanders knew that they had a staunch champion at the helm in London.

ELEANOR LAING

MP FOR EPPING FOREST

Eleanor Laing was elected MP for Epping Forest in 1997. She had previously worked as special advisor to John MacGregor.

જ્જ

A great compliment

Attending a Conservative Women's Conference just before I fought my first, unwinnable, parliamentary seat as a very young, inexperienced and shy candidate, I was introduced to Margaret Thatcher and dared to make a comment about a particular matter of government policy. On hearing my comment the Prime Minister swung round, caught me in her gaze and said with her inimitable authority, 'You are absolutely right.' At that time I thought it was the greatest compliment that anyone had ever paid me – and I still think that now.

SIR NORMAN FOWLER

CABINET MINISTER 1979–90

After a career in journalism, Norman Fowler became the MP for Sutton Coldfield in February 1974. He served in Margaret Thatcher's Cabinet from 1979 as Minister of Transport, subsequently becoming Secretary of State for Social Services and later Secretary of State for Employment. He was Conservative Party Chairman under John Major from 1992 to 1994 and a member of William hague's Shadow Cabinet from 1997 to 1999. This extract is taken from his book Ministers Decide *published by Chapmans in 1991.*

ॐ

Ministers Decide

In 1975 I was also not at all sure whether Margaret Thatcher was electable. That was not because she was a woman. I had never regarded that as making any difference one way or the other in electoral terms. It was because in the mid-1970s she appeared to the public as aloof and most certainly not one of them. Although she had come up the hard way, she gave the impression that she was to the manor born. This was not an accurate picture of the woman but that was how she was seen. In the years after her election she was given media advice which she was wise enough to take, but above all she began to project her real self. A much grittier Margaret Thatcher emerged.

So what was the secret of a leader who had won three elections and survived crises that would have toppled a lesser person? Stamina obviously; courage certainly; but if I were to choose one factor, it would be professionalism. Her attitude to the televising of Parliament is a case in point. She was a strong opponent of televising the House. She thought it would change the character of Westminster and, I suspect, put more power in the hands of the media, including her bête noire the BBC. At times I felt that she regarded me – a supporter of television and a former journalist – as personally responsible for this invasion. Yet when the decision was made and a majority, including half the Cabinet, voted for television she settled down to work. Most of the rest of us took the view that there was not much you could do. You would either come over well or not. Margaret Thatcher studied the angles of the cameras, considered how the pictures would be appearing in sitting-rooms all over the country, and emerged as the undoubted star of Westminster. Whatever may have been Neil Kinnock's hopes of this new opportunity – and remember that Kinnock made his first national reputation on television – he lost. It was the same professionalism which took Margaret Thatcher from an Opposition leader without experience of foreign affairs to one of the world's best-known and most respected statesmen. It was the same professionalism which drove her into the early hours of the morning working on the multitude of red boxes produced by the departments of Whitehall. The same quality took her into the tea-room and the dining-room of the House of Commons, rather than taking the night off; and at party conferences she was entirely tireless as she went from one function to another. She did not much like the annual trial of her speech at the Conservative Party Conference. She would sit there all week listening to her best lines being used by other speakers but knowing that the delegates would expect a sparkling performance at the end. With her speech writers she would be up half the night preparing her text. It was the price that the Leader of the Party had to pay and she paid it willingly. It was this complete professionalism which set her apart.

Margaret's family provided the indispensable background rock of support, and a clear and uncomplicated instinct about what was right and wrong provided the certainty of direction. She had a strong feeling of what was honourable and what was not. She was intensely loyal to the officials who most closely worked with her. If she ever lost her temper it was because of attacks on advisers like Bernard Ingham or Charles Powell. She regarded an attack on officials who could not answer back as basically cowardly. Critics were trying to get at her through her advisers. To her this was a particularly despicable example of dishonourable conduct.

Her view of ministers was more complex. She was loyal to them in the midst of a dispute and under attack but she also felt that they should be capable of looking after themselves. However close she might be to a minister (for example, Nicholas Ridley), if the minister insisted on digging himself into a hole then ultimately he had to live with the consequences. The interests of the Government took precedence over the interests of an individual minister. The same is true in a rather less stark way of the frequent reshuffles. Ministers were moved out of jobs in the interests of keeping the Government's face fresh. In the process quite a number were roughly treated. Leon Brittan should not have been moved from the Home Office; Patrick Jenkin should have been moved from the Environment Department, not sacked; Peter Rees should not have had to suffer the entirely avoidable fate of reading about his demise in the papers for week upon week before it happened. All the Thatcher Governments would have benefited had ministers stayed both longer in jobs and longer as ministers.

Ultimately, however, success as a political leader is not measured by skill in the television studio or how you appear to your colleagues. It is about what you achieve. Political leaders have to win elections, but it is much more important that they win respect for doing the right things rather than an easy reputation for geniality. Margaret Thatcher's achievement was to take over a country which gave every appearance of being down and very nearly out and turn it round. The change was slow and at times painful but the chances are that much of the change is permanent. She took over a country which had been brought to its knees by uncontrolled trade union power and presided over a decade of reform. Any party which seriously tampers with that record does so at its electoral peril. She took over a country where too much industry and too much activity was controlled, not very successfully, by the state. Virtually no one today believes in widespread renationalisation and a reintroduction of controls. She took over a country where millions of people were excluded from ownership. With the sale of council houses and wider share ownership important steps were taken to extend the traditional Conservative aims of one nation and a property-owning democracy. And she also took over a country where for decades tax rates had been too high but where it had become accepted that that was the inevitable way of things. Tax rates came down and my estimate is that most people in Britain would now like to keep them that way. These were real and substantial reforms which singled Margaret Thatcher out as one of the most successful political leaders this century.

LORD WADDINGTON

CABINET MINISTER 1987–92

Raised to the peerage in 1990, David Waddington had served in Margaret Thatcher's Cabinet as Chief Whip and then as Home Secretary. In 1990 John Major appointed him Lord Privy Seal. He was Governor of Bermuda from 1992 until 1997.

తికల్ఫ్

She was right

In October 1984 an IRA bomb in the Grand Hotel, Brighton nearly killed Margaret Thatcher and half her Cabinet. The next morning, at her insistence, the Conservative Conference continued with its business and over lunch I was behind the platform with her as she waited to go on stage to give her keynote speech. She said three bishops had just called in to pray for her and had had her on her knees, but when she added crossly 'as if I had nothing better to do' I knew the old spirit was there and she would put on a great show. She did.

Moments after arriving at my desk in the Home Office on the morning of the 30th July 1990 I received a call from the Police telling me that Ian Gow, Margaret's Parliamentary Private Secretary when she first became Prime Minister, had been blown up in his car. Margaret had been very fond of Ian and he of her, and when I got to Number 10 a few minutes later she was telling her staff, 'Give me work. Cancel no engagements. I have got to keep busy.' And she forced herself to carry on with her normal programme.

On the morning of the 22nd November 1990 the Prime Minister, visibly distressed, told her Cabinet that after her failure by four votes to be re-elected Leader of the Party she intended to resign. But that afternoon she was in the House of Commons replying to a censure debate and to all appearances enjoyed herself hugely as she laid about her, demolishing the Opposition case. Words seemed to come easily, but she had sat up half the night preparing for that last great occasion.

Margaret Thatcher, still then Leader of the Opposition, came up to help me in the Clitheroe By-Election in February 1979, and at lunch my nervous Chairman opened the conversation by suggesting it was about time the Country adopted proportional representation.

'Well,' said Margaret, 'I suppose it is an excellent idea if [a pause and a sniff] you don't want the Conservative Party to ever win another election.' Save for purposes of consumption my chairman did not open his mouth again.

And she could be intimidating, having little time for those who did not stand up to her and never suffering fools gladly. But she loved an argument which usually took the form of her trying to test to destruction every proposition advanced by others than herself. On most matters she was convinced she was right, but who can blame her? She usually was. Two hundred and eighty-four economists wrote to *The Times* saying her policies would not work. They did; and Britain is benefiting to this day. Many doubted whether the Falklands could be retaken. She said they had to be and they were. Everyone said the Government could not beat the National Union of Mineworkers: Margaret Thatcher knew better. The Treasury told her Britain had to enter the ERM. She felt in her bones it would end in disaster, and it did. She knew that those opposed to her in her government and in her party were risking the end of Britain as an independent nation state. That was something she was not prepared to countenance, and the fact that she was brought down for that principal reason is something of which she can be immensely proud.

Margaret Thatcher had great qualities of leadership which stood the Country in good stead in times of peril, and she was a giant on the world stage. In those days it was somewhat difficult to describe her save in adjectives familiar to the reader of Jane's Fighting Ships – Indefatigable, Indomitable, Intrepid, Courageous.

Her determination to resist every threat to peace from the Soviet Bloc, her willingness to face any amount of unpopularity at home if that was necessary in order to see her own country properly defended and the West secure, led to the deployment of the Cruise missile in Britain. That in turn gave her the moral authority to speak for the West and made the Soviets realise that they had no hope with their own far more limited resources of forever preventing democracy in Eastern Europe, let alone extending their particular brand of tyranny further west. Margaret Thatcher deserves much thanks from the British People and all who love Freedom.

It would not be right to finish without a word about her family and Denis in particular. I think it was during the summer of 1988 that I, as Government Chief Whip and Peter Brooke as Party Chairman, were having supper with the Prime Minister in Number 10 to talk about possible Ministerial changes. We had just sat down when Margaret said: 'Poor old Denis upstairs in the flat, eating all on his own. He must be very lonely and fed up.' 'Oh!' I said, glancing at Peter and having a good idea which way the wind was blowing, 'we can't have that. He must come down. We want to see him, don't we, Peter?' 'Do you really?', said the Prime Minister. 'I promise you he won't say a word'. Well, it did not work out quite as the Prime Minister promised, but it brought home to me what a marvellous relationship she had with Denis and how much she depended on him. I think he was her great strength in moments of appalling strain. We also owe *him* a lot.

VISCOUNT TONYPANDY

SPEAKER OF THE HOUSE OF COMMONS 1976–83

Secretary of State for Wales under Harold Wilson, the distinguished parliamentarian George Thomas was elected Speaker of the House of Commons in 1976. After his resignation in 1983 he was created First Viscount Tonypandy and sat in the House of Lords until his death in 1997. This extract is taken from his memoirs Mr Speaker, *published by Century in 1985.*

☙❦❧

Test of her mettle

In mid 1982 the Queen gave a state banquet for the Reagans at Windsor Castle, where I renewed my acquaintance with Mrs Reagan, whom I had met at the wedding of Prince Charles and Lady Diana the year before.

The banquet itself was a considerable strain for Mrs Thatcher and those of us who knew that there had been very heavy losses in Bluff Cove as Welsh Guardsmen were being landed prior to the taking of Port Stanley on the Falklands. The news had not yet been released and that was the only time I saw Mrs Thatcher show any real sign of strain during the whole Falklands campaign.

I think that had a man been Prime Minister, he would probably have lost his nerve long before. Any man would have gone back to the United Nations to make sure he was not going to be ostracised by the world community, in much the same way as the Opposition were putting themselves in the clear if things went wrong. Britain would have lost all influence in international affairs if Mrs Thatcher had submitted to the pressures and gone back to the United Nations. It would have meant that never again would Britain take any decisive action to defend her people. The Prime Minister showed remarkable courage and determination throughout the whole of the tragedy, and she knew tragedy was inevitable once the islands had been invaded by Argentina. But by her action she saved the good name of Britain.

The whole exercise showed that British youth, who never thought they would have to do that sort of thing again, could respond magnificently to the challenge. The Falklands affair reinforced my belief that the British character has not really changed, despite all the troubles that we face with violence and sometimes appallingly selfish behaviour. We are still a tough little race, and now the world knows it.

BARONESS COX

DEPUTY SPEAKER OF THE HOUSE OF LORDS

Caroline Cox worked as a sociologist and in nursing education before being raised to the peerage as Baroness Cox of Queensbury in 1983. She has been a deputy speaker of the House of Lords since 1986.

かや

Surprise call

In December 1982 I received a telephone call 'out of the blue' asking me if I could spare the time to come down to Downing Street to meet the Prime Minister. With a mixture of excitement and terror, I asked if I might have some idea of the purpose of the meeting. With the prospect of meeting this formidable lady, I said that I would be very happy to come with an open mind but preferred not to come with an empty mind! I was advised that it was not possible to indicate the reason for the meeting but would I please be at Downing Street at 4.45 pm the next day. Knocking on the black door with the golden 10, my knees were shaking; by the time I reached the waiting-room my mind was a 'white-out'. The only possible reason I could think for this invitation was a furious letter I had written to my MP about nurses' pay. At that moment I could not even remember a ward sister's annual salary!

Suddenly the doors opened and a charming man said, 'The Prime Minister will see you now.' I steered myself through the doors into 'the Presence'! Margaret Thatcher welcomed me graciously. She then said, 'Please sit down. I will come straight to the point because I believe in coming straight to the point.' I braced myself and she said, 'I am drawing up a list of names to go to Her Majesty the Queen for recommendations for life peerages. May I have your permission to put your name on that list?' It was a good thing I was sitting down or I would have fallen over backwards with astonishment.

She then said, 'In the Lords, I hope you will support us on education; I know you do not always agree with us on health. However, you always have freedom to speak and to vote according to conscience.'

She then said, 'I must ask you to treat this conversation in confidence until there is a press release next week. However, I expect all your family know you are here. You had better think of something to tell them. Why don't you just say that we had a little conversation about education?' She added 'but you can tell your husband about the peerage, because spouses are different!'

I appreciated her thoughtfulness, thinking of the reception committee waiting for me at home. My children, their friends and neighbours all knew I had been to Downing Street and would be waiting eagerly for my return.

Lady Thatcher's anticipation of this situation enabled me to forestall the persistent questioning from my family. And by telling my husband I was able to come to terms with the shock of this offer which would transform my life.

I always profoundly respect Margaret Thatcher's principle of granting me the freedom to speak and vote according to conscience. Subsequently I took her at her word and not infrequently spoke and voted against the Government's policy. I believe that this principle is essential for the effective fulfilment of the role and responsibilities of the House of Lords as a refining and a revising Chamber. Without it, it becomes merely a politicised rubber stamp for the House of Commons.

I hope that present and future Prime Ministers will follow Lady Thatcher's example and respect the principle of the spirit of independent thinking and voting, for without it the importance and fundamental significance of the second Chamber is so profoundly diminished that its raison d'être will be destroyed!

LORD YOUNG OF GRAFFHAM

CABINET MINISTER 1984–9

David Young served in Margaret Thatcher's Cabinet as Minister without Portfolio, then as Secretary of State for Employment and finally as Secretary of State for Trade and Industry before retiring from the Cabinet in 1989.

৵৹

Persuading the PM

I first met Margaret Thatcher when she spoke at a lunch I chaired in the late seventies. Many of the guests came up to me afterwards and said 'If only. . .' None thought that she had any real chance of winning the next election.

At that time I was already working for Keith Joseph but I did not meet her again until some time after the '79 election when, as Special Advisor to the Department of Industry, I would accompany Keith to occasional meetings at Number 10. However, observing Margaret at work from the far end of the table was one thing, dealing directly with her when she felt strongly about something was quite another.

Keith left Industry for the Department of Education and some time later I went to the Manpower Services Commission. Eventually in the autumn of 1984 she invited me into Cabinet as Minister without Portfolio with responsibilities for employment.

I chaired a number of sub-committees, one of which was engaged in developing a two-year YTS and in due course we agreed the terms of a new scheme. One of the issues was the benefit of £16 per week payable to unemployed school leavers and many of my colleagues, myself included, thought that this early indoctrination into the welfare state was quite wrong. I persuaded my committee that we should abolish this benefit but give the YTS entrants £25 per week, which they would be expected to earn.

Our White Paper was due to be published just before the Easter recess. When the Prime Minister was in Beijing the previous December to sign the Accord on Hong Kong she announced that I was to bring a trade delegation of some of the biggest UK companies at the beginning of March.

I was busy selecting and inviting my delegation when the bombshell dropped. I received an invitation to call on the Chief Secretary who gave me a simple message. Since the Treasury thought that many more young people would be attracted into our new scheme than collect benefit, it would cost £200m more of public expenditure, and where was the additional money coming from? Now, I had no department, thus no budget to cut, so I was told that if I wanted this scheme, I must persuade my colleagues to find the amount for me. No one volunteered, so I went back to my committee and persuaded them to restore unemployment pay provisions once again.

Then the day came when I had to obtain the Prime Minister's agreement to our Paper. As soon as the meeting started I knew that I was in trouble. She was adamant that we should stop paying school leavers benefit if they wouldn't enter the scheme, and nothing I could say would change her mind. The scheme in full, or nothing.

The following day was my last before I left for China. I asked for a meeting to raise the matter again and she met me in the morning with a small number of colleagues. Again nothing I could say would change her attitude. Paying benefit to school leavers was wrong, when they had the chance to earn more by entering YTS and that was that. I had rarely known her so adamant.

My White Paper, my first, was in ruins. I asked to see her, one to one, and she saw me in the middle of the afternoon. No matter what argument I used she was would not budge. The terrible thing was that I knew that she was right, but I also knew that without my White Paper, the chance for a two-year scheme was gone, probably for good.

I had to take the Committee stage of a Bill in the Lords that evening and I went through the motions in the House in a deep depression. At about eight o'clock I slipped a note to my Private Secretary to see if the PM would see me later that evening. She would, and at eleven o'clock after the business in the House I went over to Number 10.

The discussion ranged back and forth for about an hour and I did not appear to be making any progress. The clock struck and I told the Prime Minister that it was now my birthday. Suddenly she changed and reluctantly, but with good grace, agreed to the amended scheme. I left as quickly as I could before she could change her mind. I still had my boxes to do, I still had to pack and we were leaving at the crack of dawn but I was happy.

We introduced two-year YTS and the year after we were able to abolish benefit for school leavers.

BARONESS SECCOMBE

CHAIRMAN OF CONSERVATIVE WOMEN'S NATIONAL
COMMITTEE 1981–4

Baroness Seccombe was raised to the peerage in 1991 after many years of loyal service to the Conservative Party having served in numerous positions including Chairman of the Conservative Women's National Committee and Vice-Chairman with special responsibility for women.

࿇

Sensitivity and compassion

In 1982 I was Chairman of the Conservative Women's National Conference. It had been the custom for the Leader of our Party to be the speaker at the last session. On assuming office as Prime Minister Margaret Thatcher continued the practice much to the pleasure of our members.

On this occasion the country was embroiled in the battle to regain the Falkland Islands following the Argentinian Invasion. It was a particularly sensitive time as earlier in the day there had been loss of life and two British ships had been sunk. There was enormous concern as news of the action was being released continually. This led to a barrage of media assembled to hear the British Prime Minister give an up to the minute account of the situation.

I accompanied Baroness Young, then Party Vice-Chairman with responsibility for Women, to greet Margaret outside the Conference Hall. It was immediately clear that she was deeply moved by the happenings 8000 miles away. She talked of the families of our servicemen and the sadness of those bereaved. At the same time she knew that in the Hall it was not only the Conference Representatives who were going to hang on every word. It was the national and international media who were waiting to beam her words round the world.

As we approached the time for her to enter the Hall I was acutely aware of the demands she had to make on herself in preparation for her expected powerful message. When she spoke I marvelled at her remarkable capacity to speak with such brave resolution.

In private she had shown us her sensitivity, compassion, misery and vulnerability but then drawing on an inner strength she was able to speak in such an authoritative and robust way.

On that day I saw the two sides of Margaret Thatcher – the warm, caring, sensitive woman and the International Statesman. It was a privilege I shall never forget.

MAJOR GENERAL JULIAN THOMPSON

BRIGADE COMMANDER DURING THE FALKLANDS CONFLICT

*Julian Thompson served with distinction in the Royal Marine Commandos for
many years, eventually rising to the rank of Major General. He is currently a
Visiting Professor of War Studies at Kings College.*

ॐ

And the lady loves . . .

Following the march past of the representatives of the Falklands
Task Force at the Mansion House in the City of London in
Autumn 1982, a luncheon was held in Guildhall, hosted by the
Lord Mayor of London attended by sailors, marines, soldiers and
airmen of all ranks. After lunch, the Prime Minister, Mrs Thatcher as
she was then, rose to speak. Before she began, there was a prolonged,
spontaneous standing ovation, cheering and clapping for her, led by
the junior ranks in Guildhall without any encouragement or lead
being given by the officers present, but quickly taken up by all of us
with the greatest enthusiasm; we wanted to show our affection for her.
I was sitting opposite some of the members of her cabinet, who were
open-mouthed in astonishment. We adored her, and would have done
anything for her. In all my years service, I have never seen anything
like it. In the last hundred years, I can think of no politician except,
Winston Churchill, who struck such a chord with servicemen, who
usually have no time for politicians.

Some years later, Margaret Thatcher, still Prime Minister, attended
an exercise involving the SBS boarding a 'target' ship. There was an

advertisement around at the time featuring a man overcoming a series of difficult obstacles, all with the aim of carrying a box of Cadbury's Milk Tray to his lady love. I decided that the SBS would follow his example, and they entered into the plot with enthusiasm. The storming of the target was a great success, culminating in an SBS operator stepping forward, unzipping the top of his wet suit, and presenting the Prime Minister with a box of Cadbury's Milk Tray. She was surprised but delighted, and when one of her aides tried to take it off her, she rebuffed him, saying that the chocolates were for her, and no one else. We all loved her for calmness in the face of one or two potentially unnerving moments on that particular exercise, her enthusiasm, and, dare one say it, because she is an extremely handsome lady. We appreciated that too.

JOHN BLUNDELL

GENERAL DIRECTOR, INSTITUTE OF ECONOMIC AFFAIRS

John Blundell has been amongst the most prominent and influential thinkers on modern economics of recent years. He has worked for, and contributed to, numerous think tanks both in Britain and the USA.

ॐॐ

The IEA (The Institute of Economic Affairs) archive contains an interesting exchange. On the 24th October 1969 the IEA Editorial Director Arthur Seldon wrote to Geoffrey Howe as follows: 'May we hope for better things from Margaret?'

Geoffrey Howe replied: 'I am not at all sure about Margaret. Many of her economic prejudices are certainly sound. But she is inclined to be rather too dogmatic for my liking on sensitive matters like education and might actually retard the case by over-simplification. We should certainly be able to hope for something better from her – but I suspect that she will need to be exposed to the humanising side of your character as much as to the pure welfare market monger. There is much scope for her to be influenced between triumph and disaster!'

Drugs

One evening in the late '70s a group of younger members of the Conservative Party took Lady Thatcher to dinner in a private room at the Café Royal to brainstorm policy ideas. Two of us were very firmly trodden on.

First I suggested that all council housing be given away to current tenants. I was a newly elected Lambeth Borough Councillor and I had figures to show we would be much better off if we could simply tell our Director of Administration and Legal Services to mail out every single deed. Just mail them out and get rid of them I argued.

'People will not value it properly unless they at least pay something for it' she observed, quickly moving on.

Next went a colleague destined for the Cabinet who said that she was putting too much emphasis on economic freedom and not enough on personal freedom.

'Take cannabis,' he said 'It is available freely everywhere. Why not recognise reality and legalise it?'

'What do you mean by available freely everywhere?' she said in a tone of voice that should have told him to back off.

'Well, for example', he ploughed on 'my flat mate always has some and knows lots of places where he can get it!'

She turned her gaze on him.

'Peter (not his real name)' she said. 'My detective is standing outside that door. I want you to call him in now and give him your friend's details.'

I forget how Peter managed it, but he ducked and dived, weaved and wriggled, and she let him off the hook.

No, Prime Minister

In 1990 I was living outside Washington DC. It was early summer and I was planning a trip to Munich and Moscow for early September. One day the mail brought an invitation to the Social Affairs Unit's 10th Birthday Party at the Reform Club. I was about to say no when I realised that I could fly Moscow to Vienna to London, go to the party and fly to DC the next day.

I turned up on time. As I walked up the steps in lounge suit I realised Sir Antony Jay, co-writer of *Yes, Minister* and *Yes, Prime Minister*, was next to me in Black Tie. We fell into conversation and entered the event. An hour later we joined up again as Margaret Thatcher was working the room. She turned from the group next to us and spotted Tony in his DJ – the only one in the whole room.

'Ah Tony' she said, 'you must be going somewhere important later!'

'No, Prime Minister,' he replied contritely. 'I mis-read the invitation!'

So I heard the author of *Yes, Prime Minister* say to the then Prime Minister 'No, Prime Minister'.

When I became General Director of the IEA I found we had already published a collection of speeches by my predecessor Lord Harris under the title of *No, Minister*. So when Ralph turned 70 and I published the best of his articles, I had no hesitation in calling them *No, Prime Minister*.

Fifty Birthday Roses

When Michael Forsyth was national Chairman of the Federation of Conservative Students I was his national Vice Chairman responsible for publicity. Mrs Thatcher's approaching birthday seemed to me to be a wonderful opportunity for us.

About a week before the big day (October 13th 1976) we started brainstorming in The Marquis of Granby, just off Smith Square, as to what we could/should do. Eventually we settled on the idea of turning up at her Flood Street home with a very very large bouquet of fifty red roses at about 7.30am. Michael would present these to her against a backdrop of enthusiastic young students that I would recruit.

Everything was quickly arranged and the media alerted. On the morning of the big day I first picked up Michael and then this huge display of roses from a florist in Berkeley Square. The arrangement could barely fit in the taxi and we lost several heads en route.

When we pulled up there was a huge bank of cameras and a solitary policeman but not one student. 'Wait here' I told Forsyth. I jumped out, scanned the street again and finally walked up to the policeman.

'I wonder if you have seen any students?' I asked.

'Oh yes, Sir' he replied, 'Mrs Thatcher saw them out here twenty minutes ago and invited them in for a cup of tea!'

'Should I say you are ready, Sir,?' he finished.

The students duly emerged and formed a cordon. Michael presented the roses and the photos went out all over the world.

Speak Up, Young Man

I was at a round-table dinner of 40 people with Lady Thatcher some years ago. After dinner we enjoyed remarks from a distinguished guest. Then came questions. Most present were fairly senior types from the media, the civil service, industry and politics. At 45 I was pretty young but there was an even younger 35 year old representing his boss. To be accurate this young man was actually the leading expert in the room on our topic for the night.

Into the vacuum of space and time immediately following the guests' remarks the young man proffered an interesting question.

The problem was nobody could hear what he was saying. 'Speak up, young man,' commanded Lady Thatcher.

He tried again but clearly did not measure up.

'SPEAK UP, YOUNG MAN,' she commanded again.

He started a third time. It still did not measure up. She glared down the table.

'Young man', she said. 'Stand up and throw your voice. We want to hear what you have to say.'

Turning bright red he stood; he threw; they listened and at the end they applauded.

Grace You Fool!

From March 1973 to March 1974 I was Chairman of the London Region of the Federation of Conservative Students.

My year finished just after the February 1974 general election with a dinner at the House of Lords sponsored by the historian Lord Blake. My Guest of Honour was Margaret Thatcher. She had been invited nearly a year earlier as Secretary of State for Education. Now she was appearing before us as Shadow Secretary of State for the Environment.

Everything had been meticulously planned and at the appropriate moment the head table of eight trooped in. Some 200 people were standing staring at me as I thought to myself, 'we've forgotten something here. Oops, something's wrong. Why is everyone standing up. Why aren't they sitting down?'

Just as I was about to panic Lady Thatcher's left foot kicked, yes kicked, me on the outside right ankle.

'Grace, you fool,' she muttered.

Nobody had been lined up to say Grace!

I stuck my head down, said grace, and we all sat down. Whew!

Over dinner she discovered that as retiring Chairman I had personally paid for the wine for the top table.

'Oh, I can't have that,' she said and quickly passed me some folded money under the table.

Nobody Told Me!

I was hosting a dinner once for a famous politician from overseas. Lady Thatcher's office asked if she and Sir Denis could attend and I replied yes.

On the night, Sir Denis failed to show and I faced having an empty chair at dinner.

I quickly recruited a Tory MP friend who is a generation younger than Lady Thatcher, tall, straight and, my wife tells me, handsome in a battered kind of way.

We sat down to dinner. I tapped on a glass to get attention and made a few announcements.

I concluded by saying that Sir Denis's place had been taken for the night by Mr X MP.

'Really' said Lady Thatcher in an arch voice. 'Nobody told me,' she concluded.

DAVID DAVIS

MP FOR HALTEMPRICE & HOWDEN

David David was first elected to Parliament in 1987 as MP for Goole. He has served in the whips' office, as a junior Minister in the Cabinet Office and then as Minister for Europe. He is currently chairman of the Public Accounts Committee.

ॐ⚬ॐ

Building Rome

Soon after my election to Parliament in 1987 I happened to be walking through the Members' Lobby when I suddenly observed an old friend, Michael Forsyth, a well known Thatcherite and later to become a leading light in the No Turning Back Group.

Michael had been elected in 1983 and by now had become a junior minister. He was running, literally running. His hair was dishevelled and he was carrying not only his box, but somehow balancing a full tray of papers on his arm.

'Slow down,' I called out. 'Rome wasn't built in a day', I added as an afterthought.

'Yes,' cried Forsyth over his shoulder, as he swept passed me. 'But Margaret wasn't the foreman on that job.'

ALAN DUNCAN

MP FOR RUTLAND AND MELTON

Alan Duncan has been the MP for Rutland and Melton since 1992. He became Opposition spokesman on Health in 1998 and then became a front bench Spokesman for Trade and Industry in 1999.

శ్రం

Winning the war

In June 1996, I hosted a summer drinks party in my London garden for the No Turning Back group of Conservative MPs. Mrs T was the guest of honour as President of the NTB group and Michael Portillo, then Secretary of State for Defence was among the guests.

There was much debate at the time about the review of Defence budgets and Mrs T assailed Michael Portillo with questions about what would be left of our Defence capability.

Hoping to settle her down by assuring her of our adequate equipment in the future, Michael said: 'Don't worry, Margaret, we have lots of invitations to tender.'

She exploded: 'Invitations to tender – invitations to tender – you cannot win a war with invitations to tender!' and then she paused, quietened down and said: I am so sorry, Michael, I must not, I must not'. She then turned around as if to speak to someone else, the conversation having finished and, just as everyone thought that peace had broken out, she swivelled vigorously on her heels, pursed her lips, pointed her finger right at Michael Portillo and said in a determined and pointed manner: 'Michael, have you ever won a war? I have!'

ANDREW ROWE

MP FOR FAVERSHAM & MID KENT

*Andrew Rowe was the Director of Community Affairs at Conservative
Central Office from 1975 until 1979. He became MP for Mid Kent in 1983
and Faversham & Mid Kent in 1997.*

ॐ

Rally for Maggie

As Director of Community Affairs in Conservative Central
Office from 1975–9 I was responsible for arranging many of
the annual conferences she attended. In those days the Party
had a Federation of Conservative Students which was in control of
over 100 student unions. It also had a lively and effective Young
Conservative organisation and a growing Trades Unionist group.

The Community Affairs department suggested to the Chairman
and to Mrs.T that as part of the general election campaign of 1979, we
should try to destroy the allegation that the party was anti trades
unions by staging a rally of Conservative trades unionists at the
Wembley Conference centre. We had the advantage of having as one
of the members of our team, Harvey Thomas who had been trained
by the Billy Graham organisation. We also had in every Tory party area
young members of the Community Affairs team who, under the leadership of John Bowis, had been fostering good relations with the
trades unions for several years.

It was a gamble, of course, and the enormity of it was borne in on
me in the early morning of the day itself when the news came that

two of our planned busloads from the North West would fail to arrive because of a strike by transport workers. My immediate thought was that this was the TUC's response to our initiative and that instead of the 3500 people we expected we should have only the office staff and the 180 people from Scotland who had arrived by train the night before. Mad schemes of throwing them round the Conference centre and pretending that they were a Militant tendency picket came and went in my anxious mind.

All went well, however, and soon the Centre was filled with enthusiastic trades unionists. We had taken great pains to ensure that everyone present had a current membership card since we were sure that the Press would be checking.

Inside the Hall, under the skilled control of Dick Tracey a lively programme unfolded until at last Maggie herself appeared. At that point into the Hall came a long procession of men and women each carrying a placard declaring: ASTMS for Maggie, TGWLJ for Maggie and so on. It was impressive and Maggie herself was clearly delighted. She made a rousing speech, was enthusiastically received and went on her way rejoicing.

It was, in many ways, a landmark event. Not only did it secure a prime spot on the 6 o'clock news, but its verve and glamour made it a precedent for subsequent political campaigns. Maggie herself wrote a very warm letter of appreciation to me for the whole team.

I need not dwell here on the agonies to which it led. Our suggestion of a similar rally called 'Youth for Europe' to help with the European elections, met with such a long hiatus before a decision was finally taken, that we were given about three weeks in which to organise for 3000 young people to appear in the National Exhibition centre. But we managed and a new form of British electioneering was firmly established.

SIR DAVID MITCHELL

CHAIRMAN, EL VINO

David Mitchell was the MP for Basingstoke from 1964 until 1983 and MP for Hampshire North West from 1983 until 1997, serving as a Minister in Margaret Thatcher's government. He is currently the Chairman of the wine company El Vino.

༜

An act of kindness

I recall an elderly constituent coming to one of my 'surgeries', as UK Members of Parliament like to call their constituency advice sessions. It was a Saturday morning, he was last in my queue and stayed on to recount his wartime experiences.

He had been shot down over the Channel coastline and burnt on his arms. At that time Basingstoke Hospital was the major burns unit in southern England. After some treatment there he was sent to Newcastle by train for further specialist treatment.

As the train stopped at Grantham the sirens sounded for an air raid. Shortly after the 'all clear' sounded it was announced that the train would go no further until morning. Everybody got out and organised themselves as best they could for a somewhat uncomfortable night.

An air-raid warden approached my bandaged constituent asking where he was spending the night, to which he gave the reply 'I'm okay I've got a place on the ticket office floor.'

'No you haven't,' came the rejoinder, 'you are coming home with me.' This total stranger took him home, and he had a comfortable bed for the night.

Next morning breakfast was cooked by the blond pigtailed daughter in the house who then picked up her school satchel, kissed her parents goodbye and left.

He had had his breakfast cooked for him by a future Prime Minister – and that tells you something important about the home in which Margaret Thatcher grew up.

EDWINA CURRIE

NOVELIST, BROADCASTER AND FORMER MP

Edwina Currie was the MP for Derbyshire South from 1983 until 1997 and served as a junior minister at the Department of Health. She currently works as a bestselling novelist and broadcaster.

࿂

A magical experience

I first saw Margaret Thatcher in 1975 at the party conference, her first after she had defeated Ted Heath. She was our new party leader, a pretty young (49) married woman with young children, a scientist, a brain. I was a recently elected Birmingham City Councillor. I put in slip after slip to speak and was turned down. Eventually I was told, 'You're not important enough.' I went away, determined to return when I was.

Yet our paths were very similar. Some were coincidences I exploited to the full – for example, that we had the same birthday. Others were not chance. We both came from the provinces, had fathers with small businesses who loved talking politics, mothers who were quiet homemakers: our fathers were the models. We both went to state grammar schools, and on to Oxford to read chemistry. The old universities were looking for provincial girl state school scientists. It was much easier for an ambitious girl to win a place in science than in anything else.

So it meant I knew about her, and that it was possible to leap over all the barriers and become an MP like that. We were both outsiders. It also meant that I worshipped her, as did all the young Turks of the day.

I first came across her face to face at a new MPs' tea party in her room at the Commons in the summer of 1983. My colleague Robert Jackson was at that time still an MEP, and rapporteur of the budget committee in Brussels. Margaret turned to him sweetly. 'When will we get our rebate back, Robert?' she asked. 'Oh, Prime, Minister, it's not our money . . .' the unfortunate man began to explain. 'Not OUR money?' she squawked, and proceeded to demolish him, until nothing but a smoking heap of ash was left in his seat.

She turned to me. 'How are you getting on, dear?'

I decided to choose an anodyne subject. 'Fine – except with 158 new Members, accommodation is a bit of a problem,' I began (we didn't have the spanking new parliamentary building then).

'Really?' the eyebrows shot up, 'Do you have a desk?'

'Yes, I found my predecessor's.'

'Good. And a secretary?'

'Yes, I brought one from Derbyshire.'

'And a phone?'

'Yes, we . . .' my voice began to falter.

'And a filing cabinet?'

'Yes, Prime Minister, I have two . . .'

She sat back, 'Well, you've only been been six weeks, I should say you're doing rather well. When I arrived in 1959 it was six months before I had anywhere to sit. . .'

An important early event in that Parliament was the defeat of the unions, and of Arthur Scargill's miners in particular. With a mining seat (it used to be George Brown's) I was at the coal face on this. It was a meticulously planned operation. Scargill had piqued the government by threatening strike action in 1981, before Ministers were ready for him. Nick Ridley was put to the task. Soon, mountains of coal were piling up at the power stations – as we could observe daily, since five coal-fired power stations were visible from my own home. After the 1983 election, Scargill was finessed all through the winter, and bounced into calling the strike as spring started. That meant he would have to stay out at least six months to have an effect.

My miner constituents took a postal ballot. Over 90% voted, with 85% voting to continue working. The UDM was born. What they hated most was the use of the strike weapon to try and bring down a government – as it had Jim Callaghan's in 1979 – just after another election. It seemed anti-democratic to them, an impression reinforced by Scargill's refusal to ballot his own members, as the rule-book required. 'What's this about rolling back the tides of Thatcherism, Edwina?' one miner said to me. 'We voted for the tides of Thatcherism. That's why you're here.' The tide had turned, and washed Mr Scargill and all the strikers away with it.'

It was a famous victory – more so, and more enduring, than the Falklands. With it went any hope of a union bringing this country to its knees again. The effect on our reputation abroad was dramatic and beneficial. When Toyota wanted to come to Europe in 1989, there was no question: it had to be strike-free Britain. And it was no accident that they chose a spot away from existing car factories and in the middle of a strike-free country – again, within view of my house in South Derbyshire.

The story of Margaret Thatcher's later years included both remarkable success such as the ending of the Cold War and her friendship with Gorbachev and ignominy and failure. I voted against her in 1990, knowing full well that had she continued as Party leader we would have lost my marginal seat and many others with it. By then, voters other than committed Tories had had enough.

But serving with her was a magical experience, one which could never be bettered. We are a stronger, finer country for the standards she set, and the leadership she gave.

ERIC FORTH

CONSERVATIVE MP

Eric Forth served as a junior minister in Margaret Thatcher's and John Major's governments in various positions, ending his government career as Minister of State at the Department of Education and Employment. He was the MP for Mid Worcestershire from 1983 until 1997, when he became the MP for Bromley and Chislehurst.

৵৵

Tribute

The organisation of which I am Chairman – 'Conservative Way Forward', dedicated to perpetuating the principles and policies of 'Thatcherism', organised a dinner in 1999 to celebrate the twentieth anniversary of Margaret's first great general election victory.

Throughout the evening, tribute after tribute was made to Margaret and to Thatcherism. At the close, another one seemed unnecessary, so instead I was able to pay tribute to Sir Denis – 'without whom Thatcherism could never have happened.'

I think it pleased both Margaret and Denis!

৵৵

I am proud to be a member of 'No Turning Back', a group of Conservative Members of Parliament set up in 1984 to support Margaret Thatcher in her determination to challenge the bastions of socialism, public ownership and Trade Union power in Britain in the late 1970's.

Margaret attended one of our dinners in, I think, early 1986. During a rare lull in the conversation, Margaret asked if I had anything to say. To my colleagues' horror, I opined that there were too few sound 'Thatcherites' in her government, not least among NTB members present!

There was a stunned silence – and Margaret quickly moved on to another subject without comment.

By the end of 1986, at least three of the members present were in the Thatcher government – and by 1990, nearly half the group!

HOWARD FLIGHT

CONSERVATIVE MP

Howard Flight became the MP for Arundel and the South Downs in 1997. He is the Chairman of Guinness Flight a fund management business.

ৡৎ

Attractive and vital

D uring the great years of Margaret Thatcher's Premiership I was actually doing one of the things she advocated and set British citizens free to do, being an entrepreneur and building Guinness Flight as a successful Fund Management business. As a result, I cannot claim to know the great lady well, but have admired and supported her from afar for 20 years.

The first time I met Lady Thatcher socially was at a reception at Number 10 in the 1980s, where I was the guest of an MP friend. His wife commented on introducing us to Sir Denis and Maggie, that Denis looked just like my father – while remarkably true, Maggie was not amused!

In 1988 I wrote a book about currencies with the rather pretentious title *All You Need to Know About Exchange Rates.* I sent a copy to Lady Thatcher but received no response – I think my diagnosis for the purposes of the book were too financially clinical.

Just prior to the 1997 General Election I was pleased to be invited by Maggie to a reception for those known to be of sound views on Europe and the Euro. I recollect Denis interrupting while Maggie was holding court on the ghastlinesses of the EU, to the effect 'We should get the hell out.' Maggie continued without drawing breath. At the same occasion, Nick Gibb took photos of us all with Lady Thatcher, but with a pair of curtains in the background – I felt Maggie did not feel it appropriate for her to be contrasted against a pair of curtains!

At a more recent and equally enjoyable reception given by Lady Thatcher, I was talking with her when in particular it struck me what a very attractive and vital woman she still is.

LAURENCE ROBERTSON

CONSERVATIVE MP

Laurence Robertson became the MP for Tewkesbury in 1997. He had previously been an industrial consultant and a charity fundraising consultant.

そ๑๗

Hearts and minds

M argaret Thatcher changed attitudes. That was her greatest achievement. Without that accomplished, none of her other achievements would have been possible.

She changed hearts and minds. When she came to office, the country had just struggled through the Winter of Discontent. The snow had been deep on the ground; everyone, from lorry drivers to industrial workers to hospital staff had been on strike; even the dead were left unburied. Industrial strife had been a dominant influence in the 1970s. Management had lost the will and the confidence to manage.

But worst of all was the fact that few people actually believed that things could be changed or could be any different. Margaret Thatcher believed differently. She believed in the intrinsic determination and spirit of the British people, but she realised that it had to be reawakened, just as it was in 1939.

Achieving this was no mean task, but achieve it she did. She had the courage to introduce tough budgets which set the country's finances right. She had the courage to tackle the trades union barons and hand the unions back to their members. She had the courage to set free the ailing nationalised industries. She trusted the people and sold them the homes they were living in.

People began to believe in Britain once again and the rest is history. It sounds simple, but the confidence we now have in our country is down to her. To her foresight and her courage. It was difficult to understand exactly what was needed in Britain during the 1970s, but a few people did realise. But she was unique in that she was the only person who was prepared to actually do what was necessary; to have the ability to do it; and have the courage to refuse to turn back.

Now, attitudes have changed and the country is one of the leaders of the world again. What a transformation. What a Prime Minister. I only wish I could have served under her!

LORD DENHAM

GOVERNMENT CHIEF WHIP IN THE HOUSE OF LORDS
1979–91

Lord Denham served under Margaret Thatcher as Chief Whip in the House of Lords throughout her time as Prime Minister. He is also a successful novelist, his most recent novel Black Rod *was published in 1997 by Bellew.*

৯৵৻৶

Winning in the Lords

L ike most members of the House of Commons, Margaret Thatcher was never quite able to understand what the House of Lords was all about. Until she reached it herself, that is. But throughout her twelve years as Prime Minister, it fell to me, as her Chief Whip, to try and put this right.

'Why is it,' she asked me once, 'that you are always being defeated in the House of Lords, whereas we never are in the Commons?' The short answer was that, the House of Lords being a revising Chamber, without regular defeats of a Government of whatever party, the system simply wouldn't work. But I gave the more practical one. 'Because, Prime Minister, you have an overall majority of over 140 in your House, whereas in ours we haven't got an overall majority at all.' It was absolutely true, both on paper and in practice. Even at that time, if both the official Opposition and the Liberals voted against us, we still needed the support of a majority of Cross Bench Peers if we were ever to win a division. But Margaret somehow couldn't be persuaded of that at all.

'Why,' she asked me on another occasion, 'don't your revise the procedures of the House of Lords so that you can get our business through more smoothly?'

'I can't do that, Prime Minister.'

'Why not?' 'Because next time there's a Labour Government,' I said, 'we're going to need those very procedures to prevent whatever enormities they try and inflict on us.'

There was an awful silence, at the end of which I couldn't help feeling that I was lucky not to have been taken out and shot as a traitor for the very suggestion that there could be a Labour Government again.

One of Margaret's great charms, however, was that she had the most beautiful manners. There was an awful occasion when a Housing Bill was going through the Lords and a Memorial Service for Lord Dilhorne, a highly popular former Conservative Lord Chancellor, had been scheduled for that same afternoon. It was attended by almost every back-bench Tory peer. The Opposition had divided the House on one of their early amendments and, much to their surprise, had inflicted a crashing defeat on the Government. Highly delighted, they thereupon called division after division and won three more amendments in quick succession, before enough Government peers to stop the rot had managed to filter back in.

It so happened that the Prime Minister was holding one of her periodic parties for the hired help in Downing Street that evening, and I reached the top of the stairs at Number Ten just as she had been informed of the fourth defeat. I was her guest and she gallantly contrived to make a joke of it . . . but any one could see that in reality she didn't think it funny at all. My only consolation was that Reggie Dilhorne himself would have enjoyed – and I like to think indeed was enjoying – the whole thing quite enormously.

LORD HARRIS

FOUNDER PRESIDENT OF THE
INSTITUTE OF ECONOMIC AFFAIRS

Raised to the peerage in 1979, Lord Harris of High Cross is amongst the most respected political and economic thinkers of our time. He was a founder member of the Institute of Economic Affairs and of Buckingham University. He has published numerous works on economic policy and political economy.

಄ೞ

No, Prime Minister

I had met Margaret Thatcher a time or two before, in the 1960s. Once was over dinner with a bevy of businessmen including a rather self-important Arnold Weinstock – whom she made seem pretty feeble. Another occasion was over lunch with a motley bunch of back-bench Tory MPs who were lamenting the difficulty of putting across the complex case for free markets – which she resolved brusquely by suggesting they should ask their constituents whether they would rather shop at Marks & Spencer or the Co-op!

But the first personal encounter I recall more vividly was in the twilight days of Ted Heath, at the Department of Education of which she was then Secretary of State. She had agreed to meet informally with a small deputation of academics, including Sydney Caine and Max Beloff, to hear about our plan to establish an independent university – once we could raise the first million or so for start-up costs!

A sudden cabinet crisis over the Middle East prevented her prompt arrival so she had arranged for us to be met by a junior colleague named (Bill) Van Straubenzee. Not for nothing was he nicknamed 'strawberry tea'. Beautifully turned-out in suit and matching waistcoat (probably with lapels), he received us in a slightly scruffy office, but with a contrived pomp and ceremony more suited to a state occasion. He invited us to sit around him in a small semi-circle and, with appropriate solemnity launched into a discourse on the importance of higher education, periodically stretching out an elegant leg in order rather elaborately to adjust the crease in his immaculate trousers.

Suddenly, the door burst open and in rushed Margaret Thatcher, complete with handbag and a striking hat, which was allowed those days. Explaining that she might be called away again in a few minutes, she perched on the edge of a chair and told the junior minister to carry on. He had hardly completed his opening statement – to the effect that there was 'no hostility' in the Department to the broad concept of an independent university – when the lady broke in: 'No, no, William, can I put that differently?' She then proceeded to declare with deliberate emphasis that there was positive enthusiasm for the idea of competition from an institution of respected academics independent of the state.

Leaving the deflated van Straubenzee with little better to do than contemplate the crease in his other trouser leg, she emphasised with a candour new to me from a politician, that we would not receive – nor should we expect – any subsidies or special favours. What she would promise was to remove any bureaucratic obstacles that discriminated against the new enterprise. [It was precisely such equal treatment which that famous social democrat, Shirley Williams, refused to grant a few years later as Secretary of State for Education. Thus when one of Buckingham's first graduates applied for an army commission under a special system of graduate entry, Mrs Williams refused to support the appeal of Max Beloff, our first Principal, for equal treatment that was automatically granted to equivalent products, of state universities.]

In 1976 when the University College of Buckingham was ready to welcome its first intake of 60 students, it was Margaret Thatcher who performed the opening ceremony and in 1983 it was her Government that awarded the institution its royal charter as the University of Buckingham, of which she was to become Chancellor in 1992.

My second, more personal memory of Maggie's decisive style was at Chequers just two weeks after her election victory in May 1979. My wife and I had been totally astonished to be invited for Sunday lunch and to find ourselves guests of the Thatcher family – Denis, Mark and Carol plus Douglas Hurd and wife, Lady (Janet) Young and husband – who all lived nearby.

I was further amazed to find myself at the table placed on the Prime Minister's right and almost dumbfounded when she suddenly leant across and confided her decision to put me into the House of Lords. I managed to get out the words: 'Do I have any say in the matter,' to which she answered shortly, I thought almost sharply: 'No,' and with an impatient shrug of the shoulders proceeded to complain of the delays of official procedures before my name could be checked and formal marching orders issued.

I still recall the irritation, bordering on anger, with which she added: 'I sometimes think I'm the only one trying to get anything done.' I recall those exact words simply because they came into my mind so often thereafter as she struggled against cabinet colleagues, departmental committees, civil servants, journalists and no doubt many others, in her sometimes lonely mission to subdue the trade unions, check the money supply, curb government expenditure, and resist the rising tide of mischief from Brussels. I was therefore not in the least surprised that she saw off the Argentine junta and got Peter Walker to stand firm for months against Scargill's militant miners. I can think of no previous British PM this century, Churchill always excepted, who regularly stuck to his guns and displayed in Keith Joseph's words,' such personal, moral courage.'

I had scarcely been introduced as peer in July when her PPS, the incomparable, late Ian Gow, sounded me out (at a celebration party in his Eastbourne constituency) on whether I would consider quitting the cross-benches in the Lords to accept a ministerial appointment. I did not hesitate even for one second before replying: 'I'm afraid not, in no circumstances,' adding: 'I beg you not to put our friendship at risk by ever raising that dangerous question again.' Dangerous for me because I knew if I became Maggie's political leg-man, I would never be able to refuse her anything – even when I might think the great lady was, conceivably, in the wrong. Only my immediate family should be able to call on such absolute loyalty!

A more light-hearted memory, although second-hand, was told me with a chuckle by Geoffrey Howe in the days when he still basked in Maggie's favour. At an early cabinet meeting, he had a strong impulse to smoke. Seeing no-one else had lit up, he stealthily extracted a packet of cigarettes from his pocket, followed by a box of matches, before looking round to see if anyone was noticing. The prime minister leant across smiling and whispered: 'Go on, Denis smokes!'

LORD TEBBIT

FORMER CABINET MINISTER AND CONSERVATIVE PARTY
CHAIRMAN

*Norman Tebbit served in Margaret Thatcher's Cabinet from 1981 until 1987,
most famously as Secretary of State for Employment. In 1985 he became the
Chairman of the Conservative Party, a position he held until 1987.*

ॐॐ

Under Pressure

During Margaret Thatcher's time as leader of the opposition her twice weekly clashes at Prime Minister's Question Time, first with Harold Wilson, then with Jim Callaghan, often set the political agenda. It was essential in those clashes – in which the Prime Minister holds all the best cards, including the inestimable advantage of the last word – that she, not him, should emerge the winner.

Her success depended in considerable part upon briefing not only on matters of fact but on tactics to wrong foot her adversary. I was privileged to be a member of her briefing team which consisted of Airey Neave, Michael Dobbs – then a Central Office researcher – George Gardiner and from time to time others such as Nigel Lawson. Naturally our existence became known and we were dubbed by a Labour journalist 'The Gang of Four' and the name stuck.

It was during these years that I came to know and understand Margaret Thatcher. It was a privileged position but it sometimes had its downside.

I doubt if speech writing for anyone is all honey – certainly it was not so in her case. As in most things, Margaret Thatcher is pretty much a perfectionist about speeches and a good many drafts finish in the waste bin before she is satisfied with a script. I soon learned that holding back my preferred phrases or paragraphs improved their chances of finding their way into the speech rather than the bin, but sometimes the writing sessions went on far too late for my liking.

I well remember being approached in the division lobby at 10pm. 'I've just got a draft of a speech – and it's awful – would you be able to look at it for me Norman?' she asked.

'Of course, when is it for?'

'Oh good,' she replied, 'tomorrow lunchtime – do come round to the office'. Somewhat taken aback I followed her to the office where fellow speechwriters were assembling with pads and pens in hand. We were soon at work but it was hard going to hit the right note. Somewhere about three in the morning I was beginning to wilt and was caught in the midst of a great yawn.

'You're not very bright tonight, Norman,' she commented.

'It's not tonight,' I said rather huffily, 'it's tomorrow bloody morning.' Somehow that night we got a decent draft for her and I concluded that, like me, Margaret Thatcher works best under pressure – pressure that causes more discomfort to one's aides than oneself!

PATRICK MINFORD

ECONOMIST

The Professor of Economics at Cardiff Business School, Patrick Minford is amongst the most respected economists of recent times. He has published numerous books and papers and his work was highly influential upon the development of Thatcherite economic policy.

ॐ≺

Good policy

For me Margaret Thatcher was the epitome of thorough hard work on policy. A big issue would be centre stage – monetary policy and inflation, unemployment and benefits, for example – and the basics and the prejudices aired, the hard work would begin. The civil servants would of course produce their briefs and reports, and that would be the start for a general canvassing of views around those with the same aims as her. But the critics' views too must be synthesised and dealt with convincingly – how long would the monetary policy take to bring down inflation? Would cutting unemployment benefits have enough effect? The whole process would often come to a grand climax in a Chequers seminar, as it did in the case of these two topics – where she presided, heckled, or intervened with more dramatic emphasis, reducing strong men to quailing silence. But the objective was to test the preferred policies to destruction (sometimes too literally, as the burden of proof was on the effectiveness of change – political capital would be used up and there must be the probability of noticeable results). I remember on one occasion someone (one of her wets, or one of her closest advisers? I forget; it could easily have been either) said something limp and silly; this provoked one of those fearsome diatribes (a 'handbagging') which became legendary. Then later on I was the object of her ire – I fought back, which got me into even deeper water. But the fact was that she didn't care what feelings were trampled on in the process of getting to the nub of good policy – only those (men typically) with too much sense of personal pomp and worth would not understand that vital objective; and she had no patience for people who couldn't take it in such a cause. To those unfamiliar with the usual brutal seminar methods of reaching truth this was all pretty hard; but I noticed that among those close to her the survivors were a tough intellectual breed. When the country had become so used to failure in policy after policy, it was indeed vital that pretty stringent tests were applied to the new ones; they could not be allowed to fail. The Chequers seminars were rounded off by her chivvying everyone to eat properly; one got the impression that if she had only had the time she would have cooked it too. One minute the hectoring platonic dialogue, the next the attentive host bringing round the soup. The point was this: we men had settled for second, third and fourth best for her country and a small woman was going to see us and such pathetic compromise with mediocrity off, once and for all. It was startling, wonderful stuff; and how badly we needed it and how much hard work and bruised amour-propre it took.

QUENTIN DAVIES

MP FOR GRANTHAM AND STAMFORD

Quentin Davies was the MP for Stamford and Spalding from 1987 until 1997 when he became the MP for Margaret Thatcher's home constituency of Grantham and Stamford. He is an opposition frontbench spokesman on Treasury matters.

ôôô

Plunging in

I am not widely thought of as a Thatcherite, but I would certainly have described myself as that when I was first elected to Parliament in 1987. I regarded – and still regard – Margaret Thatcher's first two terms of Government as a period of heroic achievement – the economic successes, the end of the 'British Disease', the privatisations, the Right to Buy, Personal Pensions, the creation of a property-owning democracy, standing up to bullying from any quarter, and historic victories against trade union power, Argentinian invasion and the Cold War. Until the Bruges Speech I never found myself in anything other then enthusiastic agreement with her. Her personal attitude to politics – conviction, consistency, unstinting and tireless conscientiousness, setting the highest standards for herself and her ministers, absolute integrity – I still regard as a model for any age. And her period of office transformed, at least temporarily, the attitude of the British electorate to politics itself. In retrospect it was a shining oasis between the Wilsonian cynicism and national decline that preceded her, and the drift and scandals that followed. One of my proudest moments was when I was made a PPS at the end of my first year – sadly for me on the eve of the shattering Bruges speech!

Two recollections – which illustrate both one of her weaknesses and one of her outstanding strengths. Six months after my election I was invited to her room in the Commons with a dozen other new arrivals. We sat around the table. She made a few introductory remarks and then asked for our comments on how things were going. Everyone said 'wonderful, Prime Minister' or words to that effect – indeed she was at her apogee and there was little enough to criticise. 'Well, come on,' she said, 'something must be less than perfect.' I thought that an admirable approach. So I plunged in. I said that I thought we ought not to fight the next election without being able to point to something we had done for the old age pensioner – it had been the one serious difficulty during the 1987 election.

I didn't make it into a second sentence. She flew at me with a string of well remembered statistics. Didn't I know that average pensioner household incomes had increased by 50% since 1979, that now two thirds instead of one third of those retiring had some income other than the National Insurance pension etc, etc.? (As it happened I knew most of this almost as pat as she did – but it didn't really meet my point). The monologue lasted perhaps twenty minutes and began to cover the whole issue of Treasury controls and how essential they were. My colleagues sat motionless, as if paralysed, as the diatribe gathered in intensity. Some surreptitiously moved their eyes towards me though without daring to move their heads – glances of horror or fascinated anticipation rather than of sympathy. Clearly I had committed *lèse-majesté*, and now fully deserved to be thrown to the lions. Then finally the energy of the volcano seemed spent. There was neither time, nor inclination, nor I suspect breath left to discuss anything else. We filed out in silence – I, and to a lesser extent I suspect all of us, feeling a little giddy.

Of course I had misjudged the invitation to express dissent – however respectfully or tentatively I had endeavoured to do so. I had fallen into the trap set by Mao Tse Tung when he launched his Hundred Flowers Campaign and begged loyal Party members to speak up with any complaints or criticisms they had. The difference was that Mao's victims were rapidly physically liquidated. Margaret remained utterly friendly in the lobbies – and clearly did not veto my promotion to PPS. Nor was that the last occasion when I ventured some comment or suggestion. But the response was always of a predictably binary kind – either she had already thought of the point herself, or it was a very silly idea. Perhaps it often was. But for all my great respect and admiration for Margaret I began to pity her Cabinet colleagues. And I started to fear that with Margaret bearing such an immense burden of work, and taking alone such a vast range of short-term and long-term decisions, some terrible mistake might one day be made.

My second recollection comes from the end. It was well known in the Party that I was supporting Michael Heseltine in his bid for the leadership. I had never disguised my views from Peter Morrison, Margaret's Private Secretary, from the Whips or from anyone else in the House. But I felt it cowardly to leave it there, especially as I genuinely admired so much that she stood for, and was conscious of the historical greatness of the personage, and the somewhat awesome gravity of the decision we were about to take. So I wrote her a personal letter. I expressed the sincerest admiration but I explained why I had found it necessary to vote and campaign against her. I said I thought her European policy had split the Party irredeemably, was inconsistent with her own Single European Act, and while we remained in the European Community (as it was then called) inhibited us from exercising any real influence within it, thus inevitably preventing us from optimising the national interest. I might have added that we had lost a historic opportunity to take the lead in Europe.

Of course I never expected any reply. Under the emotional stress and trauma of the moment any other political leader I feel sure would simply have flung the letter into the nearest waste-paper basket – I do not doubt I would have done so myself. But two days after the second round, when there was no conceivable political or ulterior motive in conciliating me, I received a courteous hand-written response. I recall the surprise I felt as I opened it. My conflicting emotions were I think, once again, though for rather different reasons, almost giddying. But this time, as I thought of Margaret Thatcher the human being beneath her public greatness, I could only marvel.

SIR RICHARD BODY

MP FOR BOSTON AND SKEGNESS

The veteran backbencher Sir Richard Body has been a Member of Parliament since 1955, initially for Billericay until 1959, then for Holland and Boston from 1966 until 1997, and since 1997 for Boston and Skegness.

҂

In court with Margaret

I t was in 1949 when I first met Margaret Roberts, then with ICI at Manningtree in Essex. She came to help me as the Conservative candidate in the London County Council election when I was standing for Deptford.

Television was yet to dominate our electioneering; canvassing was limited and public meetings were held every day, indoor in the evenings and outdoor ones in the daytime.

Margaret came to speak outside New Cross station in the rush hour to scores of commuters on their way home, and I well remember her standing with microphone in hand beside the loudspeaker car.

The memory does not fade. It may have been her first open-air meeting, but any nervousness was difficult to detect. She spoke with modesty and sincerity and observers might have thought her demure and earnest. Her speech perhaps was rather too intellectual for a transient audience, yet quite a number delayed their journey home to hear the reasoned arguments.

In those days almost any meeting had a lively amount of heckling. It was in many ways a far more democratic form of electioneering than is the case now, because the speaker had to be on the ball and if unable to get the better of the heckler the audience would soon lose interest, whilst in open air meetings it would melt away. It is much to her credit that that was not the case on that evening outside New Cross station.

I much regret that we did not invite her to speak at one of the many indoor meetings we held throughout the constituency, as she was so obviously in command of her subject I have no doubt that she would have been a match for any heckler.

I met Margaret many times in those days. We were both YCs and Prospective Parliamentary Candidates and attended regularly the monthly meetings we used to have in the Candidates' Association. At one subsequent supper Ted Heath and she once sat beside each other. I remember he was cheerful to all while she was taciturn yet attentive to everything said around our table.

There were many other occasions too. I remember her as unfailingly considerate towards other people, whoever they were and whatever the circumstances.

We later went on to practise at the Bar and both of us became pupils to masters who were 'in crime'. In those days there were only five sets of chambers that were of criminal specialists with an aggregate membership of no more than sixty.

Now, it might be added, it is about twenty times that number.

Only four courts sat at the Old Bailey then and seldom a brief for a young barrister, so it meant going to London Sessions, by the Elephant and Castle. Going down to grubby cells to take instructions from old lags was not to her liking. What was worse were the occasions when they sought a dock-brief. This required all barristers who could not escape the court to sit in the front row of counsel benches – usually there were about a dozen of us there, for other young hopefuls would crowd in – and the old lag would emerge from the cells and shuffle to the well of the court to stand in front of counsel clutching his £2.4s.6d. Then he would run his eye up and down the rank of newly made wigs, usually pointing his finger along the line as he looked and then cry out 'I will 'ave 'im' or in Margaret's case it would have been 'I will 'ave 'er.'

So naturally she turned her back on that sort of life and moved to the more intellectually congenial world of tax chambers.

In obtaining a seat for the 1955 general election I had better luck than her, and when I decided to stand down from Billericay, choosing to concentrate on the Bar instead of Parliament, she applied to take my place in the constituency, despite my advice not to go there. She was one of the twelve chosen for interview, but fortunately rejected. She went on to be adopted for Finchley but had she been successful in Billericay her future might have been different, for a subsequent defeat in that seat would have been inevitable.

ROBERT KEY

MP FOR SALISBURY

Robert Key has been the MP for Salisbury since 1983. He served under Margaret Thatcher and John Major in a number of ministerial posts. He served on the Defence Select Committee and since 1997 has been a Shadow Defence Minister..

಄

Matron?

Ifirst came across Margaret Thatcher when I was a master at Harrow School and her son Mark was a pupil. She was one of a galaxy of Conservative politicians whose children were entrusted to Winston Churchill's old school. In the 1970s, in addition to the Thatchers, Harrow pupils included young men bearing the names Macmillan, Heseltine, Maudling, Churchill, Onslow, Oppenheim and others. The former MP Bobby Allen (whose son served for many years in the Private Office at Number 10) was a Governor of the school, as was Mary Soames. To varying degrees they all encouraged and assisted the development of my political leanings.

As a House Tutor at Harrow, I had a lot of contact particularly with the senior boys and with their parents. Margaret Thatcher's son, Mark, was in Bradbys and his House Tutor, Alan Sankey, was charming, assiduous and courteous. After lunch one day he walked into the entrance hall at the house to find a woman waiting to see the House Master. He enquired whether she had come about the job of house matron. What a pity he did not recognise the Secretary of State for Education! This tale does say something about that generation of politicians who placed huge faith in the schools they chose and their teachers – and who expected no special favours.

I was accepted onto the Candidates List in 1975 and I fought Frank Dobson in Holborn and St Pancras South in 1979. Our long suffering daughter Helen was born just before the General Election that year and her second name is Margaret! Helen met Margaret for the first time on the day before polling day in the 1983 General Election. The Liberals had declared Salisbury in their top ten target seats (as they always do!) and since I was a new candidate in my home town the powers that be at Central Office ordained that the Prime Minister should pay a flying visit to Salisbury. She landed at Old Sarum Airfield by helicopter and came by coach into the Guildhall Square where over 10,000 people were waiting for her. In the middle of the square was a Land Rover provided by my farming friend Richard Crook. On it waited the Key family including four-year-old Helen. Margaret made magnificent progress through the throng and as she climbed aboard a friend asked Helen what was special about today. 'After this, I'm going swimming,' she piped. We won the seat with a healthy majority!

In the autumn of 1984 I received a mysterious message on the Members' Letterboard in the House to contact the Chief Whip urgently. What had I done? He explained that in the Tory Party there was a long tradition of an honorary PPS being provided for former Prime Ministers. Would I look after Ted? I knew the dangers of acceptance.

I took the risk. It would not be true to say I never regretted it – it was misconstrued by some of the press and it was certainly misconstrued by quite a lot of people in Salisbury! However, I learnt a huge amount not only about Ted Heath and his beliefs and vision – but also about Margaret Thatcher. One of my duties was to act as go-between. On one occasion there was a confidence motion put down by Labour. Ted was in Israel, adding to the political round by conducting a major symphony orchestra in Jerusalem. The message came from the Chief Whip that I must tell Ted to return to London. The Whips could not contact him.

I did! He was out in the desert and somehow I managed to speak to him. He said he would not come back. I asked if I could tell Number 10 that if he had been able to come back he would have supported the Government in the no-confidence motion.

He agreed and he also let me put out an appropriate press notice. I telephoned Number 10 and spoke to Margaret's PPS. We agreed there was no alternative!

Margaret was always approachable. She would always listen to a good argument with terrifying attention and total concentration as she fixed you with her laser-beam eyes. She would listen and if she decided you were right she would back you. She did this twice for me.

On the first occasion, a group of us were absolutely convinced of the basic injustice of no financial provision to help haemophiliacs who had been infected with the HIV virus from contaminated NHS blood transfusions. A distraught mother in Salisbury came to me to tell me that her little boy at primary school had become infected this way. Other parents had found out – and they would not allow their children to attend the same school. The Head was forced to tell the mother her child must leave the school. It was absolutely terrible. I joined with a small band of Conservative MPs and we went from Junior Health Minister to Secretary of State for Health – all to no avail. John Hannam persuaded us that we must go to the top. We did. Margaret met us in her small upstairs study at Number 10. She clipped her famous handbag shut, put it on the floor, and gave us her total concentration as we put the case. In spite of all the briefing from the Number 10 Policy Unit and the Department of Health, she had never seen it or thought about it in our terms. She knew we were right. The next day there was a statement in the House announcing a substantial ex-gratia payment to establish a trust fund to be administered by the Haemophilia

Society. Many of us know that at heart Margaret is a compassionate woman.

On the second occasion, in the never-ending saga of what to do with Stonehenge (in my constituency) – a problem that has defeated Margaret Thatcher, John Major and Tony Blair – I was convinced that she had been given faulty briefing by the Ministry of Defence who are big landowners near the site. The location of the current English Heritage favourite for a new visitors' centre was unacceptable to local people and I had battled through the Whitehall machine and the PM had agreed to see me. We met in her room at the Commons. I came equipped with maps – and she was soon on her hands and knees on the carpet as I explained the problem. She agreed with me. The site was dropped.

That degree of access, concentration on detail and compassion was all part of the magic that made Margaret great. That was at the height of her power. Towards the end of her term she became less accessible and I am sure that led to disenchantment with her style. She had set impossibly high standards to maintain for as long as ten years. Incidentally, that degree of accessibility was never matched by her successor, John Major.

Having served Ted Heath as unofficial PPS, then Alick Buchanan-Smith and subsequently Chris Patten as PPS for four years, my moment came. In 1990 I was the lay member of the Medical Research Council. In spite of my duties to Chris Patten (who was Secretary of State for the Environment) I really had to attend a Medical Research Council meeting in London even though it was the middle of the Party Conference in Bournemouth. I had caught the train up to London and arrived at the MRC in Park Crescent to be told by the receptionist to phone Chris Patten's Private Secretary immediately. He was already on the way to collect me in a Government car. When he arrived, the Private Secretary bundled me straight into the car and took me to Waterloo where I caught a train back to Bournemouth. I would be met at Bournemouth by the Chief Constable who would take me straight to the Prime Minister. What on earth was all this about? The Private Secretary stayed mum. I was indeed met at Bournemouth by the Chief Constable who took me in his Jag to the Highcliffe Hotel. There I was ushered up to Margaret Thatcher's modest suite where she asked me if I would be prepared to join her Government. What can a man say? 'Yes, Prime Minister. Thank you very much. I will not let you down.' Nor did I. Within a couple of months she had been challenged for the leadership of the Party – and of course I voted for Margaret.

By the time I got downstairs in the hotel, slightly numb at the thought that I was now a Minister of the Crown, however humble, the world had already been informed of the appointment and I was surrounded by the press. Suddenly the sea of cameras parted and there was Ted Heath. He walked up to me, grinned broadly said, 'Congratulations – you poor sod!' and stumped off.

SIR JOHN STANLEY

MP FOR TONBRIDGE AND MALLING

The Rt Hon Sir John Stanley MP was Parliamentary Private Secretary to Margaret Thatcher from 1976 until 1979. He was subsequently Minister of Housing and Construction, Minister for the Armed Forces and Minister of State for Northern Ireland.

లచ

Where's page seven?

Contrary to her handbag-wielding image, Margaret was the best boss I have ever had.

Know your boss by your bad days, not by your good ones. My nadir came during a weekend tour in East Anglia, deep in the Fens. At mid-day on the Saturday, Margaret was due to give her weekend speech for the Sunday papers in a Town Hall in the Isle of Ely constituency, then represented by Clement Freud. Shortly before noon we set up camp at an adjacent hotel so that Margaret could have a final page by page run through of her speech.

Suddenly she looked up and said: 'John, my page seven is missing.' My blood chilled. 'I'm sure it's here Margaret' I replied with misplaced confidence. Frantic searches through everybody's briefcases produced no trace of the delinquent page seven. 'I'm terribly sorry Margaret,' I blabbered pitiably, page seven seems to have been left behind in London.' 'In that case,' Margaret replied, not unkindly but changing gear effortlessly into the Royal We, 'We will have to remember it then, won't We.'

Minutes later we were off to the Town Hall. I slunk in behind Margaret feeling pin-head high. She launched into her speech with her customary confidence and fluency, but my trepidation mounted as she strode purposefully towards the yawning abyss of the missing page seven. Of course, I need not have worried. Without a glimmer of hesitation or faintest change of delivery, page seven was perfectly recalled from Margaret's extraordinary computer-like memory and, in moments, she had reached the *terra firma* of page eight and beyond.

I awaited my sentence, fully deserved. Summary despatch to the backbenches perhaps – the equivalent in British politics to being shot at dawn. But no shot rang out and Margaret never once mentioned my Fenland incompetence that weekend, nor at any time subsequently – true magnanimity indeed.

For those of us who were privileged to be The Leader of the Opposition's staff, it was Margaret's personal kindness and consideration, as well as her inspirational political abilities, that impelled us to work for her night and day until that unforgettable moment came in May 1979 when, already inside Number 10 we were able to welcome her back from the Palace and greet her for the first time as 'Prime Minister'.

JOHN WHITTINGDALE

MP FOR MALDON AND CHELMSFORD EAST

John Whittingdale was Margaret Thatcher's Political Secretary from 1988 until 1990 and her Private Secretary from 1990 until 1992. He is currently Parliamentary Private Secretary to William Hague.

჻

This parrot is no more

O f all the demands on the Prime Minister's time, the one that occupied the most was speech-writing. Every speech went through at least ten drafts and major speeches many more. As Margaret Thatcher's Political Secretary, my job was to co-ordinate the preparation of speeches to Party audiences. My year was divided between fixed points: the Central Council meeting, the Scottish Conference, the Local Government Conference, the Women's Conference and most important of all the Party Conference in October.

Work would start on the Party Conference speech at least a month in advance. At a preliminary meeting, the Prime Minister would set out her ideas as to the areas that the speech should cover. This was usually done in a unbroken flow of raw Thatcher thought which our in-house speech-writing team, and those that I would commission from outside, would have to turn into draft speech form. Subject areas would be allocated between speechwriters and they would then be sent off to prepare paragraphs on each topic for inclusion. Once we had collected a number of contributions, these would be tacked together in a rough structure and the process of refinement and polishing would begin.

It was an immensely time-consuming process and at least once in the preparation of every speech, the Prime, Minister would lose confidence in the whole process, tell us that it was all useless and demand that we start again from the beginning. The next few hours would be spent slightly tweaking the sections and then reinserting them while assuring her that they were completely different from the original. At the early stages, we would be meeting once a week. This would then increase to everyday and then the whole of the weekend before the Conference would be spent working on the text at Chequers.

Once we got to Blackpool, Bournemouth or Brighton, the whole time would be spent in the Prime Minister's suite surrounded by paper, with a core team which was boosted by those drafted in to make suggestions and improvements. A single critical word at the wrong time could undo weeks of work and my job was as much to keep well-meaning but destructive critics away as it was to bring in and encourage contributors. The average length of a Party Conference speech is about forty minutes. I worked on three and in each case Margaret Thatcher spent at least eighty hours working on the text: two hours for each minute of the speech. Those actually writing the speech spent much more.

The hardest and most important parts of the speech to write were the jokes. Margaret Thatcher is not naturally a joke-teller although she has a dry sense of humour, However, she recognises that without jokes, a speech is flat and dull. A good joke-writer was therefore valued above all others. On our core team, we had two principle joke-writers: the late Sir Ronnie Millar and John O'Sullivan, a journalist and commentator who had been brought in to the Number Ten Policy Unit. They had very different styles and each brought a different kind of humour. However, in each case, Margaret Thatcher frequently required persuasion that what they had written was indeed funny.

In 1990, the Party Conference speech was particularly important. Margaret Thatcher was under heavy attack and had recently suffered the resignation of her Chancellor, Nigel Lawson. Her speech had to be as good as she had ever delivered. A few weeks earlier, the Liberal Democrats had unveiled their new Party symbol. It was supposed to represent a bird taking wing, but in the mind of John O'Sullivan it immediately became a dead parrot. He decided that he would write a section of the Speech devoted to mocking the Liberal Democrats and would include a section of Monty Python's Dead Parrot sketch. To anyone familiar with Monty Python it was a terrific idea and very funny. Unfortunately, the Prime Minister had not even heard of Monty Python.

When we came to read through the draft of the speech, Mrs Thatcher paused when she reached the dead parrot section and looked at John O'Sullivan as if he were completely mad. We knew that this would happen and so had prepared our strategy in advance. 'This is', I explained, 'one of the most famous comedy sketches ever written. It will be instantly recognisable to every person in the audience.' I was slightly less certain of this latter point, knowing Conservative audiences, but all of us present insisted to the Prime Minister that it would be the highlight of her speech.

The joke survived that read-through but I knew that she was not convinced. On each subsequent occasion, whenever we reached the parrot section, she stopped and said: 'Are you sure that this is funny?' After about the third or fourth occasion, she tried a new tack. 'I need to see the sketch,' she said. 'If I am to deliver it then I need to get the inflexion absolutely right.' As it happened, I had at home a video of the Python film *And Now for Something Completely Different*, which contains the dead parrot sketch. I therefore brought it into the office the next day.

One of the more surreal moments during my time at Number Ten followed. Sitting in my office watching the dead parrot sketch were

Margaret Thatcher, John O'Sullivan, Robin Harris who was also helping with the speech, Peter Morrison her PPS and myself. At any time, it is a very funny sketch. But the absurdity of the situation made it all the more amusing and I and the three others found it so hilarious that we had tears rolling down our cheeks. Margaret Thatcher, on the other hand, was all the more mystified. It was not her type of humour and she found it difficult to see why we were laughing so much. However, given that we all were, she accepted that it must be funny and so, true professional that she was, she attempted to master the emphasis and inflexion of John Cleese's delivery. She did so brilliantly and was soon able to deliver faultlessly the famous lines: 'This parrot is no more. It has ceased to be. It has expired and gone to meet its maker.'

In the days leading up to the Conference, the Prime Minister required constant reassurance that people would find the lines funny. She was clearly still full of doubt. However, I was able to get to enough people in advance whose opinion she was likely to ask that she was eventually persuaded. Every time we ran through the speech, I found myself laughing at the passage which simply added to the Prime Minister's puzzlement.

Finally, we got to the day of the speech. The text was finished, it had been typed up on to the autocue and we had completed the final rehearsal at which she practiced her delivery and the inflexions of the speech. However, as we waited for her to go on to the stage to deliver the speech, she was still worrying about the passage and looking for reasons that it might not work. Just as she was about to go on, another doubt arose in her mind. She looked at me and said anxiously: 'John, Monty Python – are you sure that he is one of us?'

To try to explain to her that Monty Python did not really exist would have been to risk disaster. I therefore did not even try and instead said to her: 'Absolutely, Prime Minister. He is a very good supporter.' Thus reassured, she went on to the platform to give the speech. She did so perfectly and received the biggest laugh of all when she delivered with perfect comic timing the words of the dead parrot sketch.

ANN WIDDECOMBE

SHADOW HOME SECRETARY

Ann Widdecombe has been the MP for Maidstone since 1987. She served as a junior minister in John Major's government, and joined the Shadow Cabinet in 1998. She currently serves as Shadow Home Secretary. Her first novel The Clematis Tree *was recently published by Weidenfeld and Nicolson.*

৵৵৵

Photo opportunity

In the 1980s when the issue of CND was still a very live one, I helped Lady Olga Maitland set up an organisation known as Women and Families for Defence. My contribution to the group was to write a booklet entitled. 'A Layman's Guide to Defence'. The group, deciding that it would like a photo opportunity, asked to see the Prime Minister. Margaret Thatcher agreed to see us but in her usual way it was before breakfast on an extremely dark winter's morning. We trudged along to 10 Downing Street scarcely past dawn and were received by the Prime Minister looking as if she had just walked out of a beauty salon. She was very lively and interested in what we were doing.

After we had been there about ten minutes the door bell of Number 10 went and Edwina Currie arrived on the doorstep wearing a hat! She had never been active in the group and none of us was quite sure what she was doing there, and a very embarrassed Olga, who had had to turn several people away as the invitation limited the numbers very stringently, had the job of turning away this formidable lady from the doorstep of Number 10.

We had expected a five minute audience but Mrs Thatcher gave us the best part of an hour.

MICHAEL BRUNSON

ITN POLITICAL EDITOR 1986–2000

Now a freelance broadcaster and journalist, Michael Brunson is best known for being ITN's face of current affairs for fourteen years. This passage is adapted from his autobiography A Ringside Seat, *published in April 2000 by Hodder and Stoughton.*

છે∼જી

Have you got that, Mr Brunson?

My first-ever encounter with Margaret Thatcher, a little over a year before she became Prime Minister, was explosive, and therefore memorable. I had just returned to the United Kingdom after a spell as ITN's Washington correspondent, and I had already been told that I would be the reporter assigned to cover her eventual General Election campaign.

In January 1978, as Leader of the Opposition, she gave a wide-ranging television interview, during which she was asked about the issue of immigration. She replied with what she later described as some 'extremely mild remarks'. What she actually said was this: 'People are really rather afraid that this country might be rather swamped by people with a different culture.' Others immediately found her remarks, and particularly her use of the word 'swamped', as anything but mild, hearing in them an echo of Enoch Powell's notorious 'rivers of blood' speech almost exactly ten years earlier.

The following day, Mrs Thatcher was due to conduct a morning's campaigning for the Conservative candidate in a by-election in the

Ilford North constituency to the east of London. I immediately suggested to the news editor at ITN that I should go and cover it. The Conservative campaign headquarters for the by-election turned out an old café, the former, though still appropriately named, Seven Ways Restaurant, since it was right next to the massive Gants Hill round-about. The news conference was to be held in a large and unusually depressing room, hung from floor to ceiling with the faded maroon curtains which had presumably once been the establishment's glory in its heyday.

The news conference was surprisingly poorly attended, with no more than five or six other journalists present. I was therefore able, at an early stage, to ask about the previous evening's interview, and I thought it perfectly natural to ask whether she had not regretted having raised the issue.

A volcanic eruption followed. She had not raised the matter. How could I possibly say that she had raised the matter? She had simply been asked a question, and she had replied to it in a perfectly honest and straightforward manner. What on earth was I talking about? How could I possibly put such a question to her?

Stunned into silence, I left it to others among the equally aston-ished press corps to take up the running, and they quickly turned to local matters. The news conference drew to a close and I assumed that that was the end of the matter. But I was wrong.

During some closing remarks, the volcano erupted again. Mrs Thatcher announced that she wished to say a word or two about the media. As she did so, what President Mitterand is once said to have called 'the eyes of Caligula' swivelled menacingly in my direction. She wanted journalists to know that she always did her homework, and that if we were to be regarded as true professionals, she expected us to do ours. Of course, she wanted good relations with the media, and she was perfectly prepared to answer any and every question. She always had, and she always would, with one proviso. They had to be accurate questions, properly based on facts. Had we got that? Was that quite clear? The tirade delivered, she swept from the room.

Blimey! Was this the woman that I would have to deal with during the rigours of a General Election? I soon realised, however, that it had been an exceptionally useful experience. It gave me, at our very first meeting, a clear insight into the way Margaret Thatcher operated. Above all, it showed me how strongly she believed in the old adage that the best form of defence is attack – seizing, that morning in Ilford, for example, on the tiny technicality of whether or not she had raised, or had simply responded to, an issue in order to defend herself. It was all to stand me in good stead not just during the 1979 campaign, but during the many times over the following years when we were to meet again.

SIR EDWARD DU CANN

MP FOR TAUNTON 1956–87

The distinguished former Conservative MP Edward Du Cann represented the constituency of Taunton for over thirty years. During that time he served in numerous positions within the Conservative Party and on many House of Commons committees. He received his knighthood in 1995.

∂∾∽

Formidable

Having been a strong supporter of Margaret Thatcher from the moment she became Leader of the Conservative Party in 1975 and Prime Minister four years later, I have a thousand clear memories of her.

Many people, MPs and others like me, will have watched her with admiration on public and semi-public occasions – standing resolute and indomitable at the dispatch box in the House of Commons, facing down the barrackers; evoking the enthusiasm of Conservative Party members at Party Conferences; and (how well I remember those occasions) her presence at meetings of the 1922 Committee, the back bench Tory MPs, where prima inter pares she solicited, deserved and obtained their loyal support all the years that I was their Chairman.

And, in her early days as Leader, and even when she won the General Election in 1959 and became Prime Minister, that wasn't always easy.

Her achievements as Prime Minister were formidable. The memories of her successes, which were also our country's successes, will endure to her credit.

There are a multitude of personal memories, also, which I sometimes recall. Most are private recollections, and should remain so. But not all.

I remember when we first met, at a meeting of prospective Conservative Parliamentary candidates in 1950, a dominantly male group. All of us were recently demobilised after our wartime experiences in the armed services. The late Airey Neave, fresh from his duties as a prosecutor at the Nüremberg trials, was our secretary and convenor. She was young and attractive. Naturally, she made a great impression on these lively men. And yet – she showed an exceptional keenness and capacity for self-advertisement, which was somehow daunting. Certainly it was untypical of her fellows.

Later, those of us who became MPs learned that her thrustfulness was one of her enduring strengths.

When I was a Treasury Minister, she came once to my constituency to open an old peoples' home. This was when she had her first ministerial appointment. I remember how my friends in Taunton were impressed by her seriousness, and slightly in awe of it. Here was a paradox which would endure: the truth was that she cared deeply about social issues, and yet that reality was not as widely believed as it deserved to be.

When she first became Leader of the Conservative Party, it took her a long while to settle into that position. The House of Commons then, like the Party, was also very much a masculine society. (Blair's babes hadn't yet been invented). I am not sure how easy it was for her to fit into the smoke room camaraderie that was the style of the Conservative Parliamentary Party at that time. Nor did she always find it easy in those early days to shine in the House, but her determination, her chief characteristic, carried her through. Her hard work led to an apparently easy style to fell her argumentative opponents with her oratorical handbag, full of the notes of the careful preparation that was her habit.

I remember thinking in 1975 that it would reflect well on the Conservative Party to elect a woman as Leader, the first political party in Britain to do so; and even that it would be more creditable if she were to become Britain's first woman Prime Minister. (Not that the feminists in our society ever appeared to find her remarkable success attractive). Her sex, on occasion, was an advantage to her. I have seen Tory MPs sit on their hands when Eden or Macmillan or Heath entered the room. When Margaret came in, they always stood up, to a man.

Sometimes she could be dictatorial – too often perhaps. In the end the Parliamentary Party revolted, following the example of one of her long term Cabinet colleagues – who owed his career to her. It was his personal attack on her in the House that marked the beginning of the end. Gratitude is not often the hallmark of politics. (I often wondered why some of her close Ministerial colleagues were apparently supine under the criticisms which she never held back. She liked an argument. I suspect they found it hard to argue with a woman.)

She and her immediate predecessor, Ted Heath, were in one respect in the same mould: they could be aloof, even with their close colleagues, self-contained, in a way which their predecessors in my experience, Eden Macmillan and Home, were not. My good friend Airey Neave, who had masterminded her election as Leader of the Conservative Party and became the head of her private office before his murder in the House of Commons by the Irish, told me, to my astonishment, that he was less close to her than he had expected. Leadership can be a solitary business.

As Chairman of the 1922 Committee, I was privileged to have a close relationship with her. Never was I received with anything but courtesy. Even when I had private advice to offer on matters of concern to the Conservative Parliamentary Party, including advice for which she did not care, she would hear me out with attention, take note, and, more importantly, take action.

There is one of our meetings, which I have most often looked back on, our last private meeting in the House, when I told her it was my intention, after 31 years, to retire as an MP. Typically generous, she pressed me to change my mind. I reflected aloud that it was sensible to retire early: perhaps then one's supporters might express regret; it would be foolish to wait to be pushed. I told her that she might consider this herself in due course. That advice, I remember, seemed to upset her. Now I wish I had pressed the point harder. Had she taken it in due course, she would have been spared the pain of her, eventual, unpleasant dismissal by the electorate of Tory MPs. Matters could have been, and should have been differently arranged.

She was badly counselled at that time. I hope that, while I had responsibility in the House of Commons, I never gave her poor advice: whenever we disagreed, which was rare, I still (after all these years) believe that I was right. Perhaps I learned that self-confidence from her. If so, it was a good lesson for a politician to absorb.

BARONESS NICHOLSON

MP FOR DEVON WEST AND TORRIDGE 1987–97

Emma Nicholson famously defected from the Conservative Party to the Liberal Democrats in 1995. She was raised to the peerage as Baroness Nicholson of Winterbourne in 1997. Her memoirs Secret Society *were published in 1996 by Victor Gollancz*

৯৽৽৾

Four Westminster winters: 1976, 1982, 1984 and 1990.

I believe that unlike the most successful Tory Prime Ministers of the 20th and 19th Centuries, Mrs Thatcher lost her way on the road to a new, liberal, radical synthesis. She lost her way, I believe, because the Brighton bomb effectively locked her away in a Nixonian bunker, staffed by overzealous, ideological activists and cut off from the voters she needed to see and hear and touch. The IRA won a more profound victory than was immediately apparent from her survival. Her isolation led her to harden policies which destroyed the post war political consensus that she inherited and helped develop a climate of acquisitive greed.

Four winters will be sufficient to watch her trajectory: 1976, 1982, 1984 and the five days from Thursday to Tuesday in November 1990 when it all came falling down.

In 1976, after an extended struggle, I was selected for the role of sacrificial lamb in Blyth, Northumberland, to fight the second strongest Labour constituency in the country: the scene of my own father's triumph in 1931 as a reforming Conservative. Facing sure and certain defeat I called on the new Party leader for advice in her office in the Palace of Westminster.

This first meeting with Mrs Thatcher revealed to me a pacing Tigress, full of warmth and reformist resolve, overflowing with a fighting spirit and a zeal for conquering socialism by going directly to the people. Eyes flashing bright blue, golden hair, radiating a feminine energy unknown outside the home to the Tory male establishment. She got right down to business: "Go door to door, Emma, let them know you, as a person". I moved north every weekend and lived at a £3 a night bed and. breakfast on the High Street while my principal opponent, the Labour MP stayed in the nearest five star hotel way outside the constituency issuing press releases headed "Blyth Working Men's club". I went, alone, door to door dressed in my best to honour the electorate in wind and snow through the Council estates promoting her vision of freedom from socialist control, and I polled the best Tory score in half a century.

1982 marked the bleak winter in a different hemisphere which had a major impact on her career, threatening to plunge her political trajectory perpendicularly downwards. I refer to the Austral Winter of 1982 when General Galtieri's invasion of the Falkland Islands came just when her political rating stood historically low, restored only by the professionalisrn of the British armed forces in a particularly 'close-run thing', which cost a thousand lives, and many more wounded. From pacing tigress she turned to Viking mode, conquering, scorning the vanquished enemy even in death and victory. She spurned aside the Archbishop of Canterbury's prayers for all the fallen and their families.

By Winter 1984 I was Tory Vice Chairman with special responsibility for women with regular private access to the Prime Minister. But something was changing in her: she was moving more and more swiftly away from her Methodist Liberal roots to the consensus of the nouveau riche grandees of the Monday Club and the seriously rich of her North London constituency. Cabinet and junior ministers, nearly all male, worshipped, genuflected and deprived her of the perspectives, the arguments that kept her democratically alert. Ever the scientist, Thatcher was gradually losing her intellectual challengers. She lost the opportunity to talk around all facets of an issue and was starved of real debate inside her own party, Eventually she would, resist my reasoned arguments on poll tax relief for nonworking married women, telling me that the nature of marriage was that women should be financially dependant upon men. I saw then that the modern world had grown away from her as her supplicants kept her in ignorance.

The Brighton bomb was the turning point. Crouched behind military security and Special Branch police, forbidden on real pain of death to act as a normal politician and work the street, she fell slowly into the warm, cuddly routine of being the House Goddess to the blindly ambitious of her immediate official circle. Bit by bit the new Party donors became the glitzy circus from whom she only received supportive views and approval. She stopped reading comment about herself in the newspapers, finding it too hurtful.

Thursday to Tuesday: November 1990

It was intensely clear to me that Mrs Thatcher had lost her hold over her strongest potential allies in the Cabinet. She was trapped in a room with enemies, with those bright eyed young men such as those who passed through junior Minister posts in Education could see that the scientist PM wanted to destroy the levelling influence of learning in our country. She was, indeed foolishly pulling up the ladder, as Reagan had done in Sacramento and the White House, strangling the access of new talent to the top. And these young Tories could see it happen: they became the inner core of the mutiny, waiting only for the courage of a Heseltine or a Howe to trigger the overthrow.

I tried three times, finally in public statement, to tell Mrs Thatcher that I was going to vote against her. Neither she or her circle were able to grasp my message. They lived in a cocoon of mutual admiration and the passing out of considerable public wealth.

When they finally appreciated my determined stand although it was too late, they instantly treated her with such disloyalty that I was appalled: all they could think about was when to find a new post, a better job, not to see her out with the dignity she deserved.

The day before the vote, I convinced two fellow Tories: one would vote with me, against her, and the other would abstain We made the determining two-vote margin by which she lost She left behind a Party unreformed, slavishly following transatlantic models, out of touch with a Britain packed with diversity whose talents were struggling to break out of the government controls that she, a partial Liberal, had mercilessly imposed.

SIR BRIAN MAWHINNEY

CABINET MINISTER 1992–7

Brian Mawhinney served in the Cabinet as Secretary of State for Transport from 1994 until 1995 and Minister Without Portfolio from 1995 until 1997. He was Chairman of the Conservative Party from 1995 until 1997. His memoirs: In the Firing line *were published by HarperCollins in 1999.*

❧

Empathy

Those of us who worked with Margaret Thatcher, and many others, knew all about her strength, her fixity of purpose and at times her partisan combativeness. Everyone knew that she was forthright in expressing her strongly held views.

Many fewer knew of her sensitivity to and empathy for individuals. My family and I had a first hand experience of this personal thoughtfulness.

Early in the 1980s the Peterborough Conservative Club decided to expand its lounge. I was fortunate enough to persuade Margaret, then Prime Minister, to do the official opening. My widowed mother, who had recently crossed from Belfast to live with us, came to Peterborough with us for the celebration, not least because she had never before met a Prime Minister.

The event created great excitement and there must have been a couple of hundred people in the Club when Margaret arrived. They gave her an ecstatic welcome, applauded loudly when she did the formal opening, laughed at her jokes and were enthused by her rousing call to political action in support of her government and its ideals. After the formal opening, the plan was that she would mingle with the guests and in anticipation many moved forward to greet her.

While I was introducing the family and my mother, Margaret heard that she had just arrived from Belfast. She then spent about five minutes talking to her and asking her questions about her life in the Province and the current state of difficulty there. She was oblivious to the pressing crowd and talked to my mother with great sensitivity, as if she was the only person in the room. Her ability to focus on an individual and to make that person feel important and the only one of any consequence to the Prime Minister at that time, was both remarkable and impressive.

It is just a pity that more people did not understand what a warmth of care, concern and interest she could share with ordinary members of the public, even at times of pressure.

When I hear people talk about Margaret's toughness, I am able also to reflect that she has a generosity of spirit toward individuals which is quite remarkable.

MICHAEL HOWARD

CABINET MINISTER 1990–97

Michael Howard is Conservative MP for Folkestone & Hythe. He was first elected to Parliament in 1983 and joined Margaret Thatcher's government in 1985. He was appointed Secretary of State for Employment in January 1990. Two years later he became Secretary of State for the Environment before being promoted to Home Secretary in 1993, a position he held until the 1997 general election.

I first saw Margaret Thatcher in action when, as Secretary of State for Education in the Heath Government, she addressed a dinner at the Coningsby Club, a Conservative dining club of which I was Chairman. She was very impressive, in complete command of her subject and, I thought, radiating authority.

Even so, I am not sure that I then saw her as a future Prime Minister. But, following events from outside the House of Commons, I was delighted when she was elected Leader of the Conservative Party in 1975.

People forget the state of the country at that time and in the years which led up to 1979. The air of defeatism which was the prevailing climate of the time was the economic and social equivalent of Munich. I remember hearing Peter Jay, then regarded as the rising guru of his generation, analyse: "Either", he said, "we shall have a government determined to tackle the causes of their weakness, in which case it will have to take such unpopular measures that it will never be elected for a second term, or we shall have a government not prepared to take these measures in which case weakness and failure will continue and accelerate."

The measures which Margaret Thatcher took were certainly unpopular. But from the beginning she displayed the resolve and determination which made her, to my mind, the peacetime counterpart of Churchill. I had relatively little contact with her after that first encounter, even after I entered Parliament in 1983.

She was then at the height of her powers with a majority of 144 and an Opposition that appeared to be in terminal decline. Her encounters with Neil Kinnock were so one-sided as to be embarrassing – in sharp contrast with the performance of the present incumbent in Downing Street.

In September 1985 I was asked to join the Government. That is a moment no-one forgets. I was at home in Kent at the time and was asked whether 1 would be free to take a telephone call from the Prime Minister. Then I received another call and was asked whether I could go to London to see her,

"Why does she want you to go to London?" asked my wife.

"Perhaps her telephone's out of order" suggested my eight year-old daughter.

My first job was Minister for Corporate and Consumer Affairs in the DTI. It was there that I began to have first-hand experience of the Prime Minister's interest in, passion for and mastery of detail.

We were discussing some complicated point I think related to, the Financial Services Act, in her room at the House of Commons. She asked me the meaning of a reference in a footnote to the brief she had been given. I hadn't a clue. I can't pretend that I made sure that I was the master of every footnote from then on but I had certainly been given a powerful incentive to prepare very thoroughly for meetings with the Prime Minister.

It is always dangerous in politics to have very specific and particular ambitions. But I had one, I desperately wanted to enter the Cabinet while she was still Prime, Minister. I only just made it. In

January 1990 She Made me Employment Secretary. In November of that year She was gone.

I have often been asked, and often thought, about the fateful events of that November. The advice I gave her and my thoughts and emotions have been described in full elsewhere. I told her that if she decided to fight on I would fight with her to the last ditch. But I also expressed my view that she would lose in the second ballot, possibly by a large margin.

I still think that honest advice was right though, of course, we Shall never know. But I do not share the view of those who say that even if She had survived she could never have won a fourth general election. I think she would have won again and we can all speculate endlessly on the difference that might have made to the history of the last ten years.

For my part I shall always regard it as a great privilege to have served, for five years, under one of, and perhaps the, greatest peacetime Prime Minister our country has seen.

PAUL ELLIOT

FORMER FLIGHT LIEUTENANT, ROYAL AIR FORCE POLICE

⁂

Flying with Maggie

For two years, I was privileged to be one of the numerous people who are needed to support the busy schedule of the Prime Minister. I was a serving Flight Lieutenant in the Royal Air Force. Police. My role was to implement the aviation security arrangements for senior Government Ministers whenever they travelled overseas on official engagements, Prime Minister Thatcher especially. Some of these trips were highly publicised, notably when we carried a large contingent of the Press as well as the official party on the aircraft. Others were much less well written up, on occasions when it became necessary at very short notice for the Prime Minister to engage in a 'one to one' meeting with her foreign counterparts.

Except on one long Flight from Ascension Island to the Falklands, when Margaret and Denis Thatcher travelled in a caravan which was anchored firmly to the floor of a Hercules VC10 freighter (and the rest did their best to be comfortable in the cargo bay), we all invariably flew in the relative luxury of a VC10; the pride of RAF Support Command. My work was only made difficult by the few "VIP" (and middle ranking) passengers whose arrogance forbade them from obeying simple security instructions such as those appertaining to items which were unacceptable for carriage in the aircraft. We searched everyone's personal luggage each time it was loaded and I remember worrying about how I was going to achieve this in the case of the 'Iron Lady', on the first occasion I flew with her.

I need not have feared. Margaret Thatcher was the most under-standing of all the passengers and that was my experience on every occasion that my team dealt with her. It was my responsibility to be the first down the aircraft steps whenever we arrived at a destination. Depending on the security climate, there were different procedures for the way in which I, followed by the Prime Minister, would descend towards the inevitable red carpet and the rows of host foreign dignitaries who waited to greet her. Each time, I briefed Mrs Thatcher immediately before we left the safety of the aircraft and on every occasion she listened attentively and did exactly the right thing. Other senior people who I escorted for similar reasons were often flippant and reckless. The Prime Minister was never like that; of course she did not suffer fools but to me and the other junior people who did our best to get things right, she was always most understanding.

Between the ceremonial and the pressure of events on the ground, the aircraft often acted in a place of sanctuary for our VIP passengers. It was inevitable that everyone on board relaxed after take off; the cabin was not enormous and offered little individual privacy. Obviously there were many private moments shared and these should never be discussed in public. However some VIPs were especially distant, verging on pomposity, but Mrs Thatcher was never the 'icicle' in these circumstances which I know that many people imagine her to have been. She did also engage in pleasant small talk during long duration flights, always accepting that the majority of her time was consumed by the Affairs of State punctuated by cat napping from which she had an amazing ability to awake without a call according to the timetable of events. Impeccable timing and very tight schedules were a feature of these journeys across the world; it was always our aim to arrive and depart exactly on time but sometimes political negotiations were extended and we had to wait on the tarmac for several hours longer than anticipated for the principal passenger to board the aircraft. I remember this happening in the stifling heat of a Middle Eastern country and again in the intense cold of winter in Norway. On both occasions the Prime Minister apologised to us all on her late arrival – something that none of her male ministers ever did when we were transporting them in similar circumstances.

We did not always bother the Prime Minister with the understandable operational difficulties which were experienced from time to time and I remember wondering if she would be annoyed if this were to be revealed. I got my answer over a problem which occurred with a vengeance. We had taken of from London one lunchtime in the Autumn of 1992, en route to Tokyo (and thence to Peking for the purpose of Mrs Thatcher signing the agreement to release Hong Kong to the Chinese). A couple of hours later we were cruising towards the North Pole, with Mrs Thatcher enjoying a break in the captain's seat on the flight deck, when the navigator was notified that the authorities in London had received a claim that we had a bomb on the aircraft. This was most disconcerting, although I was convinced that our tight security arrangements made the probability highly unlikely. Nevertheless the aircraft captain (a fellow RAF Flight Lieutenant) decided that we should make an unscheduled landing to check. He told the passengers that we needed to refuel due to unexpected head winds. We landed at a remote United States Air Force Base in Alaska, off loaded everyone and surrounded the aircraft with service vehicles so that no one could we what we were doing from the terminal building. I am assured that Mrs Thatcher spent the time being perfectly charming to a USAF major who, was the senior officer at the base and was in a blind panic having received such an unexpected visitor.

In the event, we experienced no explosions but I remained unsure as to whether or not the Prime Minister would explode if she found that we had not revealed the real reason for our unscheduled fuel stop to her. It was left to me to tell her some five weeks later, long after we had returned safely to the London and were being entertained at a reception in Number 10 Downing Street. She listened carefully to my story and simply said 'thank you'. I am sure that her calm reaction was absolutely genuine. I reflected again how worrying it must be for people in public life whose lives are under constant threat. If she felt the danger, Mrs Thatcher did not show it.

In September 1983, I was in Germany with Mrs Thatcher's party on another State Visit. The aircraft captain received the message that my mother had died suddenly in England. I was of course distressed and unable to return home to see my family as quickly as I would have liked. I did not expect any of the senior party to learn of my loss and was extremely surprised when Mrs Thatcher sought me out and spoke to me with great kindness. I am sure that Mrs Thatcher does not remember me for I was just one of many. From a personal point of view I shall never remember Margaret Thatcher as an 'Iron Lady'; I think that she had a remarkable ability to blend ordinary human qualities with the need to represent herself as 'the boss' whenever that was required.

MICHAEL COCKERELL

DOCUMENTARY FILM MAKER AND AUTHOR

The award winning documentary film maker Michael Cockerell has been involved in the production of political television for over 25 years, most famously as the BBC Panorama's chief political reporter. His acclaimed study of prime ministers and television, Live From Number 10, *was published by Faber & Faber in 1988. His most recent films have been profiles of Tony Blair and Alastair Campbell.*

৵৽

Maggie's Prime Time

My relationship with Margaret Thatcher did not always run smooth. Some years after she had left office I filmed Lady Thatcher and Lord (Bill) Deedes at a Foyles Literary Lunch for a BBC TV profile I was making of Deedes. 'You know Michael Cockerell', he said to her mischievously, 'was he always kind to you when you were Prime Minister? 'No', she replied, with her special brand of emphasis, 'no he was not.'

Perhaps she had in mind a *Panorama* I had made in 1982 after the Falklands crisis broke, but before our troops were in action. On the programme, some Tory MPs had expressed their hopes that war might be avoided and an honourable settlement negotiated.It was not a popular view and in the Commons the next day, the Conservative Mrs Sally Oppenheim, asked Mrs Thatcher at Question Time: 'Will the Prime Minister take time off in the course of her busy day to watch a recording of last night's Panorama in which Michael Cockerell dishonoured the right of freedom of speech in this country.' I had not, until that moment, realised that the programme was quite as good as that.

But the PM rather agreed with the sentiments of her questioner, saying: 'there are some people in this country who do not understand their duty in a democracy to stand up for our boys.' That response marked a low point in our relationship – but she was magnanimous in her Falklands victory and agreed – after a break – to give me further prime ministerial interviews.

I suppose the high point in our encounters had come three years earlier during the 1979 general election. I was making a film for the BBC about her campaign and the Iron Lady was determined to counter Labour's charges that she was harsh and uncaring. In an interview with me, she assumed a kittenish persona.

I put it to her that there sometimes seemed to be two Mrs Thatchers: one toured supermarkets and factory floors, exhibiting endless fascination about the minutiae of people's lives and jobs. The other was the platform politician – full of zealous conviction.

'How many Mrs Thatchers are there?' I asked.

'Oh, three at least', she responded in a low, confiding voice: 'there is the intellectual one, the intuitive one and the one at home.' Her manner was so intimate – even coquettish – that the late Sir Robin Day, watching in the studio when the filmed interview went out, joked: 'the untold story of the election campaign: Margaret Thatcher is having an affair with Michael Cockerell'.

The last time I interviewed her as Prime Minister was for a portrait I was making of Willie Whitelaw for the BBC. It was May 1989 and Mrs T had just celebrated her tenth anniversary in office – but ringing in her ears was her deputy Chief Whip Tristan Garel Jones' warning: 'The assassins are lurking in the bushes waiting to get you.'

I had asked Lord Whitelaw how long he felt Mrs Thatcher would continue in office: 'Oh, she is very fit, very strong. I hope she'll go on for a very long time', he replied.

'But she is not immortal', I ventured to suggest.

'No she is not immortal', responded Willie, then added, 'but perhaps she is'.

In Number Ten, I recounted this exchange on camera to Mrs T. Reviewing the tape today is revealing.

On freezing the frame at exactly the moment she hears my intimation of her mortality, a remarkable look comes over her face for an instant: an apparent mix of panic and blinding revelation. Within a few frames it is gone and she recovers her composure on hearing of recount Whitelaw's response. 'What a sweet thing of Willie to say – no, I am not immortal and I don't know how long I will go on – and no-one does.'

Within months she was gone. And like every TV journalist I missed her. Once you had Margaret Thatcher in your viewfinder she never failed to produce riveting images and powerful quotes. A medium which in any case tends to magnify personalities had for the fifteen years of her Tory leadership been faced with a giant-sized one. Disraeli, Lloyd George and Winston Churchill became Prime Ministers before the age of television.

Happily Mrs T did not.

JULIA LANGDON

POLITICAL JOURNALIST

Julia Langdon is a freelance political journalist and former Political Editor of the Daily Mirror *and the* Sunday Telegraph. *She is the author of* Mo Mowlam: The Biography *published by Little Brown.*

రావ్

On the road with Maggie

Perhaps the most chilling moment of my relationship with Margaret Thatcher occurred at about 30,000 feet. We were in an RAF VC10 – as we so often were – *en route* on this occasion to Australia. I had looked with horror at the official itinerary when it had arrived shortly beforehand. It was long and characteristically busy and the worst thing was that we had one night in the air on the outward journey and then a row of one-night stopovers in a series of different Australian cities. I realised gloomily that we wouldn't be able to get any laundry done until we reached Bangkok, ten days or so into the journey. When the Prime Minister came back in the plane to rough it with the riff-raff on the first leg of the journey to somewhere in the Middle East, I politely asked her by way of conversational small talk what she had made of her programme. 'Well!' she said, clearly much exercised on the point, 'do you realise we won't even be able to get any laundry done until we reach Bangkok !'

It was, I have to report, quite alarming to discover that one's reaction in an unpredictable set of circumstances should be so completely identical to that of the Prime Minister. And not any old Prime Minister either.

We went around the world together several times, Mrs Thatcher and I. Entirely at her behest, of course. During her years as Prime Minister, I was Political Editor of this and that and instructed by my various employers always to accompany Her Nibs wherever she went. It was the most brilliant fun, although probably more particularly in retrospect because there were lots of endless days and sleepless nights. And when you did get into bed for the first time in what felt like weeks, somewhere on the other side of the world, you could always rely on the newsdesk to ring and say that a reader had rung in about some trivial fact they wished to challenge.

I was there when military bands turned out at midnight to play obscure national anthems at the other end of the interminable lengths of red carpet laid across some foreign airport tarmac. I have watched elderly despots dance attendance upon her and I have watched her dance. It isn't always quite as glamorous as it might sound. I have trailed her around building sites in the Middle East, a sewer works in Cairo, a mining operation in Namibia, a new mass transit system in Singapore. I have watched as she took tea in a trench with two African Presidents in a war zone on the Mozambique border and as she was unexpectedly presented with an Arab stallion in a Middle Eastern desert and didn't quite know how to explain that it wasn't quite her thing. I have winced in feminist sympathy as the light of the Jordanian sun cut through her dress and made it look as if she was stark naked as she inspected the honour guard lined up to salute her. I have watched strong men and women faint from heat in refugee camps in Israel and Zimbabwe and Jordan and Cambodia and wondered if she was going to make it – and, yes, whether I was too. Possibly not in that order. I was on her plane when we were shot at by guerrillas on the way to visit Malawi – not that I knew about it until her first volume of memoirs was published. 'Fortunately they missed,' she said, recounting the incident. Together we have attended the Bolshoi, a wedding in Tblisi, a mass in Zagorsk, a riot in Melbourne, another one in the heat and dust of a Saharan harmattan as we watched a dhurbar in Kano. It was always work. She didn't relax. There were very few opportunities for hanging around the swimming pool if there was one. She didn't like sight-seeing and she wasn't really interested in culture. She didn't want anybody to think that she was pleasure-seeking, or enjoying herself – except, of course, in a political sense. She was once prevailed upon to show that she had an understanding of these things, however. We had whizzed around the wonders of Luxor in a couple of hours, typically at midday with the temperature at 120 degrees or so, simply because it suited her programme to do it at this insane time of day. Someone told her that really she ought to show she was interested in the wonders of ancient Egypt for its own sake. So when we took off she ordered the pilot to take the VC10 down to 3,000 feet so we could admire the temples of Abu Simbel in the Upper Nile. On the next trip we circled Ayer's rock in Australia. Reader, I must tell you, that we did not do justice to these wonders of the world.

There were many wonderful moments of our travels together and I cherish some in particular. There was, for example, the time at the Expo in Brisbane when she was touring the site and many eager Australians had packed the area for a glimpse of the great Maggie Thatcher. It was terribly crowded and the public were penned away from the celebrity tour of the exhibits. There was, however, a middle-ranking reptile enclosure which contained the press. Mrs Thatcher was about to move among us and, seeing some small children who were eager to catch a glimpse of this legend of their lifetime, I offered to take one small child off her mother and give her a better view. I was holding her up to see the great one pass and Mrs Thatcher stopped at the sight of the little girl's excited small face. There were no other children around because this was the press area and the public were so much further away. Mrs Thatcher didn't realise this, however, and with a politician's instinct homed in. The horror on her face when she realised that I was holding the child was a wonder to behold. 'Oh !' she said with complete disgust and incomprehension. 'It's you!'

I think my favourite moment, however, was in Moscow when Mrs Thatcher was due to meet the armed service chiefs of the USSR at their equivalent of the Ministry of Defence. I had arrived somewhat latterly, behind the rest of my press colleagues but very slightly before the Prime Minister. For the purposes of this anecdote it is necessary to recognise that to someone in the Soviet Union one middle-aged West European woman looks very much like another. Anyway, I whizzed into the lift to go to the appropriate floor where Mrs T was due to meet the top brass – literally – of the Soviet military machine and when the lift doors opened they thought she had arrived. There was music and an attendant group of military snapped to attention, saluted and clipped their heels. A man with a lot of scrambled egg on his shoulders stepped forward to greet me. 'I'm from the *Daily Mirror*,' I said, by way of explanation. 'Mrs Thatcher isn't here yet.' They were very embarrassed. I thought it was just wonderful.

WILLIAM HAGUE

LEADER OF THE CONSERVATIVE PARTY

William Hague became the Leader of the Conservative Party following John Major's resignation in 1997. He had previously served as Minister of State for Social Security and Disabled People and as Secretary of State for Wales.

ᘏᕈᗢᕉ

Maggie's Last Stand

M any people will have memories about Margaret Thatcher etched indelibly in their political consciousness. Mine has to be the final speech she made in the Commons as Prime Minister in November 1990 following her decision to stand down from the leadership of the Conservative Party.

She had been Prime Minister for eleven years and dominated British politics. She was one of my earliest political heroes and I remember sitting there, as a junior backbencher, watching with a deep sense of sorrow that she was about to bow out.

But what a way to go! Anyone expecting her to be downbeat or subdued by the experiences of recent days was sorely disappointed as she recounted how Britain had been rescued from the spiral of decline and stagnation in which decades of socialism had left it. At one stage Dennis Skinner intervened to suggest she might become Governor of the new European Central Bank. 'What a good idea' she responded to the hilarity of the House. To Tory cheers, she went on 'I'm enjoying this'.

It was then that the Conservative backbencher Michael Cartiss spoke for many of us when, pointing across the Chamber, he said 'You can wipe the floor with these people'. It was a magical performance, never to be forgotten by those who saw it.

A few months later I saw her come into the Commons tea-room and fall into conversation with Dennis Skinner. On seeing her he had cried out 'its not the same without you, love'. Looking across at him she replied 'how are you, dear?' before the two of them sat together for about 45 minutes in earnest discussion, while the rest of us strained to hear what they were talking about. Whatever people's views of her policies she was held in immense respect right across the spectrum.

I saw that again in my own leadership election in 1997 when she went to the tea room for the first time since leaving the Commons five years earlier – much to the amazement of many new Labour MPs who had never seen her in the flesh before! All the old authority, presence and conviction that she exuded as Prime Minister came back as she handbagged any wavering Conservative MPs.

They were the same qualities that had sustained her through some of her most difficult times as Prime Minister – such as the speech on 22 November 1990. It is hard now to appreciate just how difficult that speech was to make. Yet it turned out to be her grand finale as Prime Minister, worthy of everything she had achieved in eleven years. Moreover, to many of those who were privileged to be there, it was quite simply one of the greatest Parliamentary performances that we had seen, or are ever likely to see.